DATE DUE

OCT 0 1986			
DEC 1 8 1987			
APR 20 '93			
MAY 2 6 1994			
OCT 2 1996			
DF			

America's Teacher Quality Problem

=America's= Teacher Quality Problem

Alternatives for Reform

W. Timothy Weaver

PRAEGER SPECIAL STUDIES • PRAEGER SCIENTIFIC

New York • Philadelphia • Eastbourne, UK
Toronto • Hong Kong • Tokyo • Sydney

Library of Congress Cataloging in Publication Data

Weaver, W. Timothy.
    America's teacher quality problem.

    Bibliography: p.
    Includes index.
    1. Teacher—Training of—United States. 2. Teachers—
United States—Rating of. I. Title.
LB1715.W357 1983   371.1′44′0973   83-13804
ISBN 0-03-068777-2 (alk. paper)

Published in 1983 by Praeger Publishers
CBS Educational and Professional Publishing
a Division of CBS Inc.
521 Fifth Avenue, New York, NY 10175 USA

56789 052 9876543

Printed in the United States of America
on acid-free paper

For Alma,

My aunt from Texas

—How teachers ought to be—

Contents

Acknowledgments

No book is complete without acknowledging and thanking those who helped to make the book possible.

Several individuals contributed to this book. Two of my former graduate students were of great help in the early years of this work. Charles F. Parker provided much assistance in tracking down and organizing some of the test score data on college-bound high school seniors. I am especially indebted also to Kiran Chakravarthy, who prepared an initial essay summarizing the history of American teacher certification and the supply and demand cycles. Her work has grown into the first sections of Chapter 1. I also wish to thank George Blakeslee, whose recent doctoral research on the supply and demand for science and mathematics teachers has been helpful in the writing of this book.

With regard to the computer simulation modeling work, I wish to thank Barry M. Richmond and Eric Petersen of Dartmouth College for their initial ideas about formulating equations and conceptualizing the early versions of the teacher supply, demand, and quality model. For the same reason, I also thank Karl Clauset and Alan Gaynor of Boston University. I am especially indebted to Ross Zerchykov, senior policy analyst, Institute for Responsive Education at Boston University, for patiently reading and critiquing drafts of the manuscript. Many of Ross's ideas are embedded in the policy arguments in Chapter 6.

One does not ordinarily thank institutions, but in the case of this book, several organizations (and, of course, individuals in those organizations) were cooperative and supportive in providing needed data. Thus, I wish to thank the American College Testing Program (especially Merine Farmer) and the College Entrance Examination Board and Educational Testing Service (especially Rex Jackson) for patiently and diligently digging out files and records of historical data on test scores. I also thank Frances Melone of the National Center for Educational Statistics for providing computer-generated data from the National Longitudinal Study. Martin Frankel and Vance Grant, also of the National Center for Educational Statistics, have been very helpful in answering requests for unpublished data. And, as anyone working with teacher supply and demand data knows, William Graybeal of the National Education Association is a treasure of information and generous in his willingness to help researchers in the field.

Finally, I wish to thank Richard B. Freeman of Harvard University for his initial ideas and his extremely valuable work on the academic labor market, which are at the root of the analysis in this book. Dick Freeman is one of America's foremost thinkers in labor economics, and his ideas are responsible for my initial inquiry on the relationship between market dynamics and institutional responses as these affect academic quality.

Acknowledgment and thanks are owed the following publishers for allowing materials initially prepared for them as articles to be used in this book. Parts of the materials in Chapter 2 were published initially in W. T. Weaver, "Educators in Supply and Demand: Effects on Quality," School Review 86, no. 4 (August 1978): 552-93; W. T. Weaver, "In Search of Quality: The Need for New Talent in Teaching," Phi Delta Kappan 61 (1979): 29-46; and W. T. Weaver, "The Talent Pool in Teacher Education," Journal of Teacher Education 62 (May-June 1981): 32-36. I wish to thank the publishers of Training, The Magazine of Human Resources Development, for permission to print excerpts from the October 1982 special issue, A Comprehensive Overview of Training and Employee Development Activity in Organizational America. Copyright 1982, Lakewood Publications, 731 Hennepin Ave., Minneapolis, MN. All rights reserved.

No book is possible without a typist, who often turns out (and this case is no exception) to be the difference between success and failure. I am indebted to Dana Rudoph for tirelessly typing late into the night numerous drafts of the book.

America's Teacher Quality Problem

1
Defining the Problem

This book is the culmination of a series of studies on the academic abilities of those entering and leaving teaching. The issue of
teachers' abilities proves to be extraordinarily important to a society
that annually places close to 10 percent of its total wealth on the bet
that schools make a difference in the progress of a nation. The fact
that the more general educational quality debate has recently aroused
so much attention is evidence of the public's continuing belief in the
efficacy of schooling. To even hint that those charged with developing
literacy in the young are not themselves literate causes something
akin to a national nervous breakdown; yet the accumulating evidence
suggests, if anything, that the teaching profession has attracted, not
the most, but the least academically able to its ranks. These findings
have reappeared at a time when the public is being bombarded with
reports on the decline of educational excellence.

There are all sorts of definitions of teacher quality. The definition used in this book is academic ability. Academic ability is one
measure of teacher quality, but it is not the only one and perhaps not
even the most important measure. Certainly it is not the one most
often found in the history of teacher quality debates. The reasons for
selecting academic ability are twofold: first, it would be absurd to
argue that academic ability is not or should not be at least one measure of teacher quality because that would lead to "fitness" tests of
teachers, which excludes any consideration of whether teachers can
or ought to be able to read, write, or compute numbers—the very
things, presumably, they are attempting to teach others. Regardless
of the means for measuring such abilities, no one believes that teachers should, as a matter of principle, be illiterate. Indeed, it seems
indisputable that the support of public schooling rests on precisely
the opposite belief: teachers must be at least perceived to be literate
in the subjects they teach.

1

Second, despite a century of educationists' efforts to arrive at other definitions, there is little agreement inside or outside the teaching profession on what is meant by teacher quality. This may explain in part why the professional literature is full of discussions about teacher "qualifications" and relatively barren of discussions about quality otherwise defined.

It has been argued in the professional literature, even during periods of huge teacher surpluses, that there was, in effect, a shortage of teachers—that is, too few <u>qualified</u> teachers. The problem was not simply too many teachers but, rather, not enough teachers with certain attributes. The qualified teacher argument is not new and, in the United States, may be traced to the nineteenth century. The nature of this argument allows one, by simply altering what is meant by <u>qualified</u>, to claim at any time that we have a teacher shortage or surplus. The history of this debate shows that what is meant by <u>qualified teacher</u> has generally been a matter of the level and kind of formal education courses taken by the teacher as established by the profession, required by state law, and provided by schools of education. It is also the case that the minimum qualification required to teach has constantly risen throughout this century but has been altered to adjust to supply. This debate seems to be one regarding the political system of education rather than a matter of pedagogical theory. Indeed, it has no necessary or logical connection to any theory of education. Its connection is, rather, to a system of schooling. It is addressed to the polity of education. It is entirely a question of determining how the legitimate occupation of positions within the system of education will be controlled. Before the emergence of an educational system such a question would have been moot. Those volunteers from the community who were themselves literate could and did assist in the development of literacy among children. The children, once literate, assisted other children.

No one has ever seriously argued that these kinds of attributes (that is, those that have to do with the qualified teacher) are necessarily connected to learning outcomes. James McClellan (1968) argues, rather, that they have to do with restricting a market in labor. Thus, it is not surprising that the issue emerges when jobs are in short supply.

It is not precisely clear whether the qualified teacher argument implies that certain attributes are necessary for the teacher because they are connected to (1) the direct benefits of education (attitude, skills, and so on), (2) the indirect benefits of education (presumed to be some measure of social success), or (3) some other outcome, such as the moral, aesthetic, social, or psychological development of the child. It may be argued, on the other hand, that what is meant by qualified teacher has nothing to do with any of these kinds of outcomes or outputs but, rather, with how well the teacher performs certain acts of teaching regardless of outcome. For instance, the qualified teacher may be well organized and present not only an interesting lesson but also one that is based on behavioral objectives and employs feedback and a variety of teaching strategies. The unqualified teacher, on the other hand, may simply be one who is humanistic or very articulate, empathetic, dynamic, charismatic, nondirective, or whatever. If it is the case that such attributes are not valued because they are not connected to any particular learning outcome—that is, have no particular meaning that is dependent upon their consequences—then we are speaking of something akin to ritual (compare Ryans 1970). However, if in fact the qualified teacher is one who has these attributes, and if these produce certain desired consequences, then we are speaking of something very important—what one might call praxis.

The question of quality teaching, then, becomes answerable in terms of whether action has meaning for certain desired consequences. That question may be studied empirically (compare Levin 1970; Summers and Wolfe 1975; Hanushek 1968, 1970). It is a matter of observation whether good teaching produces desired results. Thus far, few of those examining the question of teacher quality are willing to accept learning results as an indication of quality teaching. (For the skeptic's view, see Heath and Nielson 1974).

It is not clear just where the qualified teacher argument leads us. One conclusion it may lead us to is that, so far at least, those people who possess the particular attributes we seek do not necessarily come from schools of education. That is, of course, James Koerner's point. The very fact that the definition of the qualified teacher has changed repeatedly since the last quarter of the nineteenth century probably suggests that either professional educators have not been able to discover what actually constitutes the qualified, qua effective, teacher (as opposed to what constitutes the dutiful teacher) or that each act of discovery is followed by a change in condition that renders the discovery false. One may well be led to think that there are not enough qualified teachers, but this conclusion may have nothing to do with any specific conclusions about surpluses or shortages of output from colleges of education. Indeed, we may wish to conclude that no matter how many teachers are graduated from colleges of education we will not get the desired attributes except by chance, on the assumption that we know neither what attributes are necessary for effective teaching nor how to reproduce them.

This conclusion leaves us without a universally, or even a professionally, agreed-upon definition of teacher quality—a conclusion that may be of some self-serving interest to the teaching profession. It certainly makes it possible to define teacher quality in any way one chooses. If quality is whatever we say it is, then no one is account-

able. But this also leads us back, by default, to the definition of
teacher quality we started with: academic ability—undoubtedly not a
definition that educators will agree on but one that is unarguably important and of self-interest to educators for other reasons having to
do with legitimating claims for support of public schooling. Like it or
not, if there is public doubt, it will prove necessary for the teaching
profession to demonstrate that its members are literate.

Whether the dismal state of teacher quality (academic ability)
is a historical fact of long standing is not precisely clear because the
absence of national test score data before 1970 does not allow a large-
scale, systematic assessment of entry teachers' academic abilities.
The data since 1970 do allow the question of entry teachers' academic
ability to be answered, and the answer will please very few. For the
period 1970 to the present, it is apparent that those preparing to teach
and those entering teaching have been generally and increasingly
drawn from the lower half of the academic talent pool. Even more
unfortunate, the first to leave teaching are the most talented of those
who enter the profession. The problem clearly has worsened with the
previous decade-long glut of teachers, although Robert Thorndike and
Elizabeth Hagen (1960) discovered the problem much earlier.

What is new about the debate is that teacher quality has been divided into arguments about qualifications or credential standards and
scholastic aptitude. This turn of events is first seen in the literature
of the 1960s and 1970s (for example, James Koerner's The Miseducation
cation of American Teachers). Those examining the problem are no
longer content to view quality as a matter of courses taken in colleges
of education as prescribed by state law and enforced by state education departments. The more recent research (presented in Chapters
2 and 3) examines the intellectual ability of America's prospective
and newly hired teachers.

This book attempts to document and explain the teacher quality
problem, beginning with its history, and to assess policies (proposed
and implemented) that have been aimed at correcting it. It will be argued that the problem results from a combination of interacting forces.
Chief among these forces are individuals' career choices, which result
in talent flowing into areas of opportunity; fluctuating demand for talent,
which is for the system of teachers colleges confined to the fortunes
and misfortunes of the labor needs of public schools; and responses
of the preparing institutions, which result in sacrificing standards for
the preservation of jobs. The effort to regulate the talent flow problem through qualifications standards (defined as college courses and
degrees) presents itself as a history of reforms that fail to reform.
If it were possible to so reform the system, the problems of the last
decade would not have materialized. They were preceded by decades
of perfecting a system of credentialing that ended up with several
states requiring master's degrees for teachers.

The book presents evidence on, and an explanation of, the "education brain drain" (Chapters 2 and 3) and then uses the body of evidence and the explanation in defining the parameters for a computer simulation model (Chapter 4). The model is used to test policies, including teacher examinations, certification upgrading, and expansion of the client base for schools of education (Chapter 5). One of the conclusions is that teacher testing, without accountability on the part of preparing institutions, will not solve the problem. Indeed, it may worsen the problem. Changing certification standards has wide appeal but is a weak policy option (as the modeling work and history tell us).

The solution rests with disengaging schools of education from their nearly total dependence on the preparation of teachers, a solution that, in effect, would disengage them from their preoccupation with teacher certification (Chapter 6). There are several benefits of such a solution, the foremost of which would be improvement in the academic quality of those being prepared to teach in the public schools. But there are other benefits. The involuted nature of the system leaves it without a means to test the ideas of teacher educators in an "open" market. The system behaves much like a public utility. The consumers (teachers, would-be teachers, and employers of teachers) have only one source of suppliers, the accredited teachers colleges. The consumers are, in effect, stuck with whatever the suppliers say teacher education ought to be. By opening up the system to prepare educators of adults (as well as schoolteachers) in corporate training environments, colleges of education would be forced to define what they are good for in a market where consumers have other choices.

This will not be an idea welcomed by most teacher educators, nor by those in the educational establishment who think that the solution rests with testing teachers, raising and lengthening certification standards, or in other ways achieving what D. B. Waldo urged in 1919, a schoolteaching profession worthy of the respect (and economic rewards) of law and medicine. It will not be welcomed because it flies in the face of conventional wisdom. It is the purpose of this book to demonstrate why the conventional wisdom is wrong.

HISTORY: BOOM AND BUST

Three U.S. presidents (Wilson, Eisenhower, and Johnson) have made the issue of teacher shortages a matter of national urgency. Each period of "critical" shortages has been followed by a surplus, and each surplus has been followed by still another "critical" shortage. There is a sort of rhythm to this history, with a frenzied rushing about to remedy a national crisis followed by disbelief and confusion when boom turns to bust. There are proposals calling for cutting requirements and then proposals for extending them. The only consistent argument made by educators is that there never seem to be enough "well-quali-fied" or "superior" teachers and never enough money for decent sal-aries. The echo of the last great teacher boom-bust cycle, 1955-80, has only just begun to fade as a new generation of educators whispers about the impending shortages of the 1980s.

The great teacher debates are marked by a prescriptive wisdom consisting of remedies to regulate supplies through certification re-quirements. The long-term tendency has been to increase require-ments by adding to the number of years of college training teachers must have to qualify for teaching positions and to centralize and stan-dardize such requirements by vesting authority at the state level to enforce and regulate teacher certification.

During the greatest teacher boom of this century, the 1960s, the debate about quality and qualifications took on a new irreverence. James D. Koerner directly assaulted teacher education and the intel-lectual quality of faculties, courses, and students. Koerner believed that the inferior quality of teachers was a direct consequence of in-ferior college training programs and a lack of stringent standards of admission to training and to the practice of teaching. This would be a particularly unflattering portrait of the efforts of educationists who had lobbied for a century to make college graduation the minimum re-quirement for entering the teaching profession. In one bold stroke of the pen, Koerner declared the effort to have failed, or worse. The educationists' dream had resulted in an involuted system of puerile and intellectually disgraceful courses that now prevented first-rate minds from entering the profession because they would not put up with the nonsense of education requirements.

In the sections that follow, we will examine the history of sup-ply-demand cycles and the proposed remedies, including those set forth by Koerner. The phases cover periods of about two decades. The first shortages are reported from 1908 to 1928, when a surplus suddenly materializes. The surplus lasts until just after World War II, when shortages begin to appear. The period from 1950 to 1970 is one of escalating shortages and a voluminous literature of remedies. Just as suddenly as in 1928, the shortage of the 1950s and 1960s be-comes the surplus of the 1970s. It appears that the teacher surplus of the 1970s will become the shortage of the 1980s.

THE GREAT TEACHER DEBATES

The great debates over teacher shortages, surpluses, and qual-ifications are part of the history of an emerging state system of free schools. Uniform standards of certification and licensure are taken

as evidence of incipient bureaucratization of the school system by
Michael Katz (1975), who argues that much of the system was in place
in the nineteenth century but reached full flower by World War I.[1]
The history, at least as reflected in reviews of the literature, begins
to show expressed national concern about qualified teachers in the
early 1900s (Maaske 1951). With growth and further centralization
of schooling after this period, and with the beginnings of uniform certification of teachers at the state level, attention began to be focused
upon salaries, supplies, and qualifications of teachers.

The first significant indications of concern were found by Roben
J. Maaske (1951) in the addresses and proceedings of the National Education Association (NEA) in 1907 and 1908. In a report to the NEA,
George S. Davis, in 1908, summarized the existing situation as follows: "In every large city school system the provision of an adequate
supply of properly prepared teachers is one of the most difficult problems with which we have to deal."

The Early Years: Teacher Shortages

The general shortage of "adequately" trained teachers during
the early years of this century, particularly the pre-World War I
years, led educationists to recommend more and better training programs for teachers. At that time, the shortages seemed to be an
annual problem in most cities and rural areas. Reform-minded educationists, such as L. D. Coffman, began to speak out on the problems of preparing teachers. Coffman, addressing the National Education Association in 1912, believed standardization of admissions
requirements and "feminization" of teaching were keeping men away:
"Our changed social conditions have been accompanied with a multipli-
cation of economic opportunities. These have reduced the attractive
force of teaching as a vocation, particularly for men."[2] Of the men
attracted to teaching, some had a college education, but few had
teaching experience or pedagogical preparation. By contrast, a
sizable fraction of elementary schoolteachers, largely female, had
little or no college education, and many lacked even a high school
education. Only a small percentage of the total were products of
normal school training.

The war years (World War I) greatly intensified the debate about
shortages of teachers nationwide. The literature of the period suggests the following causes: the military buildup, low salaries, attraction to other fields, poor working conditions, and low public and
social recognition—themes with a familiar ring. Not all educators
blamed the problems on the war. The occupation of teaching itself
was seen as a cause of the undersupply problem. This view of the

problem was highlighted in 1919 at the NEA's annual convention by Sarah H. Fahey (1919), who stated: "The shortage of trained teachers is not primarily due to the war. For some years past a distaste for teaching has been growing among professional workers." The general teacher crisis led President Woodrow Wilson to issue a nationwide appeal: "It is the patriotic duty of all those who can return temporarily to the ranks of teaching to offer their services and to notify the School Board Division of the Bureau of Education, Washington, D. C., of the offer."[3]

Handwringing about teacher quality is evident in the postwar period. The journal of the Maine State School Department complained that the supply from normal schools was not of the desired quality for high school teaching.[4] In September 1919, School and Society reported a NEA meeting in which the "appalling neglect of the preparation of school teachers despite the progress of the twentieth century" was discussed. One estimate suggested that 300,000 teachers were improperly trained; 50,000 teachers had no more than an eighth-grade education. This added fuel to the demands for higher salaries, minimum standards, and longer periods of professional training.

D. B. Waldo, president of the State Normal School, Kalamazoo, Michigan, in a presentation to the NEA in 1919, stated, "Public school service will never be generally recognized as a profession of unquestioned dignity and position until we require of teachers preparation equivalent to that now required in the professions of law and medicine." Waldo also called for a "decent thrift salary" as a minimum and "special salary rewards for exceptional teachers."[5] These proposals have been echoed in later reformists' rhetoric up to the present moment in history.

The shortage of qualified teachers was defined as an "educationally dangerous" problem. In September 1919, the NEA estimated the teacher shortage to be close to 40,000. The supply of elementary teachers was believed to be nearly depleted.[6] "Greatly reduced numbers in normal and teacher training classes—twenty percent in the last three years—combined with a general exodus from the profession, have induced a situation so critical that, unless some adequate counteracting influence is found and immediately applied, not only will standards continue downward, but many schools will be obliged to close altogether."[7] Katherine M. Cook, U.S. Bureau of Education, stated that "thousands of teachers are not only underpaid but utterly unqualified—measured by any reasonable standard."[8] A. O. Neal estimated that only about half of the high school teachers needed were available.[9] The Los Angeles Express talked about a "one-hundred-thousand teacher shortage in the United States."[10]

The Beginning of Efforts to Regulate
the Problem

Among the stopgap remedies suggested was one by Dean Balliet, of New York University, who proposed cutting the courses of teacher preparation by half to meet the emergency. [11] More urgent demands were made to raise teachers' salaries to attract more people to the profession. D. B. Waldo, of Michigan, exhorted fellow educationists to speak out on the need for better salaries and increased state and federal aid to expand teacher training institutions: "When proper standards are established, adequate teacher-training schools provided, opportunity for social service and satisfaction assured, and just salaries are paid, the supply of teachers will rapidly increase."[12]

But another form of remedy was beginning to take shape: the press for higher certification requirements vested at the state level. A resolution presented during the North Dakota legislative hearing of 1919 captures the drive toward centralization and the state's role: "The centralizing process must proceed not only from the small 'district' to the larger 'township' unit, but to the county plan of organization. . . . In a similar way there should be a unified state board of education and administration with a Commissioner of Education who would bear the same relation to the state board that the county superintendent does to the county board of education."[13] One of the primary concerns in these hearings, and the force behind centralization, was a lack of uniform teacher standards. In 1921, four states required high school graduation and some professional preparation as minimum requirements for their teachers; 14 states required four years of secondary school but made no stipulation concerning professional training; and the remaining states had no definite requirements. In 1926, at least one education course was required for one or more certificates in three-fourths of the states. Student teaching was required in an increasing number of states after 1920. [14]

As early as November 1920, the American School Board Journal, in an editorial, was able to say the teacher crisis was "exaggerated." Remedies had been found.

> In many instances, as a matter of expediency, the school
> authorities slackened on the standards of requirements
> for those entering the profession of teaching. Inex-
> perienced teachers were more readily admitted and the
> superannuated were continued in greater numbers. The
> professional standards as a whole have suffered some.
> But the conditions are far from a calamity and a crisis.
> The schools are running, and for all we know, are doing
> well. [15]

In summary, shortages, perceived inadequacies, and contentious rhetoric appear to be the major features of the literature during this period. Economic urgency is attached to the teacher problem by the notion that it would affect the "quality of the main product of the nation in the next generation."[16] From the chance remarks of educationists to the exhortation of a president, it is obvious that the teacher shortage was seen as a major national problem with economic consequences, and a growing consensus was emerging that regulation of supplies would be necessary to solve the problem.

Reversal: The First Great Teacher Surplus

The shortages of the war and postwar periods were suddenly and dramatically replaced with a surplus. The new surplus materialized seemingly out of nowhere. One of the first references to the new situation appeared in 1928: "For the first time within the memory of living men, the schools of the U. S. have an oversupply of trained teachers. Almost overnight, the supply has become acute."[17]

The problem of imbalance and the need for regulation still existed, this time in the form of controlling an excess. Earlier voices of complaint found themselves speechless. As they recovered, editorial tones of journals changed suddenly in favor of regulations that would restrict supplies of teachers. The remedies would be stricter admissions criteria to training colleges, compulsory certification, and higher standards.[18]

Frank G. Davis (1932) reported that employment in teaching increased by about 35 percent from 1920 to 1930, and that the graduation of new teachers rose 134 percent (21,012 to 49,227). Degree graduates increased by 745 percent (1,296 to 11,073). In the meantime, preschool and elementary school age populations were decreasing. Davis stated, "Just how the surplus may be controlled I am not going to say, except to suggest that we are in a situation where standards for admissions of people to teacher training institutions can and should be vigorously enforced. . . . Regardless of the other yardsticks we may apply to those craving entrance to the profession, I submit to you that a reasonably high intelligence quotient is the only foundation upon which can be built a structure of genuine professional success" (p. 377).

Most studies during this period reported general surpluses. A few reported an undersupply in some specific fields. Among those authors who admitted a surplus of teachers seeking positions, few if any, admitted that there was a surplus of "well-qualified" or "superior" teachers. Some claimed there remained a shortage of qualified teachers, but the literature, professional and popular, was loaded with reports of massive surpluses. From a survey of Texas superintendents, it was reported, "There is no question that there is an oversupply of teachers. I am swamped with applications. Colleges have mass production."[19] Earl W. Anderson's studies (1929, 1930) showed that 30 percent of English majors who were actively seeking positions in 1928 were unable to find them. In addition to English teachers, teachers in the social sciences, language, and mathematics were oversupplied (Cowley and Grant 1929; Moritz 1929; Wilde 1927). Industrial arts, commercial studies, music, and physical education were cited as fields not oversupplied.

Then, as now, the argument persisted that "competent" teachers were in short supply despite studies reporting general surpluses. Henry Klonower (1930), addressing the National Association of Placement and Personnel Officers, stated, "I do not believe that there was ever a time in the history of public education when there was such a great scarcity of properly qualified teachers as there is at the present time." At least a dozen studies concluded that there were shortages of good teachers.

The Charge to Certification

The entire phenomenon of teacher certification appeared to undergo changes in the first three decades of the century. The shift seen in the postwar period accelerated in the 1930s into a full-scale charge toward higher college requirements and a transfer of vested authority from local to state government. Minimum certification requirements became more stringent. Attempts were made to standardize certification and to centralize the process, as reflected in the shift from local to state control. In 1911, a total of 15 states issued all certificates, with 27 states sharing the authority with local officials. By 1921, 26 states issued certificates, and by 1926, 36 states assumed authority to issue certificates. Between 1898 and 1940, according to LaBue (1960), the number of states vested with authority for certification grew from 3 to 42.

The drive toward centralization of teacher licensure was solidified by the origin and spread of the practice of accepting normal school diplomas in lieu of written or oral exams for teacher certification, a practice begun in the previous century. Indeed, the general outline of teacher preparation and certification practices was in place by the turn of the century, with certification defined by preparation consisting of degrees and coursework. The war years had temporarily derailed the process, and the severe shortages that followed the war further weakened the drive. However, the surpluses of the 1930s set in mo-

FIGURE 1.1

The Supply of New Teachers, Public School Enrollments, and
Number of States Requiring the Bachelor's Degree as a Minimum
Certification in Elementary and Secondary Education

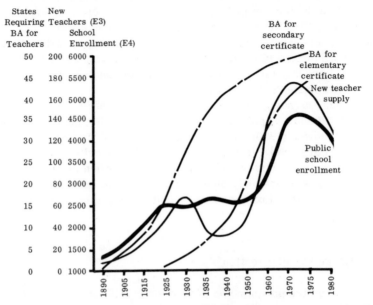

Sources: LaBue (1960); U.S. Office of Education, Bienniel Survey of Education; NEA, Teacher Supply and Demand in the Public
Schools, 1954-1980; NCES, Projections of Educational Statistics,
1971-1981; and Digest of Educational Statistics, 1972-1980.

tion a national campaign for uniform standards. The process would
be interrupted again by World War II, but, by 1955, 31 states would
require the bachelor's degree as a minimum standard for elementary
education (an increase from 14 in 1946). For high school teaching
certificates, 45 states required the bachelor's degree in 1955.

The growing pressure for increasing and centralizing standards
for teacher preparation and selection is evident throughout the literature of the period. The driving force appeared to be efforts to regulate the excessive supplies of teachers through the control of qualifications. The Elementary School Journal (1927) stated that the majority of states were raising standards to a minimum of two years of
professional preparation beyond high school, and that with these
higher standards the supply of teachers would be barely adequate.
Educationists were aware that standards affected supply, and supply
affected salaries (Wiley 1926). LaBue (1960) summarized the state

of teacher certification in 1931 as follows: More than half the states required teachers to be high school graduates as a minimum condition for licensure; several states required one year of professional work beyond high school; two-thirds of the states required one to four years of college preparation for high school teachers; 12 states required four years of college to be certified as a secondary teacher.

Figure 1.1 shows the period from 1920 to 1940 as one of maximum increases in secondary certification requirements defined as college graduation with professional preparation. (The elementary field tracks the secondary trend with a time delay of between two and three decades.) The overall picture is one of efforts, too little too late, to regulate through college requirements the supply-demand imbalances in teaching.

Other features of the teaching profession came under scrutiny during the 1930s surplus, and several prescriptions with a familiar ring appear in the literature. The "grave dangers" of tenure were noted by Clyde R. Miller (1930) and by the editor of the American School Board Journal (1930). The prescription was to revoke tenure of the "incompetent" teachers, thus making it possible to replace them with better teachers. The selections would be made by principals and a battery of selection tests. The American School Board Journal was in the forefront of advocates for higher standards of admission and higher graduation standards for teacher training institutions and it provided a ready forum for like-minded reformers of the day.

Early Reformers: The Prescriptive Wisdom

There were many presumed causes of the sudden misfortunes in education and a number of theories about how to correct the problem. Emily Guiwits (1927) believed that too many women prepared for teaching because they were unfamiliar with alternative career opportunities. She also felt that too many "floaters" were returning to teaching. A. V. Lockhart (1928) saw the cause as an overall influx of students to universities during the period and subsequent attraction to teaching due to salary increases won, presumably, during the previous period of shortages. Westward lure and laxity of certification were offered as possible causes of surpluses on the Pacific Coast. Herman Pfeifer (1930) thought consolidation of schools had reduced demand and caused the surplus problem. Pfeifer's second theory was that tenure had produced a decline in demand: As tenure increased, fewer teachers left teaching, thus creating fewer vacancies. Improper career guidance was cited as another possible cause of the surplus.

The reformers assumed that higher standards would have the effect of keeping teachers in the field for a longer period, since it would become increasingly difficult to reenter after an absence, but act as a barrier to keep the unfit out of the profession by making it difficult for them to qualify for positions.

In sum, the reformers reasoned that the problem was caused by a number of factors: great increases in college graduates, hard times and the need to earn a living, the ease of securing teaching certificates, and attractive salaries created during the previous shortage period. Those in the teaching ranks were unwilling to leave because of tenure, retirement benefits, and improved salaries. Rising standards, it was assumed, reduced turnover for the reason stated above: difficulty in reentry. Thus, raising standards would be a two-edged sword, reducing vacancies but restricting supplies.

The key to the dilemma appeared to be pretraining selection. The strategy would be to emulate the fields of law and medicine in limiting enrollments in teaching (McCain 1929).[20] The ways to implement this strategy included the more precise specification of entrance criteria (Courtis 1929); longer training periods and raised requirements (Warner 1930), including extension of training to five years beyond high school; and mergers of teacher training institutions in each state so that there would be fewer but better schools (Miller 1929). The new strategy would also include stricter codes for certification, more responsibility on the part of the state for placement, better placement (more effective matching of the particular qualifications of the applicant with positions), and careful selection and training of selection officers (Frazier 1929).

Rural education created another problem for the reformers. The prescriptions might work against improving the rural schools. J. Linwood Eisenberg (1926), in a paper presented at the Annual Schoolmen's Week Proceedings, University of Pennsylvania, worried about how to raise rural school salaries to avoid further problems of finding qualified teachers. H. M. Griffith, at the same conference, focused on problems of bringing urban teachers into unfamiliar rural areas if rural men and women failed to meet the higher standards set for certification. Clyde R. Miller believed higher salaries would prevent rural teachers from migrating in the first place, particularly men with families.

The Ebb and Flow of the First Great Teacher Surplus

By 1933, despite the persistent argument that qualified teachers were always scarce, no field of teaching was considered undersupplied. E. S. Evenden and coworkers (1935) estimated that during the peak of the surplus, 60 to 75 percent too many teachers were

being prepared annually, although there were regional differences in
the severity of the problem.

The latter part of 1935 begins to signal an improvement in the
supply-demand imbalance (a trend accurately forecast by the Educational Research Bulletin). The second half of the decade shows a
steady reduction in the reported oversupply. R. D. Moritz, of the
University of Nebraska, reported the demand for teachers in 1936
was the highest in ten years and estimated that the supply of available
teachers was dwindling.[21] Interestingly enough, Moritz, a frequent
spokesman on the supply of teachers, had argued in 1933 that the so-
called oversupply was really a case of underconsumption; with a million more pupils than in 1930, he pointed out there were 30,000 fewer
teachers employed in 1933. The NEA has for years offered a similar
argument, called the "demand for minimum quality." During the
peak years of oversupply in the 1970s this estimate portrayed a serious undersupply of teachers.

A survey of the literature of the late 1930s reveals a noticeably
lower level of preoccupation with the supply and demand problem,
perhaps a reflection of the receding problem. There is a slight note
of concern that demography might rekindle the problem. In 1939,
the Elementary School Journal warned that there would be a million
fewer elementary school enrollments in 1940 than there had been in
1930. The general outlook, however, was bullish. For instance,
R. N. Tarkington (1939) reported the demand for commercial teachers as exceeding the supply in 20 states. There were reports at this
time of some states relying on teachers from outside the state, for
example, Vermont, Wyoming, Pennsylvania, and California.

The argument lingered on that truly competent teachers were
in undersupply, especially at the elementary level. (It is noteworthy
to recall that most elementary teachers were not college graduates,
which may have been taken as the definition of "incompetent.") Nonetheless, there seemed to be general agreement among educationists
that elementary teachers were not in oversupply to the extent that
secondary teachers were, even during the peak years. The major
problem, however, was one of imbalance among the fields—too many
teachers in some fields, not enough in others.[22] Observers argued
that "needs" were there, but the selection of careers among teacher
candidates was misguided. The surplus was beginning to fade.

Lessons of the First Great Teacher Surplus

The educationists of the period were not without explanations
of the surplus once they recovered from just having explained the
shortages. The explanations of the surplus included a sudden return

of earlier teachers to the profession, more attractive salaries, a shrinkage on the demand side owing to the decreased birthrate, increased pupil-teacher ratio, consolidation of schools, and extended tenure contracts. The remedies of the problem would be directed at both supply and demand. The primary tool, among the remedies, would be teacher certification regulations. Other remedies, aimed at the demand side of the problem, included interstate cooperation, incentives for shortage areas, and a sabbatical or "stagger plan" whereby six months' to a year's leave with half pay would create employment for more substitute teachers (Hart 1934). Others recommended limiting enrollments to 25 per class. The elimination of permanent certification was seen as another way out of the dilemma.

There remained a sense that the problem had come and gone, without educationists really understanding why. No plans were made to limit growth, and a few observers worried that the problem could reappear: "The trends are in the right direction for the growth of a real profession in education. The tide of the vast oversupply of teachers has already started to ebb. . . . Let it flow, encourage it. But the sea wall of protection against a recurrence . . . will be constructed of longer and more defined preparation for teaching as a life work" (Miller 1935). The portent and the prescription seem to be confused. An already observed effect of the surplus, and one that in turn made the condition worse, had been longer tenure and less frequent turnover.

Among the most serious lessons of the surplus was the eroding effect on teachers' salaries. Richard R. Foster (1931) explained the effects as follows: "The hazard of unemployment is not limited to recruits without teaching experience. An oversupply of inexperienced teachers with a minimum of training makes the experienced, more capable teachers' position either precarious or economically unprofitable." In the "second great teacher surplus" of the 1970s this particular lesson would have to be relearned (see Chapter 4). Another lesson appeared in the literature of the period. George W. Frasier (1931) and H. T. Manuel (1932) were among those concluding that having a surplus pool of teachers would be an advantage because the choices of talent would be more ample. We will see in later chapters that this assumption, while intuitively reasonable, proved to be wrong.

Finally, one discovers the lesson that even if an oversupply exists, it is not necessarily a problem or real disadvantage to society because teachers' training is never "wasted." It is valuable in terms of personal enrichment even if the trainee were never subsequently employed as a teacher, or presumably in any occupation (Manuel 1932). This will be precisely one of the notions Koerner (1963) would attack as being preposterous. His argument would be that this is only true to the extent the student avoids education courses (see later sections of this chapter).

The Second Great Teacher Shortage

The stabilized condition of the late 1930s was followed by a new phase in the supply-demand cycle, again occurring rather suddenly. "The trend in teacher supply and demand was from a moderate oversupply in 1940 in most fields of teaching to a shortage in 1942 in almost every field . . ." (Anderson and Eliassen 1943). An early nonbeliever, Benjamin W. Frazier (1941) would argue that the shortage was imaginary: There was a reserve pool of women teachers who had left the profession after marriage and who could be induced to return, and the shortages in one community could be offset by surpluses in another. Nonetheless, the reformers began to lobby for remedies. Urgent demands were made for emergency certificates (Bowers 1941). Others urged that salaries had to be raised to attract new teachers, a now familiar idea.

During the late 1940s and early 1950s, the most comprehensive studies of teacher supply and demand were conducted by Ray C. Maul for the Commission on Teacher Education and Professional Standards of the National Education Association.[23] The period from 1950 to 1955 is marked by contrasts: a prolonged undersupply of elementary teachers and an oversupply in many secondary subjects (for example, men's physical education and social studies). Estimates suggest that only one-sixth as many qualified elementary teachers were available as were needed, whereas the total supply of secondary teachers exceeded demand by 100 percent. A reversal in secondary supply-demand imbalance would follow between 1955 and 1960. The postwar years also show a continuation of the trend toward college graduation as a requirement for teaching. In 1949, 23 states reported that slightly under half (49 percent) of their elementary teachers had completed 120 semester hours of college credits. In 1955, 32 states reported that just over two-thirds (68 percent) had completed 120 semester hours of college credits.

By the mid-1950s, the teacher shortage literature had begun to balloon with frenzied accounts of the elementary school crisis.[24] The number of live births in the United States was setting new records each year. A number of journals, periodicals, and national newspapers had begun to report teacher shortages as the "major problem of education." The tone was similar to that following World War I: desperation. Theories abounded as to the cause. Ray C. Maul provided much of the early analysis and explanation of the problem. Among factors cited were the following: birthrate, mobility of the population, industrial and military expansion, increase in high school population, sharp decline in the number of college graduates prepared to teach—particularly high school subjects, a "mopping-up" of the excess supply of previous years, and declining numbers of students enrolled in colleges.

One way to envision the size of the "second great teacher shortage" is from school census figures of the period. Total school enrollments for the mid-1960s were 30 percent more than those of the mid-1950s, which, in turn, were 50 percent more than in 1950. This enormous surge in school enrollments, accompanied by a relatively small college-age cohort, exhausted the capacity of the system to prepare and place teachers. The growing birthrate and continuing increase in school enrollments did not appear to show signs of abating. In 1963, the NEA Research Division reported that 20 percent of the U.S. population was in the school-age category and would reach 25 percent by 1970. The postwar baby boom was burying the schools and causing teacher shortages, nationwide, at all levels of the system. The equation was a simple one. If enrollments were rising a million per year, then teachers had to be added at a corresponding rate. President Dwight Eisenhower publicly urged a speedy solution to the problem in August 1960.

The remedies of this period focus on finding new sources of supplies. Included, eventually, were President Lyndon Johnson's Teacher Corps legislation, military draft deferments, NDEA loan forgiveness, a rush of MAT programs, "conversion" programs to retrain teachers for areas severely undersupplied, and a renewed clamor for higher salaries and other economic considerations (Lambert 1963). The New York Times, in September 1966, editorialized on the need "for a nationwide analysis of teacher training and teacher utilization so that all levels of education can be assured of a steady flow of high quality instructors." The NEA proposed in 1966 giving housewives short-term intensive courses in teaching and identified other schemes to prevent the problem from recurring "year after year, varying only in intensity." New York Governor Nelson Rockefeller, not to be outdone by others, announced the "teacher reserve plan," a notion similar to the army reserves. The scheme would be part of the New York State Education Department's long-range plans for coping with supply–demand problems.[25]

In the meantime, the drive toward enforcement of the bachelor's degree as the minimum standard for teaching reached its goal. In 1940, 11 states enforced the standard at the elementary level. By 1950, 21 states fell into line, and in 1964, 46 states were enforcing the standard at the elementary level. At the secondary level, in 1940, 40 states enforced the bachelor's degree as a minimum standard, and by 1960 every state complied.

The Bust

The frenzied effort to increase supplies of teachers continued right up to the point where the bubble burst—1971. By that time, the supplies of new graduates would exceed demand, which had begun to turn down, and supplies would exceed demand by various degrees of magnitude up to the early 1980s. For years, the profession would acknowledge only that the schools were no longer undersupplied. In later sections, we will show that the 1970s surplus exceeded 1 million qualified new teachers not employed by the schools. The estimate of reserve teachers (previously experienced) also attempting to find jobs that did not exist would add perhaps another million to the total numbers in the overall supply in excess of demand from 1970 to 1982 (Weaver 1978, 1979, 1981b).

Just as in 1928, when educators were caught unprepared for the first great teacher surplus, the voices of panic in the 1950s and 1960s were dumbfounded by the turn of events in the 1970s. The system had done the impossible. Supplies caught up with demand in a two-decade period of capacity building that staggers the imagination. For several years, the literature of the 1970s is barren of explanations of the new problem. One gets a sense of silent disbelief (Montgomery et al. 1973).

The great teacher boom of the 1960s was accompanied by some loud dissenters. The issue of teacher quality took on a new flavor with the publication of James D. Koerner's extraordinary book The Miseducation of American Teachers. Just as educationists had succeeded in making a century-long dream of college training for all teachers come true, Koerner rocked the foundations of the system, arguing that the college training of teachers was unworthy of the name "professional."

The Koerner Critique

James D. Koerner's (1963) study of teacher education represented a new genre of critical literature.[26] His primary target was lack of intellectual quality, by traditional academic standards, observed in educational faculties, courses, and students. Qualitative shortcomings seen by Koerner covered several things: puerile nature of course content in education; nonacademically prepared professors poorly teaching academic material; excessive specialized and redundant courses (recalling, historically, Flexner's attack on medical education—Is it necessary to teach a course to doctors on sewing simply because they someday may have to stitch a wound?); poor teaching performance by education professors; inadequate academic requirements for education majors; and general skepticism that methods courses, other than student teaching, had any value whatsoever. His general view was that these problems were even worse at the graduate level. 27

Koerner's critique, simply put, held that the preparation of teachers and other school personnel, as conducted by educationist faculties, did not meet the standard of professional training as compared with medicine and law. It seemed to Koerner that until the education profession behaved like those other professions, it received the status and compensation it deserved—or perhaps more than it deserved. And the reason the occupation of teaching is not a profession rests with the education schools and their faculties, lack of standards, and intellectually inferior students. Given this perspective, Koerner argued that teachers' salaries, based on the level of talent, quality of preparation, and workload, were about as high as they should have been (about $5,000). 28

The starting point in reforming teacher education, in Koerner's mind, was to police its standards. Thus, it would follow that teachers as real professionals would deserve and receive the same higher statuses and higher salaries other real professionals enjoy.

The most significant step toward improved quality would be a system of qualifying examinations for teachers. Examinations would screen out the academically inferior, provide school boards with a justifiable means of paying competent teachers more, and open up the teaching profession to noneducationists. To tighten up the standards of teaching practice, apart from academic skills and knowledge, extended apprenticeships were recommended. With regard to academic training, Koerner took the position that more would be better, and that history teachers, for example, ought to be historians first, that is, trained to think like historians. The same would be true in the other high school disciplines.

In summary, Koerner's reforms would enforce higher admissions standards, require teachers to major in academic subjects, greatly reduce the number of specialties represented in the schools of education (especially at the graduate level), and impose standards at the graduate level similar, if not identical, to those for arts and sciences graduates with a minimum of preparation in pedagogy.

Koerner's sentiments have been echoed for two decades, but in few respects have they been acted upon. Teacher testing is the one recent exception. But the other reforms of teacher education have not occurred; and the counterintuitive outcome in the decade just past was lower rather than higher admissions standards regarding academic quality in teacher education.

Koerner's book deserves to be taken seriously. We will summarize and then reexamine the basic premises underlying his critique of teacher education.

1. As conducted in Koerner's day, and, as many would claim today, the preparation of teachers does not justify the label "professional."

2. The professions are professions because they restrict entry by high college admissions standards; prepare practitioners through training in the competencies required of their members in advance of acceptance into the profession; police not only standards of admission to the preparation programs but also to the actual practice of the profession through qualifying examinations; and include in training a corpus of knowledge essential to professional practice. The education of teachers represents none of these.

3. Because the education "profession" lacks a legitimate basis to claim it is a profession, the status and compensation awarded teachers are justifiably below those of the true professions.

4. The essential point of reform is to change the manner in which teachers are trained (more academic subjects, less pedagogy) and impose higher entrance standards in the training programs and in the hiring of teachers.

Reexamining the Koerner Critique

Let us assume for the moment that Koerner's criticisms were, and are, absolutely correct. Does it then follow that his prescriptions would work?

Consider the salary argument. Koerner felt that salaries reflected all of his criticisms. Others assume the same thing, namely, it ought to surprise no one that those in the bottom half of the academic aptitude curve upon college graduation would also be found in an occupation in the bottom half of professional salaries.[29] Koerner said that to change that—to, in effect, accomplish what the NEA felt was a justifiable salary (75 percent higher by 1970 than the actual salary in 1963)—was absurd and would not occur unless and until his reforms in one way or another were implemented. But Koerner's crystal ball failed him. Average teacher salaries by 1970 exceeded Koerner's impossible scenario, even discounting the effects of inflation. How could this have happened, given that Koerner's most cherished recommendation, teacher examinations, was not rigorously enforced anywhere until the late 1970s, to say nothing of his proposed reforms of the teacher education curriculum?

The conventional wisdom among critics of teacher education for nearly a century has been that the cause of the quality problem is the manner in which teachers are educated and selected for subsequent employment. If the "miseducation" of teachers is the cause and inferior quality the effect, the solution must be reform of teacher education. If lack of academic emphasis is the primary illness in teacher education, then reform of teacher education that produces arts and sciences graduates who teach is the cure. Only then will teaching be able to attract high-quality candidates and prepare them in a manner that justifies the label "professional."

Although I do not take any particular exception to Koerner's thorough scrutiny of the problems of teacher education, or even his polemics, I do believe that he, and those who preceded and followed, have failed to understand how the system of education behaves dynamically as a labor market. Koerner's policy objective of higher salaries, justified only by higher-quality preparation and higher-quality candidates, is sound insofar as it went, but it failed to consider dynamic pressures that would change conditions as the ink was drying on his book. Demographic and market forces, well under way in the early 1960s, would drive up salaries and attract higher quality candidates in the years just ahead. Koerner failed to see this process as he went about examining teacher education and writing his prescriptions.

By 1970, teacher salaries had risen at a rate exceeding growth of salaries and wages paid other workers and professionals, and the academic quality of those attracted to teacher education was roughly equal to any randomly selected student entering four-year colleges. Yet none of the Koerner reforms was implemented. By 1980, salaries of teachers had fallen well below their 1970 levels, relative to average salaries, and the academic quality of students attracted to teaching was significantly below the 1970 level, as well as below the average college student in 1980.

It simply is not a believable proposition that these events had anything whatsoever to do with the Koerner proposals, because none of the things he proposed happened.[30] Indeed, the MAT programs Koerner favored entirely disappeared, once teacher shortages evaporated. Education requirements, on the whole, were not thrown out of undergraduate teacher preparation. Teacher examinations, on a broad scale in America, are of recent vintage, and still the majority of states do not require testing or enforce results of testing.

In the sections that follow, we will see that academic quality is a function of supply-demand dynamics in the total system of teacher education and employment. As Freeman (1976) has shown, the labor market for teachers behaves in many respects like all labor markets. When employers have ample choices, they will bid down wages, and when jobs exceed available labor, the wage offerings rise. This market dynamic affects institutional and individual behavior. Talent will eventually flow to opportunity. Institutions, which select and prepare people for the economy, will adjust by raising or lowering standards. These dynamics will operate independently of the Koerner prescriptions. It would make no difference (in this particular sense) whether or not teachers were arts and sciences graduates.

Regardless of which courses teachers take or how smart they are, when the market is flooded, the flow of talent will go elsewhere and salaries will go down. It appears that the arts and humanities fields are subject to exactly these pressures and respond precisely as education has: When markets dry up (as from 1973 to 1980), quality declines both in the applicant pool and in admissions. If teachers were graduated from sociology, political science, or the humanities fields in general, during the 1970s they would still be among those college populations showing the most rapidly falling academic test scores.

Koerner's identification of the problem may have been right, but his basic premises (regarding underlying causes) and therefore his prescriptions are wrong. We will see, for example, that broad-scale teacher testing, imposed as Koerner suggested, on the existing system will not, as Koerner thought (and many still do today), cure the quality problem. Indeed, teacher testing may make the problem worse, for reasons we take up later.

Redefining the Problem and Its Cause:
Talent, Opportunity, and Institutional
Response

The general premise that guides this work, and one which I believe is supported in the data and model testing to be presented in later chapters, may be summarized as follows: As market demand for new graduates in any given field declines, so too will the quantity and quality of potential students, admitted students, and graduated students. The explanation rests with individual pursuits of career opportunities coupled with institutional responses. Higher education institutions will adapt to decline by selecting the best from a shrinking pool of talent, but in so doing will sacrifice absolute for relative standards. Some fraction of those potential students who would ordinarily enter the field choose not to do so because of perceived declining opportunities. They enter other fields and leave behind those who choose to remain and those who have no choice. Student options are constrained by the minimum level of ability required for entry into various fields of study and into various colleges. For example, a student whose combined SAT score exceeds 1,200 will have more options than a student whose combined score falls below 800. Indeed, my analysis of the National Longitudinal Study data on transfers from field to field for the class of 1976 shows that the largest number of transfers between freshman and senior years occurred among students in the highest-ability fields. As we will see later, falling applications and declining test scores combined with an increase in the ratio of acceptances to applications will produce a net decrease in mean test scores among entering students relative to other fields not in decline and relative to the general test score decline. The principle holds true for both graduate and undergraduate programs and, insofar as I can determine, is passed through to college graduation, into the classroom, and out.

The underlying institutional motivation is aptly put by Myron L. Lieberman (1976): " . . . show me the professor or the college that would prefer no students to poorly qualified ones." James E. McClellan defined the observed condition as an inherent function of the educational system:

> This gives us the first clue to a functional definition of the [education] system: It is that part of the total educational enterprise of the society which automatically receives more students, or better students, or longer control over students, or some combination of the above, whenever a decision is made to upgrade educational requirements anywhere in the nation's economy.[31]

What McClellan did not say, but what follows logically, is that the education system is also defined as that part of the total enterprise that will receive fewer students, or poorer quality students, or shorter control over students, or some combination of those whenever a decision is made to downgrade educational requirements anywhere in the nation's economy, including the education system itself.

It seems obvious that the declining test scores of new teacher graduates since 1970 are, to a large extent, the legacy of the collapsing job market for educators. One hardly needs to be reminded that the public schools have generally been oversupplied with new teacher graduates and since the mid-1970s have been oversupplied in nearly every specialty.[32] Fewer than half of the total available teacher graduates were placed in teaching jobs in the last decade. Depending upon what assumptions one uses, the teacher surplus from 1969 to 1981 exceeded 1 million. The graduates who did not find teaching jobs showed higher rates of unemployment and underemployment than college graduates as a whole (Weaver 1978). As a result, dramatically fewer students are majoring in education, and among those who do, test scores are significantly lower.[33] The better students have moved to growth fields.

The education surplus and the decline in academic quality in the field are in part due to the collective adjustment of preparing institutions to the decline in demand for new teachers. Analysis of the data reveals a distinct mode of adaptation to the drying up of demand among institutions preparing teachers. The mode of adaptation was so widespread as to be considered nearly universal:

1. As applicants dwindled, a higher percentage was admitted.
2. Because the quality of the applicant pool was falling and admissions gates were being opened up, the net result was a significant drop in the basic academic skills of education majors.
3. The secondary result was to perpetuate the oversupply condition and thus make matters worse.

The forces driving this condition are just beginning to abate at lower grade levels, but will linger until middecade at upper levels of the system.[34] Enrollment will decline slightly at the elementary level until 1983-84, when a gradual upturn is expected, but declines will continue at the high school level into the next decade. At the same time, the production of new teachers, while falling annually since the early 1970s at a faster rate than demand, still remains ahead of demand and is projected by the National Center for Educational Statistics to remain in excess of demand until the mid-1980s. By the end of this decade, the likeliest scenario is a shortage of elementary, science, mathematics, and English teachers.[35]

For a few years, graduate enrollments made up for some of the losses of undergraduates. But the prospects for rising demand at the graduate level in the short term are dim for precisely the same reasons the demand arose in the first place: a severe oversupply of new teachers. As the oversupply of new graduates produced acute competition throughout the system for jobs, particularly but not exclusively in classroom positions, the demand swelled for more credentials in order for job seekers to maintain a relative advantage over others. It is reasonable to assume that as the oversupply condition recedes, as it has now begun to do, the competition will lessen and graduate demand created by defensive credentialing will decline. In addition, that group of young teachers who would ordinarily be replacing retiring teachers and those voluntarily leaving the profession, and for whom graduate school provides an economic and career incentive, are not being hired in large numbers and will not be for some years. School faculties are increasingly made up of less mobile, older tenured teachers for whom additional graduate work holds little career incentive except for picking up an additional certificate as a defensive measure against layoffs.

Strategies: Accounting for the Marketplace

In principle, it may be argued that inasmuch as the problem is caused by market dynamics, the solution must rest with strategies that account for market dynamics. It seems absolutely necessary to open up realistic new career options in education in order to attract to the field the kinds of talented persons who entered education in the late 1960s. I say this because the traditional teacher market now and in the future will not absorb all of the new teachers whom schools of education stand prepared to supply. This is not to say that there are not going to be periods of undersupply, but such periods simply produce the dynamics that cause a period of surplus to follow. The strategy for long-term correction of the quality problem must be to relieve the constraint on preparing institutions that has created an almost total dependence on the public schools and an incredibly involuted system of education. That the mission of schools of education needs to be redefined is an objective apart from the declining quality issue. The need for a redefined mission is simply magnified by the finding that schools of education are forced to shrink whenever there is a decrease in employment in the public schools and to rapidly over-expand when employment rises. The redefined mission of teacher preparation would recognize the learning needs in business, industry, government, medicine and mental health, and the military. The strategy suggested is not to abandon the preparation of personnel for the public schools but to balance the tendency to focus on that limited sphere of educational activities as the whole of education.

To illustrate briefly the significance of this proposal, consider that while the demand for schoolteachers has declined, and faculties of education have withered, the overall demand for learning in this society has vastly expanded. Without question, the demand for human resource educators is growing and will continue to grow.[36] The only question is whether schools of education are going to take notice of or in any way contribute to that growth.

From a policy perspective, it seems abundantly clear that any major movement toward a redefined mission for schools of education will be restricted by their common organizational motif and political constraints.[37] Most schools of education I am familiar with are organized around the needs, structure, and politics of controlling entrants to the public schools—needs, structure, and a politics that are poorly suited to a broader mission. The faculty and support systems needed to broaden the mission will have to come from combining the skills of faculty from several academic and professional departments throughout a college or university (a condition favored by Koerner). In addition, educational preparation programs will need to deliver the competencies training professionals employ in their work (generic, functional specializations, such as needs assessment, problem solving, evaluation, and instructional planning). To do this, schools of education will be forced to define a corpus of knowledge and skills required in professional practice.[38]

Examining the Market Strategy:
The Public Interest

Why would the strategy outlined in the previous section be of any interest to anyone other than, perhaps, education professors struggling to find students? How does this proposal lead to improvements in teacher quality, and, therefore, why would the profession, polity, or public have the slightest interest? The model-validated explanation (Chapter 4) and detailed public policy justification (Chapter 6) will come later, but here the premises of the argument are outlined.

The history of the teacher quality problem is cyclical. Periods of boom are followed by periods of bust. During these cycles, outcries for reform have been followed by actions that have attempted to limit entrance to teaching through qualification measures and handwringing about the lack of intellectual substance in education courses. By attempting to cure the problems of quality through the regulation of entry to the profession on grounds of qualifications, the short-term problem is partially solved, but the solution itself is the cause of a longer-term worsening of the problem. The training capacity expands to meet the increased qualification standards, which simply then means larger retractions are required in the next down cycle. For example, the last decade exceeded by several orders of magnitude the worst previous historical case of teacher surpluses (the 1930s). The ten-year period of the 1970s produced more than a million unwanted new teacher graduates as the preparing institutions, bloated by new faculties in all manner of specializations and programs owing to state requirements for various certificates, federal intrusion into public education, and numerous experimental programs, refused to disappear gracefully and steal away into the night. Unfortunately, the capacity also tended to expand, and then contract, without much attention to intellectual content or a clear definition of a corpus of knowledge required of teachers.

Given that the capacity to meet new requirements tends to grow mindlessly until new requirements are met and then tries to keep growing, even if demand does not, and given that demand is, initially, a primary function of demography, the system at present is self-adjusting only at very great expense. That expense is a severe downgrading of academic quality for long periods while capacity readjusts to demand. Applying the Koerner prescription (more arts and sciences, less pedagogy) only transfers the training capacity to other members of the academic institutions, namely, the arts and sciences faculties. These faculties respond in the exact same manner to cycles of demand. The problem is not solved by asking a humanities professor to relinquish his or her affinity for students any more than it is by so asking an education professor. The presumption that arts and sciences professors are somehow more noble than education professors is unwarranted (as the evidence will show later).

Teacher testing, the ultimate weapon against intellectual inferiority, will not have the expected effect of curing market problems because it simply inflates the market with teachers who cannot find jobs owing to the test score barrier, thereby worsening the supply-demand condition and driving down the size and quality of school of education applicant pools. The net result is even lower-quality teacher candidates, who of course cannot be hired. Unless coupled with admissions tests, which are equally restrictive, teacher testing will not solve the teacher quality problem. A system of restrictive admissions, in the face of declining students, ignores a vital premise of human motivation: self-preservation. [39]

A redefinition of the competencies and skills education majors can market is a long-term, feasible solution to the teacher quality problem because the problem stems from chronic market disequilibrium, which is caused by a system that confines its product to a singular occupational preparation and a singular institution (public school employment). By redefining the marketable skills and competencies graduates possess, the individual is empowered with more choices in the overall college market for people with educational talents. The overall market for educational talent greatly exceeds the singular market of public school teaching. Moreover, as a second-order benefit, the body of knowledge and specification of competencies required for successful practice outside of the public schools would have to transcend the present muddled state of the art called teacher training.

The Conditions for Higher Standards

Colleges of education will attempt to fill seats from the available pool of applicants under any and all circumstances. When that pool is shrinking in size and talent, institutional and individual self-interest dictate declining standards of admission, falling academic quality of graduates, and inferior choices for schools and communities seeking new teachers—a circumstance no one can argue is in the interest of the profession, public, or polity. Given choices of a training program that expands options for graduates, other than in public school teaching, the size and quality of the school of education applicant pool would reflect market conditions that include but are not restricted to public school employment.

The inexorable response of all academic institutions to fill seats at the expense of quality, rather than cease to exist, is not ignored, as in the case of raising admissions standards in the face of declining enrollments—a desirable but virtually impossible policy to sell to those whose livelihoods depend on students. Nor is the counterintuitive effect of graduating students who then discover after the fact they are unemployable because they fail to pass teacher examination tests—a matter of less direct self-interest to academic institutions, and therefore a matter that provides little faculty motivation to deal with the quality problem.

The expanded skills strategy will give leverage to the applicant pool constraint by making schools of education more attractive to those who wish to be teachers but do not wish to teach in public schools; therefore, admissions decisions are not driven solely by the number and talent of those at any given time who do wish to enter public school teaching. Consider the following hypothetical situation: Midwestern University has 100 seats to fill in its school of education. Under conditions in which only 100 applicants are interested in public schoolteaching careers, Midwestern may be forced to accept every applicant. But if an additional 50 applicants wish to prepare for a career in corporate training, the pool is enlarged to 150, which would allow fewer but better teacher candidates to be selected, while still filling desired capacity.

There is no guarantee, of course, that a college would not simply accept all 150 applicants, thereby defeating the strategy and sacrificing rather than conserving talent. However, I place some faith in the notion that colleges will act to conserve talent under conditions that permit standards to be upheld. If that faith were completely misplaced, then it would be the case that colleges have acted at all times under any conditions to admit as many students as possible regardless of talent. I do not find that to be the case. In Chapter 2, we will see that the acceptance fraction varies inversely with flows of students and talent. When students and talent are in ample supply, standards rise and the acceptance fraction declines. Given the opposite condition, standards fall and the acceptance fraction rises.

Creating the conditions under which colleges and universities can impose higher standards for selecting teacher candidates is enhanced by the market strategy proposed, and for the following reasons it is of immediate, direct interest to the profession, public, and polity:

• The net result would be fewer but more talented graduates entering the teacher job market—a result of almost instant benefit to those competing for jobs—and thus the professional interest is served.
• The public interest would be served by providing teachers of better quality, albeit at a higher price: as supply shrinks in quantity, but improves in quality, the wage bill will rise. But for any of the reform proposals heretofore addressed, this is an inevitable cost of improving quality.

•The polity's interest in policing, regulating, and conserving a
system of education that must compete for public resources
would be served because its underlying claim to legitimacy,
a competent teacher force, seriously eroded by the teacher
quality issue, becomes a defensible claim.[40]

Finally, the requirement for producing graduates that employers
other than public schools will hire is dependent upon a redefinition of
professional preparation (that is, training consisting of a corpus of
knowledge and skills essential to the practice setting). Such a requirement is not merely coincidental to success. It is a necessary condition.
Schools of education may claim that graduates are prepared to be
trainers, but the hard realities of business training requirements will
determine the selection of those actually prepared. The criterion
will have to change from qualification based on credits and courses
to specific skills and competencies. Such a change will undoubtedly
please even such critics as Koerner, who have long argued that the
definitions of what is a teacher and what constitutes professional
preparation are well-guarded secrets.

Conclusion

We are reminded that redefining the basis of professional preparation in education has until now eluded reformers. Any real prospects of change will certainly exceed the hope of all but eternal op-
timists. Despite numerous outrages and reform proposals over the
years, the involuted nature of the system has prevented any real
change. It is precisely the involuted nature of the system that the
market strategy attacks. There is an Adam Smith ring to this strategy,
which I readily concede. If many schools of education today want to
stay in business, their business will have to include markets other
than public schools. That choice will necessarily entail a much more
precise definition of professional training.
    In brief, I conclude that while the commonsense teacher reform
proposals contain many elements of cogent thought, they do not address the root cause of the problem, which is neither the occupational
structure of teaching itself nor the education of teachers. Policies
aimed at these targets, as the root causes, will not, as a century of
tinkering shows, prevent the problem from occurring. The problem of
talent is market driven. It seems indisputable that demand for talent
in public schoolteaching is primarily a function of demography. Political and economic responses follow, but they are not determinants
(unless one considers such features of the system as average class
size to be a political or economic feature rather than a matter of

pedagogy). Nonetheless, demand is less under the control of preparing institutions than is supply. I do not believe that the transfer of teacher supply to other units of the academic institution will produce an ennobling cure for the problem because all academics respond in the same way to market forces. I place equally little faith in raising certification requirements or in teacher testing.

It would be extremely naive to think that the market strategy proposed here will cure the problem. Whatever the nature of the academic product (engineers, chemists, MBAs, trainers, or teachers), the "cobweb" theory of supply-demand dynamics will more or less apply.[41] But the strategy at least would create leverage where none now exists, and as such it ought to dampen the extreme conditions witnessed in the past decade.

SUMMARY AND PURPOSE OF THE BOOK

The purpose of this book is to draw together the essential research on teacher quality and to examine it in terms of implications for new policy initiatives. The underlying thesis of this book is a presumption that the following conditions, observed in detail throughout the 1970s, but reported in earlier periods, are interrelated: cyclical fluctuations in the job market in teaching; a shift in student preferences away from or toward the field of education; a sharp readjustment in test scores of college-bound students and enrolled freshmen who intend to study in education and a pass-through of scores to graduating seniors and to those who find, and subsequently stay in, or leave, teaching positions; and a downgrading of status and compensation when demand falls and an upgrading when demand rises. It is these factors, and not the regulation of teacher requirements, that lie at the heart of the teacher quality problem. Any lasting solution to the problem will have to open up the marketability of teachers.

Research on this subject has even greater significance when one considers that birthrate declines (mid-1960s to mid-1970s) will exert downward pressure on college enrollment in general for at least another decade. The current academic responses to the teacher job market collapse of the 1970s may be more than a portent of coming adaptations in higher education; they may have locked many academic institutions into an irreversible course, one that sacrifices absolute standards but offers little in the way of creative policy alternatives. If my findings regarding the last decade are any indication, most, if not all, academic programs undergoing market stress have responded by lowering academic standards to attract more students—and by doing little else. In education, the result has been few if any realistic new career options for students, a significant net decline in the academic quality of students entering the field, and very little new thought about alternative policies. The situation raises some crucial questions about quality, choice, and institutional survival. It raises serious questions about the future of not only the teaching profession but other professions as well.

Chapter 2 presents data on the talent pool from which schools of education are selecting candidates and carries the analysis through to graduation and first entry into teaching. Chapter 3 presents data on the scholastic aptitude and other characteristics of the population entering and leaving classroom teaching. Taken together, Chapters 2 and 3 provide the data base for the theoretical model presented in Chapter 4. Chapter 5 presents the procedures and results of testing the model, together with conclusions from the analysis for policy initiatives. Chapter 6 presents a more detailed case for reform of education schools based on the market strategy.

NOTES

1. Procedures for teacher certification and licensure are widely evident in the nineteenth century. In the New England area, teachers have been required to have a license (defined as "allowed") since colonial days. Teachers were licensed on the basis of oral examinations, less frequently on the basis of written examinations, by public officials or school trustees. There is evidence of criticism and low quality of teachers. Licensure in the United States seems to have appeared as a government function in the early 1800s. County examining officers are found in Ohio in 1825; and in New York in 1841 and Vermont in 1845 superintendents were examining candidates for teaching certificates (Kinney 1964). By 1860 the procedure was widespread. Between 1860 and 1900, certification was shared by county or local school officials and state authorities. In the latter half of the 19th century, states began waiving examinations for normal school graduates. In 1849, New York State became the first state to prescribe by law that a diploma from Albany State Normal School would be evidence of qualification for teaching (LaBue 1960). By 1900 at least half of the states waived examinations, and 41 states issued certificates to normal school graduates. For a history of the normal school movement, see Charles A. Harper 1939.

2. It is interesting to note the similarity between L. D. Coffman's arguments and those heard today regarding mathematics and science teacher shortages—the argument now being that opportunities in high-technology firms are drawing off the talented who would otherwise be available for teaching (Useem 1981, 1982; Gaynor and Clauset 1983).

3. "To Relieve the Teacher Shortage," American School Board Journal 57 (December 1918): 47.

4. "The Teacher Shortage in the High Schools," American School Board Journal 57 (December 1918): 49.

5. "Societies and Meetings, the National Education Association, How to Secure an Adequate Supply of Trained Teachers for the Public Schools of the United States," School and Society 10 (September 1919): 299-300.

6. "Teacher Crisis," American School Board Journal 60 (January 1920): 41-42.

7. Ibid.

8. Katherine M. Cook, "Certification by Examination—The Open Door to the Teaching Profession," American School Board Journal 61 (July 1920): 29.

9. A. O. Neal, "The Shortage of High School Teachers," American School Board Journal 61 (August 1920): 72.

10. "The Salary Situation with Remedies," American School Board Journal 61 (October 1920): 40.

11. "Quotations—The Shortage of Teachers," School and Society 8 (July 1918): 52-54.

12. "Societies and Meetings," School and Society.

13. "For Busy Superintendents," American School Board Journal 57 (1918): 58.

14. "The Preparation of Teachers," Review of Educational Research 1 (April 1931): 79. Original source: Katherine M. Cook, State Laws and Regulations Governing Teachers' Certificates, U. S. Department of the Interior, Bureau of Education, Bulletin, 1927, no. 19 (Washington, D. C., 1928).

15. "Status of the Teacher Shortage," American School Board Journal 61 (November 1920): 53. Reprinted with permission from the American School Board Journal, November. Copyright 1920, the National School Boards Association. All rights reserved.

16. "Teacher Crisis," American School Board Journal.

17. "The Demand and Supply of Teachers," Educational Research Bulletin 7 (October 1928): 282.

18. "Combating the Problem of Too Many Teachers," Nation's Schools 5 (January 1930): 31-36.

19. Ibid.

20. This prescription is precisely the answer to the problem proposed 34 years later by James D. Koerner (1963). See the discussion of the Koerner critique later in this chapter.

21. R. D. Moritz, "Report of the Department of Education Service of the University of Nebraska, 1934-35," Bulletin of the University of Nebraska Series, October 30, 1935.

22. The secondary surplus was greatest in such areas as English, French, and the social sciences, while little or no "flooding" occurred

in commerce, rural education, industrial arts, and home economics. See, for example, "Commerce Teachers Needed," University of the State of New York, Bulletin to the Schools, December 15, 1931–January 1, 1932, p. 104.

23. See Maul 1950a, 1950b, 1950c, 1950d, 1951.

24. The New York Times alone carried 26 major stories between 1960 and 1966. Phi Delta Kappan replaces the American School Board Journal as the primary chronicler of bad news on the shortage. See, for example, "Teacher Shortage: Even More Severe?" Phi Delta Kappan 48 (October 1966): 95–96. For a review of the early 1950s conditions, see "Teacher Certification, Supply and Demand," Review of Educational Research 35 (June 1955): 196. For early 1950s NEA reports, see Ray C. Maul 1950a, 1950b, 1950c, 1950d, 1952, 1954. For later reports, see Maul 1960a, 1960b, 1960c, 1961; NEA 1960a, 1960b, 1961, 1962a, 1962b, 1962c, 1963a, 1963b, 1966a, 1966b, 1966c.

25. "Governor Rockefeller's Plan," New York Times, September 25, 1966, p. 1.

26. There is a sizable post–World War II literature on reforming teacher education, including Arthur Bestor's (1955) ideas, which preceded Koerner (1963) but are in concept very similar, that is, liberal arts as the curriculum for teacher education. James Bryant Conant (1963) wrote in his usual fashion about how many professors were required in order to have an elementary education department in colleges, how many credits constitute a program, and so on. Alvin Eurich (1969) called for the humanities to provide the new frontier of teacher education reform. N. L. Gage (1972) contributed to the cause his stock of ideas on learning theory and research on the teaching process as a science. More recently, Myles L. Friedman et al. (1980) have tried to prescribe a teacher education model based on competencies the practicing teacher needs to use. William E. Gardner and John Palmer (1982) place the bookend to Bestor's and Koerner's early prescriptions of more liberal arts, apprenticeships, and competency testing. Many of the themes of this literature can be found in the historical perspective reviewed earlier in this chapter.

27. Koerner (1963) saved some of his most acerbic observations for graduate schools of education: "Because the greatest deficiencies of all in education are found at the graduate level, it is here that the greatest changes are needed. . . . Graduate Education is desperately in need of a thoroughgoing overhaul from top to bottom but is not going to get it" (p. 277). Among the deficiencies Koerner cites are "wretched" dissertations (if done at all for the Ed. D.), the elimination of language requirements ("including English . . ."), "trivial specializations," and antiintellectualism. The growth of trivial specializations, Koerner felt, "reflects the history of slovenly

administration that has characterized graduate education, the manufactured professionalism that has obsessed educationists for many years, and the disgraceful abdication of responsibility by the academic faculty. However the responsibility is to be parceled out for the unhappy condition of so much of graduate education, the results of the condition are clear enough: the production of, as Flexner put it, "hordes of professors and instructors [and, he might have added, school administrators] possessing meagre intellectual backgrounds whose interests centre in technique and administration viewed in a narrow <u>ad hoc</u> fashion" (p. 164). Koerner's sentiments, and his dismal forecast of no change, seem to be prophetically echoed in a recent lament about the state of graduate schools of education. Writing in <u>Communication</u>, Eva C. Galambos states: "The proliferation of programs, combined now with declining enrollments in graduate education programs, provides a built-in incentive to make the offerings as entertaining and easy as possible to fill them up. This is unlikely to promote quality" (1983).

28. Salary, according to Koerner (1963), is the product of professional standing, which education does not have. Therefore, salaries are as high (or higher) than they should be. "When one looks closely at the education field, at the caliber of the faculty and students and training programs, and when one looks at the conditions under which public school teachers actually teach—with the myriad of incredibly trivial and demeaning tasks that administrators create and inflict upon their staff, anything from punching time clocks to collecting the milk money to taking tickets at school football games—it becomes rather obvious that whatever else teaching is, it is not yet a profession" (p. 244). To compare salaries of teachers with those of medicine and engineering is hardly realistic: "These fields are able to attract people from the upper academic ranks, who should not, in fairness to either group, be compared with people from the lower" (p. 245). Koerner was, however, very much in favor of merit pay, and much higher pay for excellent teachers, that is, those in the upper academic level, whose performance equaled that talent expectation. The evidence would be the pupils the teacher produces—another anathema to the educational establishment.

29. The data presented in Chapter 2 will show that among 1976 college graduates, those who majored in education had a combined average on the NLS test score battery of around the 40th percentile, and were near the bottom, collectively, when compared with other college majors.

30. The exception, of course, is teacher examinations. But the rise in salaries and academic quality of candidates between 1963 and 1970 occurred long before the recent rush of states toward teacher testing.

31. James E. McClellan, Toward an Effective Critique of American Education (Philadelphia: J. B. Lippincott, 1968).

32. The exceptions being physics, chemistry, and advanced mathematics at the high school level.

33. See Chapter 2.

34. The series II census estimates, used widely to project enrollments, are probably overly optimistic. The most recent data available on live births (National Center for Health Statistics) suggests that the series II-R assumptions may be closer to reality. If that proves to be the case, births will be more widely spaced, and the net effect will be a delay in reaching the upturn in enrollments expected by 1983. Our estimate, provided later, will show rising demand at the elementary level and falling demand at the high school level through 1990. There will, of course, be regional differences.

35. See Chapter 4.

36. Ironically, one of the reasons for my optimism about growth in demand for human resource educators is the failure of the public schools to teach properly basic skills to an embarrassingly large percentage of American youth prior to their entry into the work force or military. Another reason for optimism is the inevitable fact of a labor force growing older and a contraction of the flow of replacements beginning in the mid-1980s. Given these conditions, the need for job-related training and retraining is likely to increase. It also seems apparent that a declining reserve pool of youth will produce in the 1980s and 1990s an even stronger incentive than at present for mature women to enter the work force. The female sector of the work force is now predominantly drawn from among the formally educated. The learning needs of relatively uneducated women being drawn into the labor force for the first time, and the needs of their employers, will increase in the coming decade. The further integration of handicapped and disadvantaged minorities into the labor force will constitute major education problems to be resolved in the 1980s and 1990s.

37. The vested interest of schools of education in the preparation of teachers can be traced back to the nineteenth century, when normal school diplomas began to be accepted in lieu of teacher examinations for licensure (the first case on record being Albany Normal School in New York in 1849). Certified means qualified, and certified is the result of taking courses in education programs, as defined by the colleges, prescribed by law, and conducted by education faculty members who themselves are products of the same procedures. The political involution created by this system is tantamount to a closed plumbing system. Preparing graduates for markets other than public schools would seriously threaten this system, unless those markets can be so captured. To the extent they cannot be, paper credentials will not suffice. It is relatively easy to see why education

faculties are not enthusiastic about the change except as a last act of desperation. Koerner (1963) defines the phenomenon as the "centripetal nature of authority" in education. "For every move toward greater institutional autonomy, there is often an opposing one toward ever greater centralization of power . . ." (p. 19). Given this condition, it should surprise no one that the century-long literature on teacher quality is full of tinkering with the certification process (courses and state-defined standards), but almost totally devoid of any strategy that goes beyond institutional controls. The singular focus is on teachers and preparing teachers. The literature simply ignores the fact that an enormous amount of formal learning takes place beyond the education system. Perhaps that is fortunate. It leads, however, to a narrow view of the problem and omits from consideration any solution that would open up the system. Ironically, Koerner's analysis leads him exactly to that end—curing the quality problem by regulating the education system. Such a perspective, on scholarly grounds, must be judged myopic. It fails to consider that formal education is a dynamic part of a larger system of educational development in society and, in turn, is connected and integral to the total social, political, and economic life of the nation.

38. The lack of such a corpus of knowledge was presumably the reason for abolishing the Yale University Department of Education in 1958, according to Koerner. Koerner's explanation for the nonstatus of educational theory and knowledge is that " . . . like business and administration, social work, and perhaps other fields [education], reversed the procedure and came into being not because educationists had already developed a body of knowledge and research techniques, but simply because enough people thought education ought to be a separate field" (1963, p. 27). Koerner's attack, however, provides no solution except to return education to its justified place in non-academic training schools, designated as such, and limited to the practical art of pedagogy. While quaint, even Koerner acknowledges little faith that this will ever happen. A review of the American Association of Colleges for Teacher Education's (AACTE) published "guaranteed" knowledge and skills of teacher graduates would make James Koerner shudder. The guarantees seem even more nebulous and ill-formulated than the quotes from educationists' writings in Koerner's book. If graduates could be guaranteed the knowledge and skills reported in Education Times (March 14, 1983), they would have protective warranties against knowing anything that can be defined. One example should suffice: "Teacher candidates should understand laws, customs, traditions and values in relation to a variety of cultures, including the pluralistic culture of the United States and the rest of the world; the derivation of social ethics and morality; and the derivation of individual values and beliefs."

39. A quote from Education Daily (March 2, 1983) illustrates the point: "The nation's teacher educators last week moved to reassert their position that educators [meaning education professors], and not state officials, should set standards for training and evaluating classroom teachers" (p. 5). This was voiced in opposition to state-mandated teacher tests. The AACTE resolution called for all states to delegate the authority to set standards for teacher education, teacher qualification, and presumably teacher testing to the profession.

40. We will take up the legitimacy issue in Chapter 2. It should be noted that this issue is extraordinarily important. The competition for public resources rests on an assumption that those who are responsible for literacy of the young must be believed, at least, to be themselves literate. It is fundamental to the entire justification of a compulsory and tax-supported system of free schools. There is little wonder that the profession and polity are extremely sensitive to any hint that teachers are not competent in the subjects they teach or are lacking in basic academic skills. Such an admission would seriously erode the public's belief in the efficacy of schooling, and therefore threaten the system's existence.

41. See Richard B. Freeman 1971. Freeman (1971) defines the cobweb theory as applied to the academic labor market as "The fraction of students choosing these fields [narrow curriculum, lengthy training and moderate-to-long-term demand] fluctuates cyclically: a large graduating class depresses salaries and causes a relative decline in the number of entrants; when a small class graduates, salaries are increased, causing a jump in enrollments, and so on" (p. xxiii). Freeman (1971) argues that individual career decisions are the heart of the explanation and that such choices are market driven. Individual choices determine supply: "Individual career choices, not the available places in universities, determines the supply of students to diverse specialties" (p. xxi). Lags in supply, which respond to choices and salaries or job demand, are "due primarily to the length of educational programs" (p. xxiii). Students in the "pipeline" also respond and more will pursue careers in growth fields.

2

The Initial Talent Pool
for Teaching

In this and the next chapter we will examine evidence that supports the view that the qualities and characteristics of those in any professional occupation, but most notably, teaching, are determined by processes not amenable to corrections proposed in the prescriptive literature on teacher reform. The talent pool attracted to occupational preparation is a function of market conditions. Policies and processes that guide selection from the initial talent pool are limited by the composition of talents and characteristics already in that initial pool. Moreover, selection policies and processes are affected directly by availability of applicants regardless of talent and other characteristics. When available applicants decline relative to capacity, selection standards will be adjusted. Policies and processes may guide institutional decisions regarding initial selection, requirements for graduation and certification, and entrance and eventual leaving of the profession. But these policies and processes interact dynamically in response to individual choices of careers, the desire of individuals to maximize opportunities under various market conditions, and the desire of institutions to perpetuate themselves.

RECENT HISTORY

Has the talent pool for teacher education changed? More precisely, are we now selecting students from a population with generally lower scholastic aptitude than was the case ten years ago? First, what is the evidence? In this chapter national test score data are examined from the Educational Testing Service, the College Entrance Examination Board, the American College Testing Program, and the National Longitudinal Study.[1] Sources include the following:

- SAT verbal and mathematics scores (means and standard deviations) for college-bound high school seniors by intended field of study (Table 2.1).[2] Keep in mind that not all SAT takers go to college, although the vast majority do. Among those who are admitted and registered, intentions to major in a particular field change—with some predictability—over four years. These data are reported annually by the College Entrance Examination Board for the years 1972-80 and by various reports of the Wirtz Commission (On Further Examination).
- ACT English and mathematics scores (means and standard deviations) for college-bound seniors by selected fields of study, 1970-75 (Table 2.2. These data were provided by special processing and are not generally available. The same caution as with SAT scores applies here: Not all ACT test takers go to college, and student intentions to major in particular fields change.
- ACT English and mathematics scores (means and standard deviations) for enrolled college freshmen by selected field of study (identified through the ACT descriptive questionnaire) for 1975-76 and 1977-78 (Tables 2.3 and 2.4).
- ACT and SAT English and mathematics scores (means and standard deviations) of graduating college seniors in 1976 by general field of study (Tables 2.5 and 2.6). These data were obtained from the National Longitudinal Study (NLS), U.S. Department of Education, for the senior class of 1976.[3]
- SAT verbal and mathematics scores (means and standard deviations) of 1976 college graduates majoring in teacher education who did or did not obtain teaching jobs in the first NLS follow-up (1976-77) (Table 2.7).
- NLS test battery scores (vocabulary, mathematics, reading comprehension, and test composite means and standard deviations) for graduating college seniors by field of study, 1976 (Tables 2.8, 2.9, 2.10, and 2.11).
- GRE (Graduate Record Examination) quantitative and verbal scores (means and standard deviations) by selected fields of study for test takers, 1970-75.
- NTE (National Teacher Examination) test scores (means and standard deviations) for test takers, 1970-75 (Table 2.12). Data were provided by the Educational Testing Service.

Findings: National Data Sources

The earliest available ACT scores by field of study for college-bound high school seniors (1969/70) suggest that those students selecting elementary teaching majors fall roughly around the population mean in English and slightly below in mathematics. By 1976, scores for those intending to major in elementary education fall below the population mean on both English and mathematics. Mathematics scores

fall faster than English scores (about 18 percent from 1969 to 1975).
The findings for enrolled freshmen (1970-75) show roughly the same
pattern. Potential elementary education majors are closer to the
population mean in 1970 and drop slightly in mathematics by 1978.
Secondary majors fall roughly around the population mean, or slightly
above, in English and remain there from 1970 to 1975. Mathematics
scores also tend to cluster around the mean but drop slightly below
in 1975.

The SAT scores for college-bound seniors by intended field of
study are not available until 1972/73. At that time, those intending
to major in all education fields combined fall below the population
mean on average for both verbal and mathematics scores. Relative
positions show little change in verbal scores by 1980, but some continued erosion of position in mathematics is observable.

Has there been a change in SAT scores in the initial applicant
pool, that is, graduating high school seniors who intend to select education as a college major? The answer is both yes and no. Test
scores of prospective teachers have definitely been declining. Consider where the average, 1980 college-bound seniors selecting education as a major would rank on the SAT among all college-bound seniors
if they had been entering college in 1972. They would have ranked just
above the bottom quartile in both verbal and mathematics scores. But
because SAT scores of all College Board-tested students have been declining, on average, the relative rank of those selecting education has
not changed dramatically. Their verbal scores (SATV) place them on
average at about the 37th percentile in 1972 and in 1980. Their mathematics scores (SATM) place them on average at about the 37th percentile in 1972 and at about the 34th percentile in 1980. These changes in
relative position are slight and possibly due to sample fluctuations.
But in relation to other fields, consider that SATV and SATM scores of
prospective business people (that is, college-bound high school seniors)
have fallen 10 and 17 points respectively, whereas potential teachers'
scores have fallen 29 and 31 points respectively. In 1972, education
SATV scores were higher than business; in 1980, they were lower.
Demand in the two fields has changed dramatically.

Among graduating college seniors in the National Longitudinal
Study sample, class of 1976, education majors ranked fourteenth out
of 16 fields (including "other" and "undecided") on SAT verbal scores.
The only two groups of graduating seniors with lower SATV scores
than teachers were those studying in office-clerical and vocational-
technical fields. The education SATV scores were 46 points below
the average of graduating seniors. On the SAT mathematics test,
education majors ranked fifteenth among the 16 fields. Only office-
clerical ranked lower. The education SATM scores were 52 points
below the average graduating senior.

On the NLS vocabulary, reading, and mathematics tests, senior education majors as a group were below the population means. In vocabulary, only agriculture-home economics, clerical, and public service majors ranked below education majors. On the reading test, only agriculture-home economics and clerical-office majors ranked below education majors; and on the mathematics test only public service and office-clerical majors ranked lower than education majors as a group.

The average SAT scores of college seniors majoring in all education fields combined placed them in the bottom third of the 1976 graduating class (but there is a potential problem of missing cases in the SAT data). Other scores on the NLS test battery place the average education major at roughly the 40th percentile, as do the ACT English and mathematics scores.

National Teacher Examination scores also declined significantly during the five-year period from 1969/70 to 1974/75 (most recent date for which data are available). The net score decline is 20 points (581-561), significantly well beyond chance. (GRE verbal and quantitative scores, discussed later, show a similar pattern, with scores of education majors dropping faster than population mean scores.)

Comparison of Applicant Pool Test Scores

From the national data sources examined in the mid-1970s, it appears there was significant decline in the quality of potential students who intended to study in fields that were undergoing a decline in market demand for the new graduates, including education. The decline in quality appeared initially within the pool of potential applicants and then among enrolled students in the freshman year of college. The size of the various applicant pools appeared to shrink as college-bound high school students shifted career choices to fields in a more favorable demand position. The American Council on Education data on freshman career choices and the College Entrace Examination Board (CEEB) data on high school career choices corroborate this conclusion. Percentages were dropping at that time in those areas of greatest market weakness and rising in areas of greatest market strength (Table 2.13). The fields undergoing growth were business, engineering, and health and medicine. Fields in decline in the mid-1970s included biological sciences, education, foreign language, mathematics, social sciences, and psychology. The biological sciences, after growth in the late 1960s and early 1970s, had leveled off. Physical sciences and engineering, depressed during the same period, had recovered. These findings are consistent with Freeman's data (1976).

FIGURE 2.1

Comparison of ACTM Changes in Seven Fields of Intended Studies

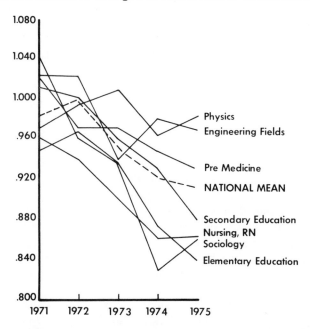

Note: Mean ACT mathematics scores for national sample of test takers designating an intended academic field of study (1970 scores = 1.0), 1970-75.

Figure 2.1 shows the pattern of changing ACT mathematics test scores in seven fields. Generally speaking, the score declines are most pronounced among those fields with shrinking applicant pools (Table 2.13). It should be further noted that in all fields the most significant deterioration in academic quality is in the area of quantitative skills. This is true at both the undergraduate and graduate levels. Verbal test score declines occurred but are exceeded by mathematics test score declines (see Table 2.2).

The career-oriented majors, including education, appear to have suffered the largest declines. College-bound students who plan majors in nursing, sociology, business, and biology show significant deterioration in English skills. Mathematics scores have fallen among majors in nursing, sociology, business, biology, premedicine, and engineering fields. However, with the exception of biology, the score declines in the science and science-related fields do not exceed overall population test score declines and are not as sharp as the declines in nonscience fields. The test score declines in biology, as the exception, are consistent with the assumptions stated earlier. The biological sciences since 1974 show a rapid falling off in student interest and potential applicants. Business is an anomaly. Test scores appear to be declining, although demand is rising. There may well be an aberration in the data due to changes in the ACT questionnaires regarding the specific careers students may select in the general field of business (American College Testing Program 1972, 1976).

Comparison of Enrolled Freshmen in Secondary
Education and Academic Fields

In this section, sample data derived from the College Student Profiles, American College Testing Program, 1975/76 and 1980/81, together with special data generated by ACT, were used to compare test scores of education and noneducation majors among enrolled freshmen for the years 1975 and 1980. The college majors were chosen by students in the ACT sample as high school seniors prior to entering college and are thus subject to the same limitations as all other ACT and College Board profile data based on high school questionnaires.

Because of the extremely small samples of enrolled freshmen selecting secondary teaching fields, especially since 1975, all of the data must be treated with caution. For example, in the 1980 ACT records, using a 10 percent sample of the ACT freshman classes, only five female students selected science education as a major. Only the English and mathematics teaching majors had 10 percent samples of 50 or more students (men and women) in 1980.

The general trends in the data, acknowledging the above limitations, suggest the following:

1. The teaching majors in 1975 and 1980 tended to attract students with somewhat lower test scores generally than the counterpart arts and sciences majors. For example, the comparative ACT English, mathematics, and composite mean scores are shown in the accompanying table for the social sciences, English, and mathematics fields for both education and noneducation majors.

	Social Science Education Majors			Social Science Noneducation Majors		
	ACTE	ACTM	ACTC	ACTE	ACTM	ACTC
1975	17.2	16.2	18.1	18.9	18.5	20.1
1980	17.4	15.6	19.8	19.9	18.6	20.5

	Mathematics Education Majors			Mathematics Noneducation Majors		
	ACTE	ACTM	ACTC	ACTE	ACTM	ACTC
1975	18.9	25.2	21.6	20.8	27.4	24.1
1980	19.0	22.2	20.2	21.0	26.4	23.5

	English Education Majors			English Noneducation Majors		
1975	19.3	17.0	19.0	20.0	18.9	20.8
1980	20.5	17.4	19.7	20.6	18.3	20.7

2. The differences between men and women seem to be consistent with well-known trends. Men in the teaching and nonteaching fields tended to have higher mathematics scores and lower English scores than women. The changes from 1975 to 1980 tend to show the mathematics score differences between men and women to be widening in the teaching fields, suggesting that women with higher mathematics aptitude may be seeking nonteaching careers. However, the samples are very small, and "inconclusive" would be the best term to describe the gender differences. Nonetheless, to illustrate the point, ACT mathematics score means are shown in the following table for men and women selecting social science and mathematics teaching fields.

	Social Science ACTM		Mathematics ACTM	
	Men	Women	Men	Women
1975	16.4	16.0	25.6	24.5
1980	17.2	13.0	24.0	20.8

3. Of the 18 college majors reported in the ACT College Student Profiles, four of the five fields that show a net decrease in mean ACT English test scores, 1975-80, are fields that traditionally attract proportionately higher numbers of women and generally fall into the humanities and fine and applied arts (education, fine arts, foreign language, home economics). The anomaly is mathematics. The decreases in mean ACT mathematics scores and mean ACT composite scores tend to be larger decreases than in mean ACT English scores —ranging in mathematics means from -5 percent to -9 percent, and in composite means from -4 percent to -7 percent.

4. The secondary teaching fields (social sciences, English, and mathematics) show declines in the ACT mathematics mean scores between 1975 and 1980 but not in the English or composite means. In

the mathematics teaching major, the ACT mathematics score mean declines 12 percent and in the social science teaching major 4 percent (see results above).

5. The college majors generally attracting students with higher test scores in 1980, compared with 1975, were the applied science fields and business administration. The following college majors show net increases in ACT English, mathematics, and composite test score means: business administration, computer science, engineering, health sciences, and social sciences (nonteaching).

In general, one is led to the conclusion, well documented elsewhere, that the last decade was one of transition, a movement of students generally away from the humanities, applied and fine arts, and education toward the applied sciences. Accompanying this shift in preference for college majors is a tendency for higher test scores to follow rising popularity of majors and declining scores to characterize majors in decline. In the next section the relationship between relative attractiveness of majors and relative changes in test scores among college freshmen is explored in more detail, together with possible effects of sex differences in selecting college majors.

Choices of College Majors, Gender, and Effects on Test Scores

Two related questions are examined in this section: Does an increase or decrease in student demand for college majors have an effect on the test scores of freshmen enrolled in various majors? Are the traditionally "feminine" careers suffering a talent drain as one of the "costs" of women pursuing new career options in fields formerly dominated by men?

It has become conventional wisdom to argue that test score declines have occurred in the humanities, education, and fine and applied arts—fields formerly more attractive to women—because bright women are choosing to enter the male-dominated applied sciences. Certainly part of the argument holds. Test scores in the humanities, education, and arts have been falling relative to the applied sciences. And the conventional wisdom that identifies female flight from these fields as the cause of test score decline may indeed be true, but it also turns out to be the case that both males and females are changing their career choices. Thus it is necessary to examine the data more closely.

In order to address the questions raised above, choices of college majors and mean test scores of freshman men and women were analyzed in a regression model. The dependent variable in the model was defined as the net change between 1975 and 1980 in the sample ACT composite scores for 18 college majors. The independent variables in the model were defined as net 1975-80 changes in the proportion of male, female, and total enrolled freshman samples choosing the 18 college majors. All data used in the model were derived from tables in the 1975/76 and 1980/81 College Student Profiles, the American College Testing Program. The actual net change values for ACT composite mean scores for each major were defined as simple ratios: 1980 means over 1975 means, adjusted for differences in the total sample means between 1975 and 1980. The actual net change values for proportions of freshmen choosing each of the 18 college majors were defined as simple ratios: 1980 proportions over 1975 proportions, adjusted for changes in sample composition between 1975 and 1980 (that is, proportion of males and females in total sample).

The correlation matrix for the four-variable model follows:

	Male	Female	Total	ACTC
Male	1.0000	-.3107	.7733*	.3953
Female	-.3107	1.0000	.0213	.1760
Total	.7733†	.0213	1.0000	.5128*
ACTC	.3953	.1760	.5128*	1.0000

*p = .015.
†p = .000.

The unadjusted correlation coefficients of statistical significance are found between two sets of factors: net change in male choice of major and net change in total student choice of major, and net change in total choice of major and net change in ACT composite mean score. In both cases the correlations are positive. The relationship between male and total choice might have been explained by a sample bias where males greatly outnumbered females, but that is not the case. The proportions in 1975 were roughly equal, and in 1980 females outnumbered males in the ACT profile sample. Further analysis suggests that both males and females moved to fields that were growing in popularity, but females were also moving into fields that were previously male dominated but declining in overall popularity (for example, agriculture and the technical trade fields).

The regression results (shown below) indicate that net change in total choice of college major has the largest impact on ACT mean score changes, followed by net change in female choices. The contribution of net change in female choices to variance in mean ACT scores is small, after the effects of net change in total choice are accounted for in the model. Net change in male choice contributes little to the R square after total and female choices are regressed and is not shown. The other results are reported below.

Variable Entered	Step 1, Total Choice	Step 2, Female Choice
Multiple R	.51276	.53868
R square	.26592	.29017
Standard error	.03615	.03663
df	1,16	2,15
F	5.70726	3.06593
Beta	.51276	
Total	.50923	.16512

For several reasons, the question of whether female flight from traditional fields has caused a decline in scholastic quality of the talent pools available for those fields obviously is not resolved by this analysis. First, the data used in the model are highly aggregated averages and are regionally biased to the ACT-tested population. Second, the majors selected by college-bound high school seniors who enroll as freshmen in college may shift considerably after such choices are made initially in high school. Third, the period covered in the study (1975-80) was a necessary constraint in order to acquire consistent data, but it may have missed a more significant period of adjustments in career choices, namely, 1970-75. Thus one may be looking at a data base of somewhat restabilized choices. Fourth, the degrees of freedom are severely constrained by the relatively small number of cases (18 college majors) and for this reason meet only minimum standards of regression analysis. Finally, there is the problem of regression analysis itself. Although the levels of association in this analysis are statistically significant even for the small number of cases, and the general findings consistent with previous studies, there remains the cause-effect issue. It is not possible to attribute direct causality to regression findings, and the choice of a career is an extremely complex issue requiring much additional research, including detailed case histories, which are not readily available. Nonetheless the data are not confirming of widely held opinion.

COLLEGE SELECTION: RHETORIC AND REALITY

It has been argued that education faculties sort out the academically weak students prior to student teaching and graduation. The NLS data do not support that argument, at least insofar as basic skills in reading, mathematics, and vocabulary are the selection criteria. Instead, teacher education is the field showing the least selectivity, from college-bound applicant to completion of degree, among the programs for which comparable data are available (greater selectivity being defined as rising average test scores).

A comparison of SAT scores for the total 1972/73 college-bound sample (College Entrance Examination Board) and the class of 1976 graduates (NLS) shows an increase in average verbal and mathematics test scores. (The SATV scores rise from 445 to 491 and the SATM scores rise from 481 to 527.) Scores in some fields reflect a greater degree of selectivity than others. For instance, the difference between applicants' and graduating seniors' scores on the SATM is greatest for students majoring in physics and mathematics, health-related fields, business, engineering, and vocational-technical fields. The fields showing the least amount of selectivity are education (ranked lowest in net change in both mathematics and verbal tests among the ten fields that could be analyzed), followed, respectively, by biology, social science, and agriculture-home economics majors. It could not be said, on the basis of these data, that selectivity or lack thereof takes place at college entry or after admission (Table 2.14).

A comparison of ACT college-bound students with enrolled college freshmen one year later suggests that the selection standards for elementary and secondary education majors may have changed between 1970 and 1975.[4] The ACT English and mathematics scores of college-bound applicants planning elementary and secondary education majors in 1969 were significantly lower than the ACT-tested elementary-secondary majors who enrolled as freshmen one year later (using data from 1,128 colleges and universities that use ACT scores; see Table 2.15). However, ACT English and mathematics scores among students in the college-bound applicant pool in 1974 (those who planned elementary and secondary majors) did not differ significantly from college freshmen (who had taken the ACT) in elementary-secondary education the next fall, 1975. In comparing other fields, it is generally the case that among the career-oriented majors, selection standards appear to have changed most significantly since 1970. Among the science and science-related fields no apparent change has occurred. With few exceptions, the sciences and engineering freshmen do not differ significantly from the previous year's applicants in either 1970 or 1975. Keeping in mind the limitations of these data, it is apparent that "soft" professional fields were admitting higher percentages of students in 1975 than in 1970, and it is among these students that the largest score declines were occurring. With the exception of psychology and secondary education, the fields that showed a 10 percent or greater decline in English or mathematics scores also showed a substantial rise in acceptances (Table 2.16).

The findings of George Nolfi et al., indicate that students are not only constrained by test scores in selection of fields of study but also in the selection of colleges.[5] Money also plays a very significant role. Poor students are more likely to choose colleges consonant with their abilities or one they can attend while staying at home.

They are not likely to select colleges with average test scores above their own. These findings may help in part to explain the lag in adjustment of preparing institutions to the widely reported surplus of teachers. College Entrance Examination Board data indicate that the majority of teacher education candidates come from families with incomes that are average or below average and that they have relatively low SAT scores. Such students tend to be concentrated in the four-year colleges. Given the constraints of institutional and college major selection among this population, many have no choice other than teacher education if they wish to attend college (see also Chapter 3).

These findings are consistent with those of the Wirtz Commission (College Entrance Examination Board 1977), which found that since 1973 students have tended to shift to occupational or career majors and that those in the career group have "consistently and markedly lower average scores on the SAT" (verbal and mathematics sections alike) than do those indicating the "arts and sciences choice" (p. 19). Furthermore, within the career-oriented fields, those suffering the greatest market weakness also show the largest score declines.

Moreover, more recent SAT scores show some "inflationary" effects. The Wirtz Commission found that while the predictive validity of the SAT mathematics and verbal scores increased between 1970 and 1974 regarding subsequent college performances, between 1963 and 1973 versions of the SAT tests show an "upward drift" of 8 to 12 points. "This means that the declines in the ability the SAT measures have been from eight to 12 points larger than the recorded and reported scores indicate" (p. 9)—a dismal prospect, given the teacher test scores reported in this and the next chapter.

Other Effects

It has been suggested that the mean verbal and mathematics test scores of students majoring in the professions, and particularly in education, might have been negatively affected by an influx of minority students.[6] The assumption is that the professions, specifically education, tend to be open and to attract larger proportions of non-white students than the arts and sciences. Analysis of the NLS data supports neither contention: There is not a larger proportion of non-white students in education than in other career fields (all career fields having a smaller proportion of minorities than do arts and sciences), and the presence of minorities among graduating education seniors has virtually no effect on test scores.

If one divides graduating seniors in the major fields into career-oriented fields, arts and sciences, and engineering, the proportion of white and nonwhite students shows the following: (1) the fields with the largest proportion of nonwhite students are the arts and sciences (10.12 percent), not the career-oriented fields (8.13 percent);[7] (2) the engineering fields have the lowest proportion of nonwhites (4.6 percent), and agriculture-home economics the highest proportion of nonwhites (13.0 percent); and (3) the proportion of nonwhites among education majors is 8.20 percent, just slightly higher than the average for the career fields as a whole (see the accompanying table).

Fields	Nonwhite	Total	Percent
Career fields	16,967	208,644	8.13
Arts and sciences	15,583	153,980	10.12
Engineering	747	16,222	4.60
Education	6,485	79,079	8.20

The effect of nonwhite test scores on population means among seniors in the various fields of study for both verbal and mathematics SAT scores is minimal and explains little of the declining test scores observed among the professions in general.[8] In the case of education majors, the removal of nonwhite scores has a net positive effect of 8.7 points on the SATM and 7.7 points on the SATV scores—in both cases less than one-tenth of a standard deviation.[9]

Responses of Individual Colleges: Case Histories

There are several crucial questions to be raised about the responses of institutions of higher education to the collapse of the college job market during the 1970s. Did colleges and universities, particularly those that train large numbers of teachers, respond to changing market demand as aggressive entrepreneurs? Or did they, as Dwayne Ward reported (1975), adopt an attitude of "benign neglect" (allowing students simply to vote with their feet)? Did shifts in market demand for new graduates stimulate changes in the intake processes of colleges and universities? Was there a significant decline in the quality of those entering preparation programs for fields in decline? Do colleges and universities function to produce a steady flow of only the "best and brightest" into the social institutions of the society? Or is their function, rather, to produce a steady flow of credentialed persons? These are entirely different questions. If institutions were to accept declines of more than 20 percent as an important measure of a student attribute, one reasonably believed to be a determinant of later professional effectiveness, the question would seem to be answered. If the institution admitted but had absolutely no intention of awarding credentials to such students, although the students had expressed a clear intent to major in a professional preparation program and believed they would receive degrees, a different kind of question is raised—one of propriety. The answers will have to do with conserving talent versus self-preservation.

Although elementary teaching had fallen from an average employment rate of 80 percent (1952-68) to 50 percent or less between 1969 and the mid-1970s, the institutional response was spread over a much longer period than in the case of engineering retrenchment earlier in the decade. In the cases examined, enrollments had fallen in education, but in eight teacher colleges surveyed (see below), the enrollment decline did not sharpen until 1974, at least five years after the market decline itself began. Projections of the National Center for Educational Statistics (NCES) show that the numbers of education majors graduating with B.A.s would continue to exceed demand into the mid-1980s (National Center for Educational Statistics 1982).

The availability of lateral program options may have temporarily worsened the problem of deteriorating test scores in education. In those cases where options were readily available (deliberate policies, for example, to expand programs in such fields as business administration or allied health), SAT scores and applications were likely to drop more rapidly. It is assumed that teacher education programs in universities in general were perhaps forced to shrink faster and earlier than teachers colleges for this reason. Ward (1975) suggested that this had been the case.

In fields that require higher than average minimum abilities, in theory it may be postulated that some threshold exists below which no student would be deemed capable of succeeding nor, one presumes, would be admitted. Engineering, physics, and medicine may be good examples, although considerable flexibility may exist in all three fields. (Engineering test scores among entering students in three schools surveyed, for example, suggest some latitude, as will be seen later.) However, in a field such as education, there seems to be little concrete evidence that any threshold exists, yet there must be some logically compelling argument for establishing a minimum. Otherwise, we would be taking the position that it does not matter how low a teacher's verbal and mathematics skills are as long as a school of education is willing to graduate such persons and a school system is willing to hire them.

Case Studies of College Admissions Practices

Nineteen postsecondary institutions were surveyed in 1977 on a case study basis. In 10 of the 19 institutions in which test scores were available for education majors, the scores show a major decline among freshman education candidates (Table 2.17). Although statistical treatment is not possible (only means were provided), the score declines are in the range of 35 to 100 points—certainly large enough to suggest statistically significant changes. Ratios of acceptance show sizable changes since 1970, with some of the institutions moving to a condition of nearly open enrollment. All ten of the institutions that provided specific admissions data in education show declining applications and substantial increases in the proportion of freshman education majors admitted relative to applicants. The institutions are regionally representative, and from the analysis of the national data, the institutional score declines are representative of national trends.

In the teacher education programs of eight state colleges examined, verbal test scores of freshmen had fallen from a combined average of 472 in 1970 to 417 in 1975 (the last year for which data would be released by the institutions). By comparison, the cumulative mean SAT verbal scores for all seniors in high school who indicated that they will major in education in college was below 400 (397 in 1976). For males choosing education, the mean verbal test score in 1975 was 362 and in 1976, 384 (College Entrance Examination Board 1972-76).

The declines in SAT scores examined in the eight state college programs exceed the national decline in overall means for all tested

Year	Eight Teacher Education Verbal Scores	Verbal Scores, National Mean	Eight Teacher Education Mathematics Scores	Mathematics Scores, National Mean
1970/71	472	455*	506	488*
1975/76	417	431	445	472

*The averages for 1966/67 through 1970/71 are estimates of the averages that would have been reported for college-bound seniors of those years if such reports had been produced.

Source: College Entrance Examination Board, 1975/76, p. 7, table a.

students. For purposes of comparison, the mean SAT verbal and mathematics scores of the eight colleges and of the national sample of college-bound seniors are shown for the years 1970/71 and 1975/76.

Note that the teacher education scores are higher than national scores in 1970/71 and lower than national scores in 1975/76.

Two Prototype University Teacher Education Programs

Two schools of education located in large public and private universities provided application, acceptance, and test score data for the years 1969 through 1975 (see Table 2.18). The pattern shown from one school in Figure 2.2 is typical of both schools of education and of the eight state colleges. Applications fell, ratios of acceptance rose, and test scores declined. For one of the two schools (located in a private university), comparative data were also available from the schools of engineering and health sciences located within the same university (Table 2.19). The pattern is consistent across schools. As applications fell, the acceptance fraction rose and test scores declined.

Sorting out the effects of admission policies from the effects of declining scores is somewhat speculative, but from the findings reported above it is clear that admissions standards were falling in the ten case study institutions that admit students who plan to become elementary or secondary teachers (when standards are defined as the ratio of acceptances of previous years' tested students).

A Within-University Comparison of Selectivity among Departments

From a medium-sized public university, applications, acceptances, and test score data were supplied for 14 academic departments for the years 1973 and 1980 (see Table 2.20). For each academic subject, Spearman rank-order correlations were run between acceptance fraction (percentage of applicants accepted) and the test score yield (applicant scores as a ratio of acceptance scores). The results are as follows:

X Variable	Y Variable	N	r	t	df
1973 acceptance fraction	1973 test score yield (SATV)	14	$-.304$	-1.004	12
1980 acceptance fraction	1980 test score yield	14	$-.463*$	$-1.807*$	12

| 1973 acceptance fraction | 1973 test score yield (SATM) | 14 | -.438 | -1.699 | 12 |
| 1980 acceptance fraction | 1980 test score yield (SATM) | 14 | -.262 | -0.941 | 12 |

*p = .05.

In all cases, as the acceptance fraction rises, the test score yield declines. The 1980 verbal score relationship is significant.

Obviously, there are limitations, not the least of which is the fact that not much change is observed in this particular university's application pool between 1973 and 1980. Given the size changes in the state colleges seen earlier, the relationships may have been expected to be larger. Nonetheless, the relationships are in the direction predicted, and one of the relationships is significant. The education department is one of those that increased its acceptance fraction, although the net change in education selectivity is relatively small. The education department in this university, in contrast to the earlier

FIGURE 2.2

Applications, Percentages, Registrations, and Test Scores for a University-Based School of Education, 1968-75

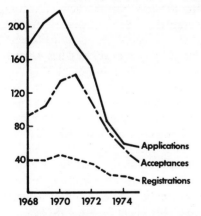
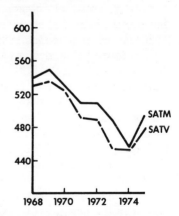

Left: applications, acceptances, and registrations (converted numbers) in a university teacher-preparation program, 1968-75. Right: mean SAT verbal and mathematics scores of entering freshmen in a university teacher-preparation program, 1968-75.

cases, did not have a rapid falloff in applications. It is significant to note that this particular education program had undergone a major reform between 1973 and 1980, merging with the social work department to form a new school of human services and education. In a sense, it represents a test of the hypothesis to be discussed later in policy testing and in Chapter 6—that is, by broadening the client base, schools of education may avoid collapse of enrollments and declining test scores.

Three Schools of Engineering

Data on applications, admissions, and test scores were supplied by three schools of engineering for the period 1969-75, a particularly difficult time for engineers (compare Freeman 1976). The results show that acceptance ratios rise over the period as test scores decline (Table 2.21). Of obvious importance in engineering would be mathematics scores. For the three schools, mathematics scores dropped 84, 20, and 28 points. It would appear, in these schools at least, that there is some latitude in selectivity given increases or decreases in demand for preparation in engineering.

The Graduate Level

Of the 15 fields displayed in Figure 2.3, six show significant declines. In addition to education, majors in aeronautical engineering, sociology, political science, and public administration show significant declines in both verbal and quantitative skills. These were all fields with market weaknesses at the time.

Figure 2.3 shows a pattern of significant decline in GRE scores among potential applicants in fields that are undergoing market adjustments, but unknown is whether declines in quality also characterize those who finally enter the graduate schools and subsequently an occupation. The data required to address those questions are inaccessible. Nonetheless, the trend in education is clear. The GRE verbal and nonverbal test scores among education majors have declined significantly since 1970. Scores of teacher majors were substantially lower than scores of majors in several other professional fields compared in 1975/76, and teacher scores have fallen at a faster rate than the overall GRE scores since 1970. Scores for 1981/82 show essentially the same pattern. Education majors rank at the bottom of the 11 majors reported on GRE verbal and quantitative scores (Educational Testing Service 1983).

FIGURE 2.3

GRE Scores for Selected Fields

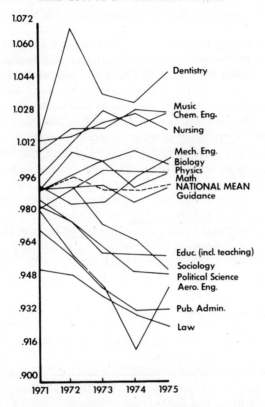

Note: Mean GRE quantitative test scores for national sample of test takers designating selected academic fields (1970 scores = 1.0), 1971-75.

Source: Martin Glaubeitz, Educational Testing Service, personal communication, 1977.

In the next chapter we will examine the academic quality and other characteristics of those entering and staying in or leaving classroom teaching. The evidence will show that the talent drain, evident in the beginning of teacher training, extends into the career choices of teachers. The basic contention that talent flows into areas of opportunity will be further supported.

NOTES

1. For the most part, data from the testing services are available in annual reports and other documents. The data from 19 colleges and universities, primarily in the Northeast, regarding admissions, applications, and test score data are not publicly available, and I have agreed not to reveal the identities of these institutions.

2. All tables discussed in Chapter 2 appear in Appendix A.

3. Note that data on ACT and SAT scores for college seniors by field show a large number of missing cases, which may distort the results. The NLS test score data by field of study are more complete and probably provide a more accurate comparative base. The percentile ranks of education majors on the NLS test battery are slightly higher than on SAT tests, perhaps reflecting the degree of distortion owing to missing cases for the SAT scores.

4. W. Timothy Weaver, "Education in Supply and Demand: Effects on Quality," School Review 86 (August 1978): 552-98.

5. George Nolfi et al., Experiences of Recent High School Graduates: The Transition to Work or Postsecondary Education (Cambridge, Mass.: University Consultants, 1977).

6. National Public Radio, "All Things Considered," December 1977.

7. The largest effects produced by the removal of nonwhite test scores are found in the office-clerical, vocational-technical, and biology fields. In the case of office-clerical majors, removal of the nonwhite scores raises the mean SATM score 17.1 points (less than four-fifths of a standard deviation). In the case of vocational-technical majors, the SATM increases 17.2 points (about one-seventh of a standard deviation), and in the case of biology majors the mean population score is increased approximately 15.3 points, or about one-seventh of a standard deviation. For these fields, except vocational-technical, the removal of SATV scores is approximately in the same range. The effects in these fields, quite small, are two or three times greater than in the other fields, and in some cases the removal of nonwhite scores lowers the population mean (physics and mathematics, agriculture-home economics, computer, professional).

8. See V. S. Vance and P. C. Schlechty 1982 for additional analysis of educational test score data for whites and nonwhites.

9. See W. Timothy Weaver, "In Search of Quality: The Need for New Talent in Teaching," Phi Delta Kappan 61 (September 1979): 29-46.

3

Who Enters and
Who Leaves Teaching

The evidence presented thus far suggests that the talent pool from which schools of education select first-year students has changed since the earliest baseline year (1969/70), when ACT test score data are available by field of study. It also appears to be the case that admissions of students into teacher education have permitted a pass-through of these changes to enrolled freshmen. In both cases (initial pool and admitted students) average test scores for students indicating a preference for teacher education have declined relative to the baseline year and relative to mean scores of the total college-bound population. The declines are sharper among elementary candidates than among secondary candidates. Mathematics aptitude for both groups has declined more than verbal aptitude. Data from the National Longitudinal Study (NLS) show that the initial changes in test scores continue to college graduation. Graduates with teacher education majors rank below the population mean and near the bottom of the list of college majors.

A comparison of the NLS sample of education majors, class of 1976, who did and did not find teaching jobs shows that on four out of five measures of competence in mathematics, reading, and vocabulary, those not teaching (presumably employed elsewhere) have higher test scores than those teaching. The exception occurs in mathematics, where NLS mathematics scores favor the teachers 55.90 to 55.80. The only differences that approach statistical significance are in the SATV and SATM scores. Nonetheless, it is important to note that the process of teacher selection and placement does not result in more academically competent teachers being selected. It is not clear whether the choice rests with the education major (more academically gifted students may not seek teaching positions) or whether the choice is primarily determined by employers. It is clear that a large majority of the 1976 education majors sought teaching positions. [1]

It is interesting to note that the teaching candidates who were hired did have slightly higher grade-point averages than those not hired (2.86 versus 2.79), perhaps suggesting the employers do use grades as a measure of academic performance and as a guide to hiring teachers.

THE TALENT POOL REVISITED: HISTORICAL DATA

In a major study for the Carnegie Foundation for the Advancement of Teaching, W. S. Learned and Ben D. Wood (1938) examined the academic ability of college students in 1928 and 1932 in Pennsylvania by field of study. Their findings show the following: For men preparing to teach high school subjects, test scores were "at or above average" on all tests except English in 1928 and 1932, whereas women were below average in social studies, mathematics, and science but above average on literary tests. In 1928, men in education compared favorably with the other professions, but in 1932 were below the positions of most other professions. In all cases, the average student in teacher training colleges had lower scores than those in "arts colleges." (The majority of teacher candidates at that time in Pennsylvania were preparing in the arts colleges.)

The comparison of men in education with the male-dominated fields of law, medicine, and engineering (fields consisting "solely or chiefly" of men) shows that the initial but not later positions of the male teacher candidates were relatively better than positions of men in the other fields, except engineering. In the female-dominated field of modern foreign languages, those preparing for nonteaching fields tended to have superior test scores in general education areas (mathematics, English, social studies, science).

Learned and Wood were able to compare the college test scores with a voluntary group of high school seniors in four Pennsylvania high schools tested with the same battery in 1934. They were disappointed with the results, which showed that 12 percent of the seniors tested had higher scores than the median of the teacher candidates; 18 percent of the seniors had higher vocabulary scores than about half of the teacher candidates; and 15 percent of the seniors had higher science scores than 40 percent of the college students planning to teach science. Looked at in total perspective, the overall median test scores of the college group (would-be teachers) was nearly double the median of the high school group and 88 percent of the high school seniors scored below the median score of the college group. Nonetheless, Learned and Wood expressed dismay.

An additional part of the Learned and Wood study compared the net gain scores of students majoring in education and engineering, matched for equal IQ scores, from sophomore to senior year. The reaction was again disappointment. The majority of educators failed to gain as much in general academic achievement as their engineering counterparts. However, an examination of the data shows that for higher IQ students (in engineering and education) the gains were about the same, but for lower IQ students the engineering gains were substantially greater. Since the majority of education students had lower IQs compared with the engineers, the conclusion was that most education majors were in effect wasting their time in college.

L. M. Sharp and S. B. Hirshfield (1975) examined the characteristics of college entrants in 1967 (graduating in 1971) who selected teacher preparation as a career choice. They found a higher-than-average stability among the education group in sticking with their career choice—71 percent of those initially indicating a teaching career retained that interest through graduation. They discovered a change, however, in the college group as compared with the 1960s: more students of higher ability defecting for alternate career choices.

> The data suggest that in the early 1970's more than in the early 1960's, able male students from modest backgrounds raised their sights and gave up teaching for more prestigious and lucrative careers. They also show that women of high ability and in comfortable financial circumstances sought alternatives to teaching careers and selected career jobs which required advanced training, such as college teaching and the professions. (p. 10)

In an examination of the hired and nonhired graduates, those hired had higher grade-point averages (see Weaver 1979): "The most compelling difference between hired and non-hired prospective teachers was grades" (p. 15). The committed teachers were described as mostly white, attenders of teachers colleges (not universities), and lower in academic ability than those not committed to teaching.

The Classroom Teacher: Academic Ability of Those Leaving or Staying

Two studies, one of women teachers (Pavalko 1970) and the other of men teachers (Thorndike and Hagen 1960), allow us to examine the characteristics of teachers entering and leaving teaching in the 1950s and early 1960s. The Thorndike and Hagen study was part of a larger follow-up research project of 10,000 men tested between 1942 and 1946 for Army Air Force training. The education subsample consisted of 658 men between the ages of 34 and 42 contacted in 1959. Of the group, 250 were still in teaching, 126 were in school administration, and 82 were college faculty members. Ex-teachers numbered 172 and ex-college faculty members numbered 28. All had qualified for Aviation Cadet Training ("equivalent to the 50th percentile of a high school senior group," p. 8). Each of the subjects completed a questionnaire on teaching satisfaction and dissatisfaction.

The ex-teachers (elementary and secondary) had significantly higher test scores on reading comprehension, arithmetic reasoning, and mathematics than those remaining in classroom teaching (but not higher scores than those in school administration). The college differences were similar but not significant. Thorndike and Hagen's conclusion: "It appears that those who were academically more capable and talented tended to drop out of teaching and those who remained as classroom teachers in the elementary and secondary schools were the less intellectually able members of the original group" (p. 10)

In examining the factors that explain leaving classroom teaching careers, Thorndike and Hagen found that financial considerations "swamped" all others; in response to the question "What do you feel would be most important in getting men into education and keeping them there?" 80 percent to 90 percent mentioned pay. Next in importance were classroom conditions (classroom crowding, materials, nonteaching duties), status, and, far down the list, promotion opportunities. For those who had left teaching, the primary factors were low pay and opportunity for another good job. Lack of promotion in teaching was a "poor third." Commitment to remain in teaching was not significantly different between well and poorly paid or intellectually more or less gifted teachers who had not already left the classroom, but pay still remained their primary source of dissatisfaction.

Ronald M. Pavalko's (1970) study of teachers and would-be teachers in Wisconsin relied on a statewide sample of female high school graduates from 1957 followed up in 1964. The study examined characteristics of women who became teachers and of women who planned to be teachers but did not enter teaching as a career. Pavalko used the Henmon-Nelson Test of Mental Ability as a measure of intelligence. Other factors included socioeconomic status and community size. Pavalko found that two-thirds of the women who became teachers were from above average socioeconomic backgrounds. Community size was not a significant factor. He also found that women entering teaching were overrepresented in the upper third of mental ability and underrepresented in the lower third. The late recruits to teaching tended to have the highest ability of the group entering teaching.

The attrition rate from teaching as an occupation was highest among the high ability group, lowest in the middle ability group, and

next to lowest in the low ability group: "Although teachers are recruited disproportionately from girls of higher measured intelligence,
it is those of lower measured intelligence who continue working"
(p. 352).

In a series of studies using National Longitudinal Study data
(Schlechty and Vance 1982; Vance and Schlechty 1982; Bethune 1981),
the characteristics of those entering and leaving teaching in the 1970s
help to complete the historical picture. The findings may be summarized as follows. For white females, Bethune found that those majoring in education in the freshman and senior years of college were from
lower socioeconomic status (SES) backgrounds, had lower self-concept,
had poorer academic performances, and attended less selective colleges than their counterparts in other fields, findings consistent with
those of Sharp and Hirshfield (1975) but inconsistent with those of Pavalko (1970). Schlechty and Vance found that those recruited to teaching
(both male and female) were drawn from among the least academically
able (SAT scores) as were those committed to staying in teaching (as
compared with those who had left or who were prepared to leave).[2]
Teaching also appeared to attract and retain disproportionately those
from rural and small town origins and of lower SES backgrounds
(Schlechty and Vance 1982). Schlechty and Vance found no dominant
effects of sex, race, or attitude in school attrition among newly recruited teachers.[3] Rather, the primary difference was academic
ability.

EXPLAINING THE FINDINGS:
TALENT AND OPPORTUNITY

Henry Levin (1970), using the Equal Educational Opportunity
(EEO) data (Coleman et al. 1966), particularly the EEO reanalyses by
Eric Hanushek (1968), estimated the cost differences in recruiting and
paying for experienced versus verbally gifted teachers. Levin's
analysis is significant for three reasons. First, his findings on attrition and ability among newly recruited teachers are consistent
with the previous studies: "The stock of teachers with three years
or more experience shows significantly lower test scores than those
with less than three years experience" (p. 33). Second, Levin con-
fronts the issue of teacher ability and student learning results directly:
Each additional point on teacher verbal test score would add .175 point
to black students' verbal scores and .179 to white students' verbal
scores. On empirical grounds, the issue of teacher quality may be
argued to be of vital importance to those concerned both with excellence
and equity. Third, Levin argues that the negative effects observed
(best and brightest teachers leaving teaching) is in effect the result
of talent flowing into areas of opportunity—an argument I find very

convincing: "This finding is consistent with the fact that the schools do not reward such proficiencies (verbal ability) while other employers do. It seems reasonable that this . . . could be reversed by a more competitive salary policy, one that did account for the teachers' verbal facilities" (p. 33). Levin estimated that it would be ten times more cost-effective to spend dollars on recruiting and retaining verbally proficient teachers than spending dollars on experienced teachers—given that the desired outcome is better learning results for students.

This brings the argument back full circle to talent and opportunity. Educationists who argue that changing the conditions of teaching (promotional schemes, inservice or preservice education controlled by the teaching profession, differentiated staffing, innovative teaching approaches, class size, materials, duties) is the solution to the teacher quality problem are ignoring the fundamental dynamics that have caused the problem we observe over very long periods of time. The documented evidence is clear. Thorndike and Hagen found that those who had left teaching did so because they were attracted to higher paying opportunities, not because the conditions of teaching were unsuitable (the majority of "defectors" did not cite teaching conditions as a primary reason for actually leaving). This finding is repeated in D. C. Turk and M. D. Litt's (1982) study in Connecticut 20 years later. The primary source of teacher dissatisfaction was pay and status. This is not to say that other things are of little or no concern. That would be a misreading of the data, to say nothing of ignoring common sense. Teachers are dissatisfied with many things, but the precipitating factor that leads actually to changing occupations appears to be pay and opportunity in jobs other than teaching. Turk and Litt found, for example, that 76 percent of the teachers surveyed cited "insufficient salary" as their reason for intending to leave teaching. The next most frequent reason cited was "poor opportunity for advancement," but it was cited by only 46 percent of the sample.

In Thorndike and Hagen's study (1960), working conditions were more important sources of dissatisfaction to those who remained in teaching than to those retrospectively explaining why they left, but pay was still the number one dissatisfaction for nondefectors.

To seize upon pay is to engage in single-cause reasoning. Pay for teachers is not the single cause of the problem, although salary (or a surrogate such as job opportunity) is an extremely important factor in the talent-flow dynamic. When that talent that is defined by such measures as verbal proficiency or arithmetic reasoning is financially rewarded by employers other than schools but not necessarily by schools, there will be an outflow of that talent from teaching. The dynamic interplay of supply and demand and opportunity, which is discussed in detail in the next chapter, will act as a parameter governing the attraction toward or away from teaching. Preparing institutions are responsible for the supply of new graduates and the advanced training of those in teaching. They may and will act to over-supply the market for teaching and by doing so they will drive down financial rewards. This will increase the attractiveness of alternative choices to those with the talent to act on the choices, and they will do so in response to the need to preserve incumbents' jobs when conditions are such as to threaten jobs.

There is an important difference in the findings on teacher talent in the Pavalko study, as compared with the studies of Bethune, Schlechty and Vance, and Sharp and Hirshfield. The initial talent flow into teaching in the early 1960s, compared with the entire period of the 1970s, shows the effects of a rising level of teaching opportunity contrasted with a long period of decline. Pavalko's findings of high ability women entering teaching in the early 1960s sharply contrast with the more recent findings of the opposite. The difference may be explained by citing social changes that now encourage more females to enter traditionally male-dominated fields, but even this explanation is consistent with the overall argument of talent moving toward areas of opportunity. However, as already noted in Chapter 2, both males and females are shifting career choices consistent with rising and falling opportunities, not just in teaching, but in fields of study generally.

Pavalko also found that those leaving teaching were proportionately of higher ability (although an examination of the data shows that a majority of low and middle ability females also left teaching). It is important to note that his study was completed before the rapid rise in teachers' salaries occurred in the mid-1960s, which may or may not have affected his results. Even with the net gains in teaching, the approaching parity in teacher salaries, when compared with other professions, was short-lived and abruptly ended with inflation and the teacher glut of the 1970s. It is difficult if not impossible to find the historically precise effect of rising salaries, but the data reported earlier (ACT) suggest the effects were present. As of 1969/70, those initially recruited to teacher training (male and female) were indistinguishable in academic ability from students entering college preparation generally. By the mid-1970s, however, test scores of the initial recruits had fallen significantly below the college-bound population mean, paralleling with remarkable precision the decline in job opportunities and the relative decline in salaries.

CONCLUSIONS: TEACHERS AND TEST SCORES

Do the findings on test scores (Chapters 2 and 3) represent a problem for the public, polity, or profession?

The decline in scholastic aptitude of prospective teachers would be of major educational significance in the long term only (1) if scholastic aptitude is directly related to the mastery of professional skills, (2) if those deficient in professional skills are not screened out prior to graduation or upon being evaluated as beginning teachers, and (3) if the employment of teachers deficient in professional skills actually produces inferior learning results or other undesirable schooling outcomes.

If the decline in scholastic aptitude of those selecting education as a major is matched against the level of marks received in college, one would be led to conclude that scholastic aptitude differences of the sort described here are not useful predictors of skill mastery within professional preparation programs, at least as determined by professors of education through their marking practices. For instance, a recent student survey in a major eastern university showed that the school of education awarded the highest percentage of A's while being ranked the lowest among the major schools in freshman average SAT scores.

The question of whether declining verbal or mathematics test scores among entering and graduating majors automatically signal diminishing pedagogical skills, or negative effects on students in American classrooms, is a question so imprecise as to not be directly answerable here. The decline in National Teacher Examination (NTE) test scores, reported by the Educational Testing Service (ETS), suggests, insofar as NTE is a useful measure of the general pedagogical knowledge required of the prospective classroom teacher, that pedagogical knowledge is declining. However, consider that A. A. Summers and B. L. Wolfe (1975) discovered a negative correlation between teachers' NTE scores and standardized achievement scores for elementary and high school students. On the other hand, the findings of James Coleman et al. (1966) show positive correlations, net effects of family background and other school factors, between teacher verbal test scores and student verbal test scores.[4] James Guthrie and co-authors (1971) state what they believe to be the significance of these findings on verbal ability:

> The findings can be construed to mean that an intellec-
> tual facile instructor is more adept at tasks such as
> finding means to motivate students, adapting materials
> to their ability levels, and communicating in ways that
> make the subject matter more understandable. This is

an interpretation that is totally consistent with observation and conventional wisdom. (pp. 70-71)

The Wrong Question

The important question is not empirical. The more important
question is normative: Should professional teaching skills be expected
to produce desired learning results? And is it a reasonable expectation that a definition of professional competency include those cognitive functions reflected in such measures as the SAT?

The first question: Is teaching practice accountable for learning
results? Can any profession be judged entirely by whether its treat-
ments produce desired results? Not on empirical grounds, because
in most cases the desired results are too ambiguous, or not observable
in the short term. Even if the results are observable and unambiguous,
it is rarely possible to show a direct and indisputable causal link from
treatment to cure whether the treatment works or does not work. One
might think of the results of counseling and psychotherapy, which are
neither unambiguous nor short term. The same presumably can be
said of teaching.

But there remains the issue of reasonable expectation. A profession would simply cease to have legitimacy at all if it never produced any results that were thought to be causally connected to competent practice. Imagine the situation in which surgeons killed all of
their patients, or every patient in psychotherapy was driven incurably
mad, or lawyers sent every client to the gallows. Given these results,
the basis of a claim to professional authority would be preposterous.
Even the rain dancer must produce rain sometime, the priest must
save a soul sometime, and the witch doctor must effect some cure
sometime. Otherwise, there would be no grounds on which to exclude
anyone from membership in the professions, ministries, or crafts.
Even in teaching, some results under some conditions must be claimed
to be connected to professional competence. The question is which
results at which time.

Is it a reasonable expectation that schoolteachers ought to instill
in students the ability to read and write sentences, recognize common
words, and add, subtract, and multiply numbers with at least minimal
proficiency after 12 years of schooling? If it is not, then the discovery
that such skills fail the test of minimal proficiency and have diminished
would be irrelevant. It seems such basics are expected—schoolteachers are judged responsible for their development, at least by the public—and the discovery that student skills have diminished is a cause
for public alarm. If the education profession wishes to make the
claim that students' knowledge and skills should be produced by teach-

ers in schools, then it must also be able to make the claim that its members are competent in the basics they teach.

To the extent the teaching profession cannot claim to be literate and to foster the development of minimal literacy in the young, it will suffer serious loss of its fundamental claim to authority. Otherwise, it would be reasonable to contest the legitimacy of the teaching profession to claim any exclusive prerogative in the conduct of schooling, or the school's authority to compel communities to set aside property rights through taxation, or the enforcement of compulsory attendance. This view seems to be implied in the Robinson v. Cahill and Pauley v. Kelley decisions, which have defined "thorough and efficient education" in terms of inputs, including the quality of teachers, and learning outputs. [5]

In this sense, the education profession must be able to claim that schooling is essential precisely because it fosters the development of certain skills and attitudes among the young that eventually strengthen the community's welfare and protect those very political rights that are subordinated through taxation so that schooling is freely available to all. Under these circumstances, it will be necessary to argue that the teaching profession possesses competencies that at a minimum are believed to be decisive in producing those learning results, even if the case can never be empirically demonstrated. Among those competencies, it is presumed, will be the ability to add, subtract, read, and write. If we discover that these competencies of teachers (adding, subtracting, reading, and writing) have declined or are low to begin with, then one should expect an enormous public outcry.

It is important to realize that defining teacher certification standards statutorily, in terms of just these kinds of skills, at a time when these skills appear to be declining, accompanied by public awareness of declining student test scores, reinforces further the public belief that student competency and teacher competency are causally linked. They may not be, or at least we may not be able to show that they are, but a public perception seems to be emerging that solving one will solve the other.

But is there really any consensus on what kinds and levels of scholastic skills competent teachers need to have? Are SAT, NTE, GRE, or ACT scores fair indicators of that skill level? Do teachers need to have proficiency levels equal to people in other professional fields? What difference does it make if in fact teachers graduating from college have skill levels below average for other graduates? Perhaps it makes no difference.

What Does the SAT Measure?

Those who spend their time on the matters discussed in the previous section argue that the SAT is not a test of minimal literacy. The National Assessment of Educational Progress (NAEP) would probably be a better indicator. The SAT is a test of high-level reading, and in the opinion of Warner Slack and Douglas Porter (1980) it tests achievement of a type not likely to be gained solely in schoolwork, although learning experiences in school are likely to have a considerable, if not decisive, effect on scores. Roger Farr and Jill Edwards Olshavsky (1980) state, "declining SAT scores tell us very little about the basic literacy of high school upper classmen, and there is no evidence of widespread lack of basic literacy for the population" (p. 528).

In reviewing sample SAT verbal items from a practice book, Farr and Olshavsky suggest that successful test takers would certainly have to be able to distinguish between definition and connotation, given such words as "saturnine," have a keen understanding of syntax and an awareness of prevailing value systems that must have influenced the test maker, and an ability to select between the obliquely correct and the somewhat more precise. On the other hand, NAEP test items, and minimum competency tests modeled after the NAEP, require some literacy, although a different level of literacy. The NAEP tests the kinds of reading typically encountered in everyday experiences requiring minimal evaluation and inference.

What do we expect of teachers? Do we expect minimal reading skills, or higher level reading skills as measured by the SAT? What do the state certification laws imply? Consider, for example, the new Massachusetts certification requirements. Common verbal standards for all new classroom teachers include the following:

The effective teacher communicates clearly, understandably, and appropriately. To meet this standard, the candidate will demonstrate that he or she:

1. Gives clear and concise explanations and directions
2. Frames questions so as to encourage inquiry
3. Uses appropriate metaphors, examples, and illustrations
4. Makes the goals of teaching and learning clear to students
5. Uses language appropriate to the age, developmental stage, special needs, and social, racial, and linguistic background of his or her students
6. Serves as an example of clear and effective oral and written communications
7. Listens to students
8. Communicates effectively with parents

Examination of common instruction/evaluation standards suggests a strong expectation of verbal and conceptual ability of the teacher. Examples from the Massachusetts law include the following:

1. Understands the needs and interests of his or her students and designs or adapts the curriculum to meet those needs and interests

2. Relates the elements of instruction sequentially to each other, to other fields of knowledge, to students' experiences, and to long-term goals

3. Understands developmental psychology, and the relationships between stages of growth

4. Teaches, as necessary, the basic academic skills (reading, communication, mathematics) related to the goals of instruction

5. Uses evaluative procedures appropriate to the age, developmental stage, special needs, and social, racial, and linguistic background of his or her students, and corrects for any ethnic, racial, or sexual bias in evaluation.

By state law, beginning September 1, 1982, new teachers must show evidence of such skills as a prerequisite for certification in Massachusetts.

If we take seriously the idea that teachers really ought to be able to do these things, and do them effectively, then we are demanding communication skills of a high level. We are not talking simply about basics.

In conclusion, it seems apparent that the average academic skills of new people preparing for and entering teaching careers do not match the standards expected in the foregoing discussion, if those standards are intended to screen people on criteria measured by such tests as the SAT. This condition is consistent over the last decade with changes in the college-bound population seeking careers in professional fields generally. The causes of this condition have to do with social, demographic, and economic factors coupled with the response of college-bound populations to those factors, plus the adjustments made by higher education institutions adapting to declining student enrollments.

We will see in Chapter 4 how supply and demand dynamics affect market conditions, what role schools of education play in that dynamic, and what the modeled outcomes may be for attracting talent to teaching. In Chapter 5 we will examine the modeled efforts to manipulate the system with the expressed purposes of defeating the dynamics that produce the teacher quality problem.

NOTES

1. Mark Borinsky, Survey of Recent College Graduates (Washington, D. C. : National Center for Education Statistics), preliminary data, personal communication, May 1977, January 1978.

2. Data were derived from the fourth follow-up, NLS, and included those prepared to teach and entering or not entering teaching between 1976 and 1979, as well as those who entered but left teaching during the time frame. The data show that 15.8 percent and 2.19 percent of those lowest and highest on the SAT were committed to stay in teaching at age 30. The comparison of SATV scores of those leaving or remaining shows a discrepancy of about 28 points (favoring the leavers) and on the SATM about 14 points (favoring the leavers).

3. Slightly more blacks were in the college population of education majors in proportion to all black college graduates than was the case for whites, but proportionately fewer blacks entered teaching and proportionately more intended to leave. Proportionately more men than women intended to leave teaching early. Proportionately more men and women of rural and small-town origins entered teaching and proportionately fewer left or were prepared to leave. Men and women of lower SES backgrounds were slightly more likely to remain in teaching and more were recruited to teaching in the first place. Locus of control and self-concept (as derived from NLS questionnaire items) did not discriminate leavers from nonleavers. The academic ability of leavers and nonleavers was not found to be affected significantly by sex, race, community origin, or attitude. Higher ability men, women, minorities, and those of higher and lower SES and large and small communities tended to want to leave teaching, while their counterparts of lower ability tended to want to stay.

4. The EEO data have also been analyzed by Hanushek (1968, 1970), Levin (1970), and others. Rosenshine and Furst (1971), in summarizing a number of studies on teaching effectiveness as related to student achievement, identified a cluster of factors that are apparently by-products of teacher verbal intelligence: clarity of presentation (making points clearly, explaining concepts clearly, effective use of voice and gesture, using a variety of teaching procedures), and task orientation (focusing on the accomplishment of specific academic tasks to be learned). W. B. Brookover et al. (1978) identified a set of "teacher climate" variables, which, when combined with overall school climate, explained a substantial amount of variance in student achievement. Among the key teacher climate variables were teachers' sense of academic futility and expectations for quality instruction. In an Irish study (reported variously by Madaus, Kellaghan, and Rakow 1975; Madaus, Kellaghan, Rakow, and King 1979) an important factor in explaining learning results across subjects was "academic

press" and degree to which scholastic success was valued by students and teachers. In summarizing the most recent literature on school effectiveness, K. H. Clauset (1982) found that attention to and teacher support of academic emphasis and time devoted to learning were keys in explaining achievement variance. These more recent findings are even perhaps more suggestive than the earlier findings on verbal ability (Levin 1970; Hanushek 1968, 1970) that academic quality is an important factor in teaching success. It would be hard to imagine how a teacher whose own academic success is suspect could effectively teach students to literally love the discipline of academic pursuits, to say nothing of delivering the clarity of presentations and explanations of academic subjects Rosenshine and Furst (1971) found to predict learning results, or to diagnose the academic learning problems essential to B. S. Bloom's (1976) theory of quality instruction.

5. See Paul L. Tractenberg, Testing the Teacher: How Urban School Districts Select Their Teachers and Supervisors (New York: Agathon Press, 1973); idem, "The Legal Implications of Statewide Pupil Performance Standards," Rutgers University Law School, September 1977; idem, "Evaluating Student Competency: The Legal Issues," paper presented at Conference on Issues in Competency-Based Education, Georgia State University, Atlanta, October 25-26, 1978; and idem, "Testing for Minimum Competency: A Legal Analysis," paper presented at American Educational Research Association Topical Conference on Minimum Competency Achievement Testing, October 12-14, 1978.

4
Supply, Demand, and Quality

We begin this chapter with an examination of the teacher job market much as the problem is treated elsewhere, that is, without regard to dynamic interactions. The data are treated as though the future is an extension of history. By so doing, we are able to see the limitations of linear models as a tool for policy analysis. Once we have examined the teacher job market from the traditional view, and the policy implications of that view, we will reexamine the problem from a system dynamics perspective. System dynamics allows the construction of a model that makes explicit and tests the theoretical premise of the book: teacher quality as a function of individual, institutional, and market forces. The literature is full of prescriptive wisdom about teacher quality but barren of theories or models that test theories. If one believes there is a direct and causal interaction among job market conditions, individual pursuits of opportunity, institutional adaptations, and talent flows, the beliefs need to be tested. I present the beliefs and tests of those beliefs in subsequent sections of this chapter and in Chapter 5.

Only those with historical amnesia would not realize there has been a teacher surplus for the past decade or that teachers colleges have been graduating people with questionable academic skills. But how exactly does one explain such a problem? What are the assumptions about causality? There seems to be a growing belief that teacher shortages are just around the corner, and that in math and science critical shortages exist now. What exactly is the basis of this conclusion?

We start with teacher supply and demand trends as they are traditionally estimated.

TEACHER SUPPLY AND DEMAND:
A LINEAR MODEL

In this section, teacher supply and demand trends in public education are examined as linear functions of historical conditions. The
data and method of analysis are briefly discussed, followed by a discussion of results.

Two primary sources of information were used to estimate baseline historical and projected demand trends for 1970-90. National Education Association (NEA) annual teacher supply and demand reports
1970-80 and National Center for Educational Statistics (NCES) data on
enrollments, percentages of teachers by subject, and student-teacher
ratios.

Teacher Demand

The NEA computes teacher demand as the product of turnover
rate, enrollment change, and student-teacher ratio change. In defining demand satisfaction, the NEA assumes that some combination
of new teacher graduates and reentering experienced teachers may
fill available vacancies. The component of demand to be filled by reentering teachers is estimated as a percentage of the existing teacher
force (varying from 1.7 to 3.0 percent). Once the demand filled by
reentering teachers is determined, the remaining available vacancies
are filled by new teacher graduates. The estimates reported in this
section follow the NEA's method of computing demand and distributing
reentering teachers and new teacher graduates to that demand.
Teacher demand, in all cases reported below, is calculated as the
sum of beginning teachers due to turnover rate, net enrollment
change, and student-teacher ratio change. The demand for new
graduates is the summed demand for additional teachers minus the
demand filled by reentering teachers.

Teacher Supply

The supply of new teacher graduates reported here is taken
directly from NEA tables for the years 1970 to 1980. Beyond 1980,
the supply of new teacher graduates is estimated by linear extrapolation based upon the average rate of change for the previous five years.
Thus, if supply shows a net decline for the period 1975-80, the 1981
supply and supplies for subsequent years to 1990 will show a continuous decline based on the slope of the curve for the prior period.
Using these assumptions, supplies, in all cases declining since 1975,
would eventually crash to zero. This, of course, would not be a

likely scenario under any but the least imaginable circumstances. Dynamic factors will play some role in determining the actual outcome. That is, as supplies begin to fall below demand, market conditions will reattract supplies given a time lag for information to spread through the system and for individuals to make career choices and prepare for teaching. But in this section, we deliberately allow supplies to decline at their historic rates in order to show what the condition would be in 1990 given no dynamic effects or policy interventions. The linear models presented are driven by demography and assumptions about student-teacher ratio, turnover rate, reentry of experienced teachers, and linear extrapolation of supplies of new teacher graduates.

Elementary and Secondary Education

In Figure 4.1, elementary and secondary teacher supply demand conditions are represented as a ratio (demand over supply). A ratio of 1.0 would mean that for each new graduate, exactly one teaching position would be available. When the ratio exceeds 1.0, people available exceed jobs available, and when the ratio falls below 1.0, jobs exceed people. The supply of teachers is the estimated total number of new teacher graduates each year unadjusted for assumptions about the percentages who might actively seek teaching jobs. The demand for new teachers is estimated as the net demand for new

FIGURE 4.1

Supply of All New Graduates in Elementary and Secondary Education Relative to Positions for New Graduates, Log. 1970-90

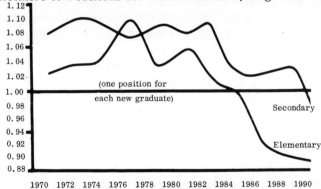

Source: Demand calculated from net enrollment, turnover, and student-teacher ratio (National Center for Educational Statistics 1982; National Education Association 1970-80). Supply estimates taken from NEA tables of teachers completing first degrees in education and extrapolated for 1980-90.

teacher graduates, after accounting for vacancies filled by reentry teachers.

Both levels (elementary and secondary) show early surpluses (ratios exceeding 1.0) and later shortages. The elementary teacher surplus, however, responds earlier, showing a decline after its peak in 1976. The secondary teacher surplus peaks in 1980 and then begins to subside ending in 1990. The differences in periodicity reflect the phased differences in elementary and secondary student enrollment fluctuations, which in turn drive demand for teachers. In both cases, supplies of new teacher graduates decline rapidly from their peak in 1972, with secondary supplies falling faster than elementary. Elementary enrollments decline first, but stabilize earlier than secondary enrollments, which explains the earlier rebalancing in supply-demand condition. Elementary enrollment increases beyond 1983, with falling supplies of new teachers, explain the sudden elementary teacher shortage by 1986. (Tables 4.1 and 4.2 show the teacher supply and demand for elementary and secondary education as estimated by the NEA and the NCES and extrapolated to 1990. *)

Secondary Teaching Fields

Shown in Figures 4.2 to 4.5† are estimated supplies of new teachers for four major teaching fields relative to the demand for new teachers in each field: English, mathematics, science, and social science. The major science fields are examined separately in a later section. The trends of the last decade in secondary teaching will surprise no one familiar with the field. English and social science were flooded with new graduates relative to jobs until 1982. Mathematics teachers are undersupplied almost from the beginning, and science teachers on the whole barely satisfy demand but are not as seriously undersupplied as mathematics. The mathematics and science condition worsens after 1982, but by 1990 all four areas of secondary teaching are undersupplied. The 1990 condition is explained by a declining rate of supply in all four areas that exceeds the rate of decline in the demand for new teachers.

Science

The supply-demand condition in science must be disaggregated to see the seriousness of the problem. Examined separately (Figure

---

*Tables 4.1 and 4.2 are in Appendix A.
† Figures 4.2 to 4.10 are in Appendix A.

4.6), one sees that new physics teachers are in short supply beginning in 1970, and the condition deteriorates rapidly after 1982. New chemistry teachers are in short supply after 1972, and, like physics teachers, would be virtually nonexistent by 1990 if conditions continue. New biology and general science teachers are generally adequate relative to demand until 1982, after which supplies, falling at a faster rate than demand, begin to signal shortages.

Discussion

The supply-demand conditions discussed above report history with as much accuracy as assumptions permit and project future conditions on the premise that nothing changes. It is important to re-examine those assumptions. The turnover rate factor is an estimate, not the actual numbers of vacancies created by retirements and voluntary separation from public school teaching. (The turnover rate estimates are shown in Tables 4.1 and 4.2 for elementary and secondary teachers.) If turnover rate were manipulated, the supply-demand condition would be changed. Because turnover rate accounts for a large component of demand, its sensitivity to error is large. The same may be said of reentry rate. The estimate is based on NEA surveys, but again the values are not actual numbers of experienced teachers rehired (see Tables 4.1 and 4.2). Both in the case of turnover and reentry, the NEA and the NCES assume net decreases have occurred in recent years: fewer teachers voluntarily separating and fewer former teachers reentering the profession.

A reanalysis of the demand estimates for 1971 (NEA 1982) based on numbers of teachers hired the previous year, holding constant assumptions regarding hiring due to enrollment and average class size changes, would suggest that hiring to replace turnover vacancies was higher than originally estimated (8.6 percent). My estimate is that turnover rate at the secondary level in 1970 was closer to 10 percent. By 1980 the NCES had readjusted its turnover rate downward from 8.6 to 3.9 percent, based on surveys of new teachers hired the previous year. If adjustments were made in the turnover rate assumptions used to calculate the trends in Figures 4.1 to 4.5 to reflect the newer NCES assumption of 3.9 percent turnover in 1980, and an estimate of 10 percent in 1970, the surpluses of the early 1970s would be smaller and the shortages forecast for the period beyond 1982 would be smaller. The baseline trends (Figures 4.1 to 4.5) use an initial turnover rate estimate of 8.6 percent in 1970, decreasing to 5.9 percent in 1980, and held constant from 1980 to 1990.

These assumptions are more than of casual interest. One can manipulate the assumptions at any time to produce surpluses or shortages. In the next section, model parameters will be allowed to readjust the turnover, reentry, and average class size baseline rates used in Figures 4.1 to 4.5. By this method, we estimate what the rates would have to be in order to balance the supply-demand equation, that is, to produce a hypothetical condition in which one job is available for each new graduate seeking a job. We do this in order to estimate the magnitude of change (deviation from initial baseline assumptions) required to equilibrate the job market in the 1980s, given the demand and supply parameters produced by enrollments, numbers of teachers needed, and projected declines in school of education graduates.

ADJUSTING THE LINEAR MODEL: POLICY PROBLEMS

Figures 4.7 to 4.10 show adjustments in turnover rate, reentry rate, and average class size required to produce an equilibrated model in which, hypothetically, a job exists for each available new graduate seeking a job. The teaching fields shown are the "worse case" conditions: elementary, mathematics, and science teaching. These fields will be seriously undersupplied after 1984 if the baseline assumptions in the linear model are taken as givens.

The policy problem examined in this section is the magnitude of change required in order to fill teacher vacancies, given (1) increasing enrollments in grades K-6 and declining supplies of new elementary teachers and (2) chronic shortages in physics and mathematics made worse by a supply curve declining at a faster rate than teacher demand in these subjects.

Turnover Rate: Retaining Present Teachers

To what extent would turnover rate have to deviate from the NEA baseline of 5.9 percent or the new NCES baseline of 3.9 percent in order to equilibrate supply and demand in these subjects (while holding constant other factors)? Figure 4.7 shows the two baselines as constants, while the required turnover rate is adjusted to balance supply and demand. The impossible case is elementary teaching, where turnover rate would have to fall to less than 1 percent by 1990 if supply were to equal demand. Imagined in policy terms, the elementary teacher shortage, given dwindling supplies, could be solved by inducing teachers not to leave teaching, thereby creating less demand; but the magnitude of that policy intervention would be very large, even given the lowest estimated baseline of 3.9 percent. Virtually no elementary teacher could leave teaching under this hypothetical condition. The practical impossibility of this notwithstanding, one may assume that reductions in turnover rate will require incentives for teachers to remain in teaching. Those incentives will have to be purchased, most likely in the form of higher salaries and better working conditions, which add up to bigger budgets and more taxes.

In the case of mathematics and physics, the magnitude of change is smaller than in elementary education, but the deviation from baseline is still substantial. The turnover rate would have to fall between 1.5 and 2.0 percent to satisfy demand by 1990. Again, the policy implication is one of incentive to retain teachers who otherwise would leave teaching. There is reason to believe that in mathematics and physics the incentives would have to be indexed, to some extent, on private sector opportunities, which are greater than in the case of elementary teaching (Useem 1981, 1982).

Reentry Rate: Attracting Former Teachers

To what extent would reentry rate have to deviate from baseline in order to close the supply-demand gap? Here the NEA baseline estimate is that a reserve pool of former teachers seeking reentry exists at an annual level approximately equal in size to 2 percent of the presently employed classroom teachers.

The elementary teacher condition, as our worst case scenario, shows an adjusted reentry rate of approximately 8 percent in 1990, compared with the constant of 2 percent (as estimated by the NEA). In policy terms, this deviation from baseline would require incentives sufficient to produce a fourfold increase in expected behavior of former elementary teachers. For mathematics and physics, the demand requirement could be satisfied with less, but less is still a significant problem. Reentry would have to increase threefold by 1990 in order to fill the demand gap by attracting more former mathematics and physics teachers back into the classroom. In both cases (elementary and secondary fields), the incentive implies salary increases and/or other inducements that cost money and, in turn, taxes.

Student-Teacher Ratio: Larger Classes

To what extent would average class size have to deviate from baseline in order to close the supply-demand gap? The baseline estimate is produced by the NCES. In elementary schools, the average class size in 1980 is approximately 21 students per teacher and, based on historical trends, would decline to just under 19 students by 1990. The average class size at the high school level is just under 17 students per teacher in 1980 and would be expected to be between 15 and 16 in 1990.

The adjusted student-teacher ratios are shown in Figures 4.9 and 4.10. The adjustments represent a condition in which the entire demand gap is satisfied by class enlargements. Thus a vacancy caused either by turnover or change in enrollment, and not filled by a reentry teacher, remains vacant. Obviously, this would mean an annual cumulative decrease in the total number of teachers employed and annual increases in students per teacher. All other things being equal, the average elementary teacher would be teaching 25 students per class in 1990, compared with about 20 in 1980. Average physics classes would increase from about 17 to 20 students over the decade, and mathematics classes would increase from about 17 to 20.

Of course, all other things will not be equal. One would imagine that if teaching load were to increase monotonically, both reentry rate and turnover rate would be affected. Increasing work load would likely push more teachers out of the classroom and discourage former teachers who might otherwise want to return to teaching. In addition, the salary demands of teachers would be expected to increase with work load.

In the short term, adjustment in average class size is the most probable policy action because of its direct and immediate effect in adjusting to teacher shortages: budget savings. The longer term effect is likely to worsen the problem, because of expected teacher dissatisfaction.

Conclusions

Two major conclusions seem warranted: (1) There will not be enough teachers to go around by mid-decade because some component of teacher demand must be filled by new teacher graduates, and that source of teachers is rapidly shrinking; and (2) the rather loose and uncertain coupling between incentives to attract more former teachers and to hold on to present teachers will have less appeal in the short term to policymakers than the immediate solution that is obvious through class size enlargement. Bear in mind that these conclusions reflect short-term conditions based on trends, not explicit dynamics of the marketplace. Those dynamics can be only implicit in linear models.

Given the normally expected and implied dynamics of labor markets, the first efforts of employers to fill demand that exceeds supply is from existing sources of labor: increasing work load, retaining employees, and attracting marginal workers (those qualified but employed elsewhere or otherwise engaged). In the longer term, new supplies will respond to the shortage condition as information reaches young people making career decisions. More will choose

teaching as market conditions improve (ample jobs and higher salaries).
However, the new supply response takes time. At the very least, it
would take two years for students in college already to switch majors
and acquire enough education credits to qualify for teaching jobs.
For those just entering college, the time delay is four years.

Since the supply-demand condition described above will begin
to manifest by 1984, the earliest one would expect new supplies in the
market would be 1986 to 1988. By that time, shortages will be severe
enough to require policy intervention. Given the period just beyond,
it would be expected that new supplies will rise to meet demand and
then recycle another oversupply.

In conclusion, this section presents a linear version of the supply-demand system for classroom teaching. As such, it serves as
a model of the near term based on history. However, the important
point is that this analytic approach is incomplete for an understanding
of how the system behaves or is likely to behave in the future. Linear
models, by definition, do not include dynamic feedback properties.
So, although economic principles and common sense lead us to believe
that all other things are not equal, we treat linear models as if they
were. As suggested above, each of the possible policy interventions
will have effects on compensation and working conditions and will not
manifest results in isolation from one another. Moreover, the dynamics of the job market, in terms of new supply and its response to demand, are not treatable in the linear model. Supplies contribute to
the shortage condition, and to the previous surplus condition, in
response to demand factors. Also neglected is attention to quality
issues, which I believe are produced by supply-demand conditions.

In the following sections we focus on the dynamic interaction
of supply, demand, and quality.

SYSTEM DYNAMICS: AN ALTERNATIVE PERSPECTIVE

There are a number of limitations in traditional correlational
models that have point-in-time prediction as their purpose. First,
there is no guarantee the future will be like the present. There is
a risk of generating misleading results just when a predictive model
is needed most—when the system is undergoing an abrupt alteration
in its traditional mode of behavior. Second, correlation is not causa-
tion. To design policies based on correlational relationships solely
is to risk attacking symptoms or effects, not underlying structural
relationships. Third, to achieve a numerically precise point-in-time
prediction requires an accurate numerical and structural specification of both the system and the system's external environment—impossible even in theory to accomplish. Fourth, historically driven

models restrict the scope of potential policy alternatives. Such models reflect only the historically known range of behavior that the system has exhibited in the recent past. This means the model cannot be validly (in a statistical sense) used to investigate policies that cause the system to operate in as yet historically unobserved regions of its operating range. But causing a system to shift its locus of operations within its operating range is precisely what an effective policy is designed to do (as will be seen in Chapter 5).

System dynamics was developed in order to overcome these kinds of problems (Forrester 1968; Forrester et al. 1976). System dynamics models are not designed to generate numerically precise point-in-time predictions. Rather, their purpose is to aid in the design of policies that are effective in mitigating problematic behavior.

Advantages of a System Dynamics Perspective

System dynamics forces attention on persistent regularities—in this case, the maintenance of self-adjusting balances among career choices, opportunities in the job market, talent flows, and institutional responses. These dynamic forces are embedded in and contribute to other regularities. For example, the teacher market is a subsystem of the larger market for college graduates. Changes in one affect the other. The teacher job market in the 1960s absorbed approximately one-fourth of all college graduates and was a major contributor to the overall boom in college employment. When the teacher market dried up, the humanities, arts, and sciences graduates who, with minimal preparation in education, might have become teachers, suddenly found few school districts willing to hire them. At the same time, government's retrenchment of employment opportunities dampened alternatives education majors may have had in nonschool employment.

The general retrenchment of both sources of college employment had a dramatic effect on wage offerings and on returns on college investment. The net effect, according to Richard Freeman (1976), was considerable shifting of college majors to fields not in retrenchment and a change in the composition of the college-bound population (fewer white males, more females and minorities). The effect on schools of education was dramatic. The percentage of college-bound students selecting teacher education fell from its 1969 peak of 24 percent to less than 5 percent in 1982. These kinds of responses, however, are not uncommon. Engineering enrollments declined by almost one-third in the aftermath of the engineering glut of the 1969-71 market.

The dynamics lesson is that these adjustments in opportunities and career choices also affect talent flows and institutional responses.

Academic departments faced with survival choices will yield to the pressure by redefining acceptance standards, in some cases abandoning, in all but rhetoric, any standards. The flow of talent from declining fields combined with institutional responses will produce the decline in academic quality discussed earlier.

The second advantage of the system dynamics approach is its internal focus, that is, it assumes that structure causes behavior. This methodological bias is especially useful in explaining the persistence of documented regularity—market shortages followed by surpluses, followed by shortages, and accompanied by talent fluctuations —despite repeated efforts to change the regularity. The literature on teacher reform describes but does not explain the persistence of these trends (Davis 1932; Bestor 1955; Koerner 1963; Conant 1963; Eurich 1969; Gardner and Palmer 1982). The literature is also unable to explain why reform efforts have failed. The logic of system dynamics —the internal focus on structure as a cause of behavior—can provide such an explanation (a theoretical model), if we conceive reforms as external inputs and cause of the problem as internal dynamics.

The internal focus of system dynamics stands in contrast to a traditional view that sees external forces as causing behavior. In system dynamics the structure is a closed-loop structure, whereas traditional models assume an open-loop structure. The difference is critical. Closed-loop structures are feedback structures; open-loop structures are models of linear effect (as shown earlier in this chapter). An emphasis on feedback structures can provide explanations for regularities seemingly impervious to intervention (Richmond 1977; Collins 1976; Forrester et al. 1976). Such a systemic, inward focus is missing from the vast majority of studies of teacher quality, which are dominated by a single view: teacher education as the cause of, and thus the point of intervention for, the perceived inferior quality of teachers.

The great teacher debate has amused and delighted some, while angering others, but the reformers have failed to reform. Missing from the debate is an overall explanation of systemic relationships that over time tend to produce the boom-bust cycle in the teacher market. By drawing boundaries and making specific distinctions between endogenous and exogenous variables, system dynamics models (such as the one presented in the next section) make explicit the assumptions in social explanations. For purposes of this analysis (to follow), the model's boundaries are coterminous with the public schools as employers of teachers and schools of education as producers of teachers. The remainder of the academic sector is not modeled, nor is the overall labor market. The model allows for choices between education and other fields of study but does not disaggregate the behavior of the other fields. Similarly, the model allows people in the teacher job market to leave that market for employment in other sectors of the economy but does not disaggregate the behavior of the other sectors.

Finally, system dynamics, by expressing effectively a set of relationships believed to be theoretically sound and by reproducing historical patterns of behavior, allows an evaluation of policy alternatives based upon the behavior of the model (see Chapter 5). In fact, the justification for model building rests with the eventual ability to test policy interventions.

In the sections that follow, the teacher supply, demand, and quality model (referred to hereafter simply as "the model") is presented in detail.

WHAT THE MODEL SIMULATES: THE PROBLEM OF DECLINE QUALITY

The teacher supply, demand, and quality model simulates the dynamic causes of the talent decline in teacher preparation and initial entry into the classroom. For modeling purposes, talent is defined in terms of scholastic ability and is represented in the model by an average SAT score (combined verbal and mathematics average). As a reference point (and discussed earlier in Chapter 2) Figures 4.11 and 4.12 show the national mean verbal and mathematics SAT scores of the college-bound high school population of College Entrance Examination Board-tested students compared with the sample of College Board test takers indicating an education major (College Entrance Examination Board 1973-80). In both the verbal and mathematics scores since 1973, there has been a more rapid decline in the sample indicating an intent to major in education than in the test-taking population as a whole.

A mathematical version of the model described in this chapter consists of a set of simultaneous equations that program the computer to produce the dynamic behavior of a supply-demand system (Forrester 1968; Forrester et al. 1976; Goodman 1974).* In this section, the computer version of the model is simplified as a set of diagrams showing the flow of people through the education system and into a labor market from which they are hired or continue advanced education. The initial diagram (Figure 4.4) shows the basic levels and rates in the model and includes a co-flow of test scores accompanying the movement of people through the system. A set of causal-loop diagrams is used to describe the feedback characterstics of the model.

---

*A mathematical version of the model is available upon request from the author.

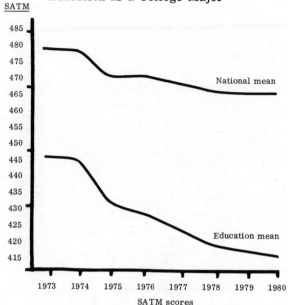

FIGURE 4.11
SAT Mathematics Means for College-Bound Seniors Selecting
Education as a College Major

Source: National College-Bound Seniors' Intended Areas of Study
—First Choice, College Entrance Examination Board, 1972/73-1979/80.

FIGURE 4.12
SAT Verbal Means for College-Bound Seniors Selecting Education
as a College Major

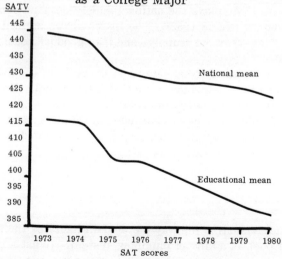

Source: National College-Bound Seniors' Intended Areas of Study
—First Choice, College Entrance Examination Board, 1972/73-1979/80.

FIGURE 4.13

Documented Teacher Supply and Demand, 1960-90

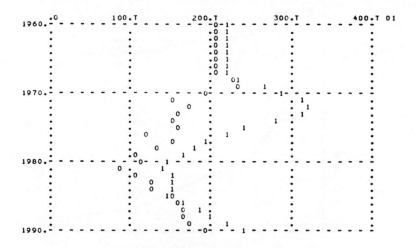

ESDAT: Documented teacher demand.
ESNTG: Documented teacher supply.

Source: National Center for Educational Statistics, Projection of Educational Statistics, 1988-89.

Figure 4.13 displays the national supply–demand condition in teaching, 1960-90 (NCES 1982). The figure shows an initial shortage, followed by a ten-year oversupply, and then gradual rebalancing in the late 1980s.

These two sets of trend data, test scores and supply–demand conditions, are the "reference modes" for the model. They are assumed to be the dynamically interrelated outcomes of school demographics, individual choices to pursue opportunities, and institutional responses. The manner in which they are interrelated is described below.

The Talent Pool

One may visualize the way the model simulates the fluctuations in the talent pool as a kind of plumbing system. (What appears in the well eventually comes out of the spigot, given various filtering processes.) The initial source of talent for teacher education is determined first by the fraction of high school graduates who seek entry into schools of education. As that fraction increases, the SATs of those seeking entry into schools of education increase relative to those seeking alternatives, and vice versa. The second-order determinant is SED selectivity. If every student in the population of SED candidates were accepted and enrolled in a school of education, the first-year classes of education schools would exactly reflect the distribution of those applying. But schools of education may choose only those in the upper end of the distribution, thus the initial scores in the talent pool would be "filtered" upward as reflected in higher scores for acceptances. The model simulates conditions under which the choices of students (as applicants) determine the parameters of choice for institutions, but institutions respond to these individual decisions by setting selection standards that either magnify or limit talent conservation.

The primary determinant, but not the only determinant, of both student decisions to pursue various careers and institutional responses to those decisions is the point-in-time attractiveness of the field of preparation. Attractiveness, in turn, is a function of job market conditions (among other things), which rest with supply-demand dynamics. When supply is increasing relative to demand, the perceived attractiveness of the field declines (given time for the perception to be formed among those seeking entrance to colleges). When demand is increasing, relative to supply, perceived attractiveness increases.[1]

The argument here is that student decisions are strongly influenced by perceived job market conditions in existence when students are choosing college majors.[2] This form of influence is not the same as "occupational outlook," that is, the reading of projected needs at the time of graduating from college four or five years hence. There may be two sources of information on occupational attractiveness: prospects at the present moment for employment and salary differentials. By the latter, I mean discrepancies among entry salaries of various fields. Although neither source of information may be precisely known by students, the combined effects of teachers' influences, the press and other media, guidance counselors, families, and peers are assumed to influence individuals' decisions. The work of Richard Cebula and J. Lopes (1982) at Illinois State University reinforces this basic assumption. Their findings suggest that changes over time in salary differentials among 26 fields are more predictive of occupational preparation at the undergraduate level than occupational outlook. Changing salary differentials are associated with changing supply-demand mix (Freeman 1971) and may be taken by students selecting majors as evidence of present-moment employment prospects. Because changes in salary differentials reflect past, not future, information, the finding that such information strongly influences selection of undergraduate majors suggests that the modeling assumptions are at least consistent with other research. In the model, the employment

FIGURE 4.14

Annual Teacher Demand Compared with Average Annual Salary of
Classroom Teachers Adjusted for Inflation, 1971-91

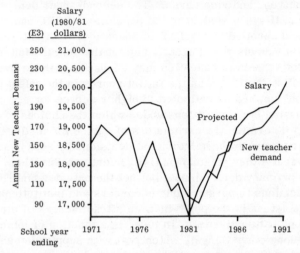

Sources: National Center for Educational Statistics (1982);
Frankel (1982).

prospects at a given time reflect average previous changes in the percentages of teachers hired from the teacher job pool. Substituting
point-in-time prospects with salary differentials would not change
model behavior in this case because teacher salaries and teacher demand are strongly correlated (Freeman 1976; Frankel 1982). Figure
4.14 illustrates this point. The relative salary gains of the shortage
years (1960-70) are entirely lost during the surplus years (1970-80).

The talent pool manifests in the model as a series of levels and
rates dynamically connected to job market and other model-generated
behavior. In the model, the talent level of those who are accepted into
education schools is the residual of the initial talent in the college-
bound population seeking various alternatives for career preparation
and the standards of selection employed by institutions. The talent
level of those graduating from education schools and entering the
teacher job market is the residual of the talent of those entering, and
continuing or not continuing, teacher education four years earlier.
The talent pool from which school districts select represents again
individuals' decisions to pursue various careers, including teaching.

The Job Market for Teachers: Individual
and Institutional Responses

One of the fundamental assumptions reflected in the model is
that individuals will pursue "careers open to talent," and opportunity

(as perceived by those pursuing careers) will dictate various levels of talent eventually finding its way into various fields. In this sense, the teacher labor market is assumed to behave like other labor markets in theory. School district employers will be compelled to select from a field of qualified applicants constrained by individuals' choices to pursue teaching as a career. When the "opportunity quotient" (demand relative to supply) rises in teacher employment, schools will have more talented candidates to select from, given time for supplies to adjust to demand, and will presumably act rationally to select the most talented candidates available to fill vacancies.

The protraction of the teacher job market imbalance (surpluses of candidates) shown in Figure 4.13 and declining test scores of entrants and graduates of teachers colleges are assumed to be the result of two factors: (1) institutional responses that reflect a willingness to lower entrance standards to whatever level is reflected in the applicant pool as that pool decreases in both size and quality; and (2) an initial pool of applicants more constrained in its choices by higher standards in other fields of preparation (Weaver 1978, 1979). The evidence seems to be clear that individual choices have resulted in lower scores in the applicant pool, higher scores for those who transfer out of teacher preparation, and higher scores for those who leave the classroom once hired.[3] What about admissions standards and qualifications? These are presumed to be decisions over which institutions have some control. The evidence seems to show that the selection fraction varies inversely with demand at the college level. How do we envision this working in the model? The following section provides a conceptual answer and subsequent sections an operational answer.

Standards and Qualifications

The qualifications route followed by eventual leaders in education begins with classroom teaching. The vast majority of professors of education begin their initial careers as classroom teachers. Kuuskraa (1978) reports that 90 percent of education professors were former elementary or secondary teachers. Certainly that is true of principals, superintendents, supervisors, and directors at the school system level, since most state certification laws require teaching certificates and classroom experience as conditions for certifying school administrators. Most deans of education are former professors of education and thus it is undoubtedly true that most were also former teachers. The development of leadership in the education profession depends almost entirely upon the initial abilities of those in the classroom.

How do we see the collapse of the teaching market affecting standards and qualifications of those entering teaching? In answering this question, let me first examine the connection between educational qualifications governing entry to the teaching profession and standards that regulate flows of people into, through, and out of educational institutions.

In the case of professional qualifications, one might be concerned with legal or professionally desired criteria for entering teaching. One would be concerned with how such qualifications are defined, how they are set, and how they change. It will not always be the case that legally required qualifications will be the same as qualifications professional groups seek to require. In fact, it may seldom be the case. But such qualifications, whether legal or preferred, will inevitably be related to the second set of standards regulating attainment of educational credentials (degrees, diplomas, and so on).[4]

As a general proposition (embodied in the modeling work discussed later), when the educational system is confronted with fewer students at any time, at any level, it will attempt to lower one set of standards as a means to generate more students, while perhaps raising another set of standards for the same reason. On the other hand, when confronted with more students than desired, the system may attempt to smooth the flow by raising all standards.

Before proceeding, it is obvious that we need to define what is meant by standards. It follows from the above that there must be different kinds of standards. One may claim that standards are falling and rising—at the same time—and not be inconsistent. Standards may have to do with degrees and credits, or with the criteria by which educators distribute degrees and credits (such as test scores or grades). Standards governing each of these may rise or fall independently, but in a general sense we define standards as "decision rules" that govern the passage of people into and out of the educational system. I will refer to these decision rules as primary, secondary, and tertiary standards.

Primary standards may be defined as the decision rules that directly govern the awarding of what Thomas Green (1980) calls "second-order educational benefits"—the degrees, diplomas, and certificates that constitute a particular institution's imprimatur of completion of a given level of the educational system. The rules apply to both entrance and exit because second-order benefits both signal the completion of a level and also serve as the basis for acceptance at the next level. It is standard practice for colleges to require some number of Carnegie units of high school credits as a requisite admissions consideration, and high schools require the same as a prerequisite for graduation. But even if that prerequisite is met, the student who wishes to be a high school graduate must still have a diploma that certifies graduation. Virtually every school and college requires some specific number of credits as the basis for graduation and the awarding of diplomas or degrees. Those that do not stand ready to translate what they do require into such credits.

Secondary standards may be defined as the decision rules that govern the evidence or criteria on the basis of which "second-order benefits" are distributed, determining when, how, and for whom credits satisfy the awarding of second-order benefits. Credits alone are insufficient. The system needs rules, policies, practices, and regulations governing both the distribution of credits and the certification of graduation. That need is satisfied by such things as marks or grades, examinations, or standardized or competency test scores, which form not only the evidence of certifiability of persons in the system but also a second level of differentiation. It is common practice for virtually all schools and colleges to set secondary standards as minimums—that level below which credits or certified units of completed work will not be awarded. Colleges may record on a transcript courses in which students receive a grade of C, but not count that course toward a degree. The grade-point average or test score may also be the direct criterion used for entrance to the next level. It may not be enough to have simply a passing mark or an average score. [5]

Tertiary standards refer to the decision rules that justify or explain the distribution of credits and degrees on the basis of attributes students bring to educational institutions. The attributes I have in mind fall into two broad categories: cognitive abilities as measured by IQ or aptitude tests and motivational traits or attitudes, such as tenacity, courage, and loyalty. Although not all educators believe such attributes are produced or changed by experiences in school and college, virtually every educator believes such attributes are decisive in differentiating the success or failure of students in achieving grades, test scores, and thus second-order benefits. Tertiary standards give meaning to the use of criteria or evidence on the basis of which second-order benefit awards are made. Credits are not awarded on the basis of students' IQ scores or motivation level, but motivation and IQ scores form the basis for explaining how grades and achievements are distributed, which does constitute the evidence for awarding credits. In some instances, tertiary standards may directly affect entrance decisions. Regardless of credits, degrees, or grade-point average, some colleges reject students on the basis of aptitude test scores. However, once past entrance, students' aptitude scores will rarely, if ever, constitute the direct cause for termination. [6]

These three levels of educational attainment standards are summarized below:

Standard	Criteria	Distribution
Primary	Credits	Degrees
		Diplomas
		Certificates
Secondary	Marks	Credits
	Grades	
	Test scores	
Tertiary	Aptitude	Grades
	IQ	Marks
	Attitude	Achievement
		scores

Teacher Standards and the Dynamic Effects
of the Job Market

Teachers, like other potential employees, seek jobs in a labor market, although a somewhat narrower labor market constrained by public policies. But even in that narrow labor market, employers bid salaries for services of qualified persons as do employers in other labor markets. When confronted with surpluses of qualified persons who can offer the desired service (call it service X), employers will bid down salaries for that service as long as all positions can be filled at lower salaries. The inverse is true: Given a scarcity of qualified service providers, employers will bid up salaries. Of course, there are limitations. Given a scarcity, employers may choose to redefine what is meant by desired service X, as in the case of hiring noncertified teachers. Given surpluses, professional interest groups will try to create the impression among employers that more of service X is needed than employers had been willing to purchase. [7]

It is not, of course, in the economic self-interest of teachers or their associations, or those seeking entry into the profession, to have salaries bid down. The expected reaction of service X offerers (teachers), therefore, will be to attempt to reduce the availability of qualified employees. One of the ways to reduce availability is to increase qualifications; another way is to create more demand for services. But these pressures emanate from offerers of service X, or would-be offerers of service X, or their supporters, that is, teachers, teacher associations, and certificating agencies at the state level, which are influenced politically by teacher associations.

The empirical evidence suggests, first, that in teaching the number of regular classroom teaching positions has declined (decline is in part offset by increases in special education positions), although, on the whole, positions have declined more slowly than enrollment declines would predict (NCES 1980). Second, states are raising teacher certification requirements. Historically, the trend is consistent. When surpluses arise in teaching, certification requirements rise. When shortages occur, certification requirements may be ignored.[8]

Preparation for the Market

Surpluses of teachers and the bidding down of teachers' salaries will be irrelevant to the economic self-interest of professional incumbents at the next level of the system—those who prepare teachers— unless and until surpluses and bidding down of service X cause surpluses and bidding down of the preparers' own service (call that service Y). The teacher surplus problem caught the attention of professors of education only when it became clear that fewer students were choosing teacher preparation.[9] If the preparation for service X is rendered less attractive due to surpluses, and if that condition causes a reduction in demand for service Y, then teacher preparers will also act to create more demand for their own services (service Y).

Because qualifications for service Y as opposed to service X are as high as they can be, raising qualifications is not feasible at the level of service Y. Thus, the proposition that surpluses cause qualifications to be raised is true only for those levels of the system where qualifications are not as high as they can be. It may be the case that "better qualified" faculty members are hired by schools of education when faculty members are in surplus. But by "better qualified," we would not mean a higher degree except in those institutions where the faculty typically has not held "terminal" degrees. It cannot be the case, however, that higher credentials are expected because there are no higher credentials.[10]

Will service Y providers (professors of education) favor raising the qualifications for service X providers? Only if raising qualifications for X produces more demand for Y. But it may not. It may actually reduce the demand by making occupational preparation even less attractive. Thus, the ambivalence in colleges of education about raising qualifications for teachers during an application drought is understandable. In short, professors are likely to favor extending credits for preparing teachers only when that ensures more jobs for professors, and disfavor when it does not.

The more likely response from service Y types is to lower entrance requirements having to do with tertiary standards (aptitude), and by similar means to attempt to retain students longer by increasing primary standards. The latter is accomplished when students who would fall below previous students on scholastic aptitude are discovered to have completed more education courses than previous students.[11] The percentage of A's awarded in a school of education may also rise under these conditions as the relative rank on SATs of its students declines (known otherwise as "grade inflation").

Counteracting Forces

Unless the action of service Y providers (professors of education) to create more demand for service Y can be effected without producing more surpluses of service X, such actions will run exactly counter to the economic self-interest of service X providers. The most immediate mechanism of adjustment and control for professors and college administrators confronted with declining enrollments will be to regulate admissions and exit standards so as to produce more students. Academic policies and rules will adjust to admit and try to retain a larger proportion when fewer apply.

These strategies when employed by service Y providers are likely to produce larger surpluses of service X, not in the self-interest of X, clearly in the short-term interest of Y, but also clearly disastrous in the long term for both. The long-term dynamic, given more rather than fewer graduates who cannot find teaching jobs, is constantly to reduce the preference for occupational preparation in teaching. As greater and greater surpluses accumulate, salaries are bid down, occupational mobility decreases, and preference for teacher preparation falls farther. The actual point at which economic self-interest of professors is injured is reached when all clients are admitted who apply and all are retained who can be reasonably induced to stay, while the pool of such clients still falls below capacity of the preparing institutions. We see such a condition now in teacher education programs.

It may then be in the economic self-interest of professors to attempt to extend credit requirements, and it will be in the interest of professors to create the impression of more demand for service X by redefining the range of occupations service X providers are told they can enter. Education professors have been slower to understand the latter than one would have thought. But those who do understand realize that the only way to maintain tertiary standards, sufficient supplies of students, and not at the same time create surpluses of teachers, is to redefine the mission of teacher preparation. It is not necessarily a bad idea. The fact that teacher surpluses coincide with growing demands in the private sector for trainers makes the idea especially appealing (see Chapter 6).

These propositions are summarized below.

1. Qualifications cannot be raised at the level of service Y in response to surpluses of service Y providers.

2. Qualifications can be raised at the level of service X in response to surpluses of service X, and pressure will arise to do so, but that may not be in the interests of service Y providers; in fact, if raising qualifications reduces the supply of students for service Y providers it is directly contrary to Y interests.

3. In which case, service Y providers will oppose raising the qualifications for service X providers.

4. Service Y providers will lower tertiary standards when confronted with fewer students to be trained in service X.

5. Thus, creating a further surplus of service X providers.

6. The long-term interests of neither X nor Y are served because the field becomes chronically oversupplied and less attractive.

7. The net result is a deterioration of quality where quality is defined in terms of tertiary standards.

Summary

We have seen in Chapter 2 an empirical case for arguing that declining test scores are the result of individuals' choices coupled with institutional responses (increasing the acceptance fraction). Here we have examined a principled argument that says institutional incumbents (in this case professors of education) will act in response to declining demand for their services in such a way as to over-supply the service at the next lower level of the system, namely, services of teachers. In this sense, we see a "tragedy of the commons"[12] whereby each college faculty's self-interest is served by recruiting and graduating additional teachers, but collectively, this results in a chronic oversupply, falling demand, deterioration of quality, and eventual collapse of some schools of education.

These propositions and empirical claims are embodied in the computer simulation model described in the following sections.

STRUCTURE OF THE MODEL

Figure 4.15 shows the movement of people through the education system and the accompanying co-flow of test scores. The diagram does not include every detail in the model, but rather is intended as a road map for convenience of the reader.

Enrollments in schools of education result from the fraction of all college-bound students applying to and subsequently accepted by schools of education. Those in the teacher job market have entered

FIGURE 4.15

Flow Diagram: Teacher Supply, Demand, and Quality Model

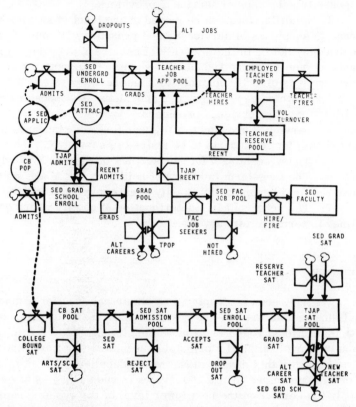

from undergraduate and graduate schools of education or from the teacher force (as either released teachers, or those reentering after voluntary absences). People in the job market may be hired by schools, attend graduate school, or leave the market for employment in other sectors of the economy. People entering graduate schools of education and eventually seeking teaching jobs have completed undergraduate education programs, except for a fraction of arts and sciences majors pursuing the master of arts in teaching. All graduates enter a pool from which those going into the teaching market are separated from those entering (or seeking to enter) educational faculty positions at the college level.

The co-flow diagram shows that scores are initially generated for all college-bound students and then are split into scores of education majors and others (arts and science and professional fields other than teaching). The next talent pool level is the school of education from which scores accompany dropouts (and transfers) and graduates. Those graduating enter the job market or graduate school and then the job market. The final talent pool is the teacher job market from which school systems select candidates. Others leave for alternative employment or graduate school.

These flows and the variables affecting them are explained in more detail in the section on model variables.

Model Dynamics

The teacher supply, demand, and quality model is depicted as a series of feedback loops. The diagrams represent, at a simplified level, the dynamic theory of the system. In this sense the model consists of three major feedback components. The first of these is illustrated in Figure 4.16. Thereafter, in successive figures, one additional loop is included.

Loop 1: Supply and Demand

Loop 1 (Figure 4.16) illustrates the simple supply and demand dynamic that, given time will respond to market conditions by a series of oscillating changes in supply and demand. The behavior produced by this version of the model would be a more or less continuous pattern of demand rising or falling in response to demography (student enrollments and teacher vacancies in the elementary-secondary schools) and being tracked over time by supplies of qualified people to fill that demand. The source of teacher demand is primarily exogenous, but demand can be adjusted by student-teacher ratio and teacher turnover rate. "Desired" student-teacher ratio is also exogenous and reflects philosophical, economic, and political conditions not modeled (represented by historical data). The actual student-teacher ratio prevail-

FIGURE 4.16

Steady State Model of Teacher Supply and Demand

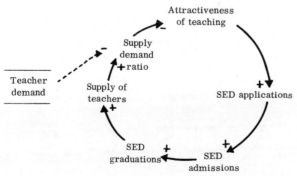

FIGURE 4.17

Steady State Model of Teacher Supply and Demand with Selection Function Added

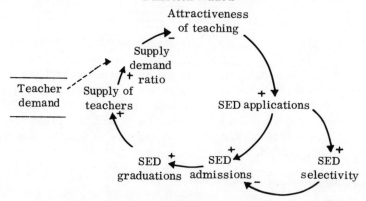

ing at any given time in the model is dynamically determined by the number of teachers employed divided into the number of students enrolled at the elementary-secondary level (which may exceed or fall below the historically defined standard).

The causal loop in Figure 4.16 shows that as attractiveness of the teaching field increases in response to demand, applications increase, admissions, enrollments, and graduations increase, and sup-

FIGURE 4.18

Model of Teacher Supply and Demand Resulting in Oversupply and Collapse

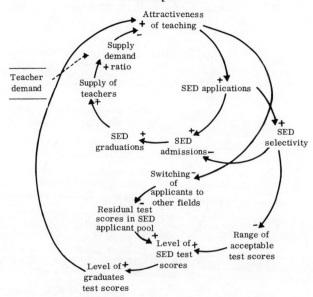

ply catches up with and eventually exceeds demand; when supplies exceed demand, the polarity of the loop reverses, driving down attractiveness, applications, admissions, and graduations—causing still another reversal of polarity. Significant time delays in the system create an out-of-phase cycle in which supplies are first too low, then excessive, followed again by shortages.

Loop 2: Institutional Response

As applications rise, schools of education can be and are more selective, thus limiting the flow of students (Figure 4.17). But as demand continues, even with more selectivity, the level of enrollments rises over time together with graduations. When attractiveness declines, selectivity is adjusted to preserve resources and temporarily the system may maintain enrollments at previous levels as well as graduations. When applications fall below previous admissions (even with 100 percent acceptance rate), enrollments will decline.

The important effect of this response pattern, apart from delaying supply-demand rebalance, is to produce a decline in the average quality (test scores) of students admitted and graduated.

Loop 3: Talent Pool

The level of talent in schools of education reflects two conditions: talent in the pool applying to Schools of Education (SEDs) and selection standards (Figure 4.18). When demand and attractiveness decline, the talent level in the applicant pool falls, and standards also fall, producing an amplified downward pressure on the net level of talent being admitted. The loop shows that the range of acceptable scores increases at a time when the overall distribution and mean scores in the talent pool are moving down the scale from a previous point when the field was more attractive.

MODEL VARIABLES

The model includes three major sectors: (1) flows of people into and out of the education system; (2) flows of people into and out of a job market for educators; and (3) a co-flow of test scores accompanying people through the education system and job market. Variables and assumptions in each sector of the model are defined below.

Education System: Levels and Variables

The education sector is divided into three levels: elementary and secondary schools, undergraduate schools of education, and graduate schools of education.

Elementary-Secondary Schools

The number of students in elementary and secondary schools is represented by an aggregate annual school population, grades K-12, generated by a table function in the model based on actual and projected public school enrollments, 1960-90 (National Center for Educational Statistics [NCES] 1982). The model does not generate students enrolled in private or parochial schools, nor does the model keep track of students by grade level or subjects.

Model dynamics generates an annual level of classroom teachers and demand for new teachers. The model does not include administrators or professional support personnel. The desired level of staffing of classroom teachers is determined initially by a desired student-teacher ratio. New teacher demand to meet desired levels of staffing is a function of student enrollment changes, teacher turnover, and historical or projected changes in desired student-teacher ratios. The actual hire rate is modulated by availability of new teachers and time to create and fill vacancies. The fire rate is modulated by time to lay off teachers due to declining demand. The hire/fire function in the model is designed to simulate a "sticky down-slippery up" phenomenon. The model assumes shorter time delays to fill vacancies than to reduce staff.

Teacher turnover rate is defined in the model as a normal fraction (based on NCES and NEA assumptions) adjusted dynamically by hiring conditions. As hiring conditions improve (from the job seekers' perspective), teacher turnover rate increases, simulating an increase in risk taking among those employed in the system who may wish to leave the system temporarily or permanently (an assumption consistent with NCES modeling efforts).

Undergraduate Schools of Education

The college system consists of undergraduate schools of education and graduate schools of education. The model does not include other academic fields. College-bound students who select majors other than teacher education are split off as a separate rate in the model, but are not accumulated in a level.

Undergraduate enrollments are determined by rates of applications and acceptances, minus the dropout (and transfer out) and graduation rates. Variables affecting these rates in the model are defined below.

SED Applicant Pool Variables. The rate of student applications to undergraduate SEDs is a function of the teacher job market conditions, given time for market information to reach prospective applicants and for them to respond to that information. When teaching jobs are in ample supply, the fraction of students in the college-bound population applying to undergraduate SEDs will increase. Conversely, when teaching jobs are scarce relative to supplies of people seeking jobs, the fraction of applicants will decrease. The model assumes that information always reflects previous conditions and is not instantaneous. It is also assumed that student choices are based on previous information, not on anticipated future conditions. Thus, while market conditions in the recent past might reflect an oversupply of teachers, students entering their first year of college could be graduating at a future time when the market is undersupplied. However, it is assumed that applicants' choices and actions do not reflect such a reading of the future market situation. The result is a phased delay in resupplying the teacher job pool, or depleting the pool, of about four years after a change in demand manifests.

SED Acceptance Rate Variables. The acceptance rate simulates institutional response to student demand. Acceptance decisions are determined by two factors: the availability of students applying to schools of education, relative to other academic programs, and schools of education capacity (both graduate and undergraduate). It is assumed that schools of education will take the best available students, but the actual talent level of those accepted is a function of the talent available combined with the decision to admit larger or smaller fractions of those who apply (see later section on test scores). Standards (acceptance fraction) are variable, not fixed, in the model, and they reflect conditions created by attractiveness or unattractiveness of the field. While standards are adjusted dynamically in the model up or down depending on conditions at a given point in time, they may be manipulated in policy testing (see Chapter 5).

Capacity is defined in the model as the present number of faculty members relative to demand for faculty members. As the present number of faculty members exceeds demands, pressure rises in the system to admit more students by increasing the acceptance fraction, and vice versa. [13]

SED Outflow Rate Variables. The number of graduates from undergraduate schools of education is determined dynamically in the model by the number of admitted students four years earlier minus dropouts and transfers (defined in the model as dropouts). The dropout rate is defined as a normal fraction of those entering adjusted by teacher job market conditions. As the job market deteriorates, the dropout rate increases. The time to become aware of job market conditions for students already in college is shorter than for college-bound students. The effect is to produce quicker responses to job conditions for undergraduate students than for college-bound applicants. The model simulates a condition in which a fraction of those admitted as freshmen can

switch their intended majors in teacher education and reduce or increase the graduation rate depending on market conditions.

SED Faculty Variables. The number of SED faculty members is generated by model dynamics and is determined by two factors: hire/fire
rate and faculty turnover (adjusted by hiring conditions). Faculty demand to meet desired staffing levels is a function of enrollment
changes, desired faculty-student ratio, and turnover rate. The hire/
fire rate is adjusted by time to hire or fire (reflecting the sticky down-
slippery up phenomenon—here reinforced by college tenure contracts).
Faculty turnover is defined in the model as a normal fraction responsive to hiring conditions. As hiring conditions improve (from the job
seekers' perspective), turnover rate increases, and vice versa, reflecting increasing or decreasing risk behavior.

Graduate Schools of Education

Graduate student enrollments are determined dynamically in the
model by applications and acceptances minus the dropout and graduation rates. Each of the rates and variables affecting the rates are defined below.

Applicant Pool Variables. The graduate schools of education applicant pool is composed of the following:

Employed teachers: The number of experienced teachers (three
or more years in teaching) applying to graduate school as part-time
students is defined in the model as a normal fraction responsive to
two factors: overall teacher job market conditions and the effect of
an influx of new entrants to the teacher force. These two factors are
related but may operate independently on the model.

Regarding the first factor, as overall job market conditions deteriorate, the dynamic effect on those already employed in the system
is assumed to be curvilinear: increased pressure to acquire advanced
credentials (the familiar "defensive credentialing"), followed by a decline in pressure if conditions deteriorate further.[14] The second factor, perceived competition from new entrants, reflects an assumption
that new entrants to teaching will seek graduate training and by doing so
affect the perceived relative advantage of older teachers (to the extent
that perceived advantage is derived from advanced credentials). It is
assumed that this pressure arises when there is a large influx of new
teachers in the system accompanied by graduate school attendance of
those new teachers, thus inducing further defensive credentialing by
older teachers. The net effect is a temporary surge in graduate school
attendance by those in the system, followed by abatement as the system
slows down its hiring of new teachers and the teacher force reaches a
point of "credential saturation."[15]

The two pressures (credentialing as a defensive response to decline in overall job prospects and credentialing owing to perceived erosion of relative advantage between older and younger teachers) may operate independently. Consider actual conditions of the past 30 years: As the teacher job market improved (as during the 1950s and 1960s), advanced credentialing resulted primarily from the influx of new teachers.[16] By the end of the 1960s this source of pressure dissipated, but overall job market deterioration began to affect defensive credentialing behavior. Thus, graduate enrollments rose temporarily while undergraduate enrollments declined, but now have begun to drop rapidly.

New BA graduates: The number of new BA graduates from teacher colleges who seek to enter graduate schools as full-time students immediately after graduation is defined in the model as a normal fraction, adjusted by job market conditions. As the teacher job market declines, in effect closing out new BA graduates from teaching jobs, there is a tendency for some increasing fraction to go directly to graduate school. The relationship is assumed to be curvilinear: pressure to go to graduate school rises with market decline, but it subsides if the market declines further.

Unemployed teachers: The number of teachers in the market defined as "reentering teachers" or "laid-off teachers" seeking admission to graduate school as full-time students is simulated in the model as a normal fraction responsive to market conditions. As the teacher job market declines, pressure arises to acquire more graduate credentials. If decline worsens, the pressure will increase and then subside.

Former teachers seeking college faculty positions: The primary source of SED faculty members is assumed to be the elementary and secondary school teacher force (see Kuuskraa 1978). In the model, a normal fraction of teachers leaving the school system (turnover rate) does so to seek admission to graduate schools as full-time students in preparation for faculty positions at the college level. The fraction of those pursuing such career training is adjusted dynamically by the demand for college of education faculty members. When demand increases, the fraction leaving the teacher force to prepare for college careers will increase, and vice versa.

MAT program applicants: The model simulates the flow of people into graduate schools of education from the arts and sciences who seek preparation for the master of arts degree in teaching. Model dynamics generate the number of such persons as a normal fraction adjusted by teacher market conditions. When the teacher job market improves, the fraction seeking the MAT increases. When the market declines, the fraction seeking the MAT decreases.

Graduate SED Acceptance Variables. Institutional response to demand fluctuations is driven by two factors: available supplies of applicants and capacity effects of the graduate and undergraduate schools. When supplies of applicants are increasing, the acceptance fraction declines. When supplies of applicants slacken, the acceptance fraction increases. It is assumed that graduate schools will respond to capacity conditions at the undergraduate level as well as at the graduate level. The capacity effect is defined as a pressure that increases acceptances when faculty members are in excess of those needed and that decreases acceptances when faculty members are undersupplied, relative to demand.

Graduate SED Graduation Rate Variables. Graduation is defined in the model as a normal fraction of the total graduate school enrollment minus dropouts. The model is initialized with one-fourth of the enrolled students being graduated (a parameter consistent with NCES data, see Projections of Educational Statistics to 1981-82). As contrasted with the undergraduate SED level, a large percentage of graduate students are part-time students and complete their studies at variable lengths of time. In the model, all graduates enter an annual pool of those who have finished graduate school and are then split into respective rates reflecting the entrance components four years earlier (the model assumes an average of four years to complete graduate studies). No distinction is made among graduate degree levels.

Graduate SED Faculty Variables. The number of graduate faculty members is generated by model dynamics and is determined by two factors: hire/fire rate and faculty turnover (adjusted by hiring conditions for educational faculty members). New faculty hiring is a function of enrollment changes, desired faculty-student ratio, and turnover rate. The hire/fire rate is adjusted by time to create and fill vacancies or to lay off staff. The model assumes a "sticky down-slippery up" phenomenon immured by tenure contracts that are normally terminated only when entire programs are terminated. Faculty turnover is defined as a normal fraction, adjusted by hiring conditions, which when favorable increase turnover and when unfavorable reduce turnover (reflecting occupational risk behavior of the faculty).

Teacher Job Market

The teacher job market adjusts in the model to two sets of factors: demand for classroom teachers and supplies of qualified people to fill demand. The model assumes "qualified" to be a function of completing degrees in education. The model makes no provision for hiring as teachers those without at least a minimum of preparation in education, but it does assume that a fraction of all qualified BAs will be minimally prepared (arts and sciences majors with the minimum qualifications to be hired under temporary certification as provisional teachers). The fraction of minimally prepared graduates increases or decreases depending on job market conditions. When market demand relative to supply is strong, the fraction minimally prepared will increase. The model does include a MAT sector that graduates in two years arts and sciences majors with a master of arts degree in teaching.

The supply side of the teacher market is defined below as a set of inflow rates from several sources. The number of people in the job market at any given time represents a dynamic balance between those being hired or leaving the market to attend graduate school and those entering the market. The number of people in the market annually rises or falls depending on whether the leaving rate exceeds or falls below the entrance rate to the market.

The market annually absorbs entrants and places a number of people in classroom teaching jobs depending upon demand. The fractional teacher hiring rate (hired teachers from the market over the total people in the market) is a primary driving force in the model, simulating in effect national teacher job market conditions.

As the pool of available and qualified job seekers rises relative to demand, the attractiveness of the teaching profession declines, causing a shift in interest in the college-bound population away from teacher preparation, but temporarily increasing defensive credentialing among those already in the teacher force. Those left behind in the job pool and not hired by school systems may leave the market by attending graduate school and returning later to the market or by taking alternative employment in other sectors of the economy. The average length of time those not hired by school districts spend in the job market is defined as a normal "dwell time" of about 14 months but is modulated by the number of people who are attempting to leave. As the residual in the pool rises, the length of time required to leave increases.

The rates affecting the market and the variables determining those rates are defined below.

Teacher Job Market Inflow Rates and Variables

People moving into the job market seeking employment as teachers include the following: new BA graduates from SEDs minus those who directly enter graduate schools, former teachers seeking to re-enter teaching, graduates from graduate school who previously left the job market, and MAT graduates.

These components of the inflow to the job market are regulated by model dynamics that increase or decrease supplies depending on recent job conditions. When job conditions are positive (job demand rising over supplies), more former teachers will actively seek to re-enter teaching. The supply of new BA graduates into the market is regulated by conditions at the time those graduates first entered college, producing a continuous and automatic time delay in response to market conditions. The flow of M.Ed. and other graduates with first professional degrees at the graduate level will be regulated by market conditions in effect at the time they entered graduate school, producing another continuous and automatic time delay. In addition, the supply of teachers in the job market may be augmented by those laid off from school systems. In the model, "RIFfed" teachers reenter the job market from which they may be rehired, or leave to attend graduate schools, or seek alternative employment.

Teacher Job Market Outflow Rates and Variables

The exit rates from the teacher job market include teacher hiring, graduate school attendance, and alternative employment. The model may be regulated in policy testing to increase or decrease the number leaving the job market for employment in the private sector. It is assumed that the attractiveness of SED graduates to nonschool employers can be increased by SED program changes that focus on human resource development as a new area of professional preparation (see Chapter 5).

Test Score Co-Flow Variables

One of the most important issues examined in this model is the conflict between conserving talent as a resource and conserving jobs of incumbents as a resource. It is a fundamental premise of the model design that an educational system must compete for and conserve talent under conditions in which opportunities for the talented are dynamically changing and are open to individual choice. The model also reflects a premise that the talented and nontalented will attempt to capitalize on opportunities when those opportunities arise, meaning that, all things being equal, the most talented students will seek entrance to fields of greatest career opportunity, but so too will the least talented. Those fields enjoying high demand will be selecting students under conditions of optimal choice, meaning that while the least talented may choose them, they will not choose the least talented.[17] Those not chosen will be forced to select less attractive fields, and those providing training in such fields will be forced to accept them or go out of business.

The model generates behavior in which talent is more or less conserved but within a system in which counterpressures to conserve institutional resources other than talent constitute the system's highest priority. For example, when opportunities in teaching are scarce, relative to other careers, the talent flow, as represented in student choices, will be away from teacher preparation. Institutional responses may then have the effect of either reducing or increasing the system's conservation of talent. Empirical evidence suggests that under conditions in which the choice is "poor students or no students," faculty members will choose the former as the lesser of two evils. What evidence there is suggests that this choice is not unique to faculties of education (see Chapter 2).

Design of Test Score Co-Flow

For each of the above-defined components of "people flows in the model," from high school to teacher employment, a test score is generated by the model as an average score for that component of the population. The test score co-flow includes four levels: college-bound population, SED talent pool, SED undergraduates, and teacher job applicant pool.

The co-flow sector is designed so that scores flowing from the first pool constitute the initial source for all subsequent pools. Scores are initially generated in the model (college-bound population) as the product of college-bound students and an annual SAT score.[18] In subsequent pools, the level of scores is determined by the interaction of student choices and institutional responses. Scores are split off for those students who apply to schools of education as a residual of all scores in the college-bound population talent pool. Scores then accompany those accepted into schools of education and are split again between those graduating and those dropping out or transferring. Scores of those graduating enter the teacher job market talent pool from which a fraction will accompany those hired as classroom teachers, leaving for graduate school, or looking for alternative employment.

The talent pool levels and variables are defined briefly below.

College-Bound Talent Variables

The outflow of scores from the college-bound talent pool is divided first by the scores of that component of the total college-bound population that will attend arts and sciences programs and professional programs other than teaching. The average test score of arts and sciences and other professional majors is a function of the attractiveness of those programs relative to education. Once the initial average scores are determined, the residual test scores flow into the SED talent pool. Model dynamics determine whether education test scores will be high or low relative to others. If teaching is an attractive choice for students, the scores of education applicants will be higher compared with others, and lower if teaching is unattractive.

SED Entrance Talent Pool Variables

The scores flowing into the SED talent pool represent the parameter of choice for schools of education. The average score of those selected (admissions) for schools of education is a function of the acceptance rate and level of scores in the pool. When the acceptance rate reflects a high standard of selectivity (smaller fraction accepted of those available), an average score of admitted students will be higher. If the acceptance fraction is high (meaning lower selectivity standards), an average score of admitted students will be lower.

Enrolled Student Talent Pool Variables

The average score of students enrolled in schools of education reflects incoming scores of first-year students minus scores of students graduating and dropping out (including transfers). The graduates' average scores, relative to those dropping out or transferring, is determined by the average scores of the entering class four years earlier, adjusted by job market conditions. When the teacher job market is strong, the average scores of those leaving before graduation will be lower relative to those graduating. When the job market is weak, scores of those leaving before graduation will be higher relative to those graduating.

Teacher Job Market Talent Pool Variables

The initial source of test scores for the teacher job market is disaggregated by the model into the following: (1) scores of new BA graduates from schools of education, (2) scores of reentering teachers, and (3) scores of graduates from graduate schools of education. The average score of each of these components of the inflow rate is determined as follows. Scores of reentering teachers are defined as an average of scores of teachers hired from the job pool five years earlier (which simulates the condition of the school talent pool five years earlier). Scores of MAT graduates are defined as an average score of arts and sciences majors in the college-bound population six years earlier. Scores of graduates of SED graduate programs are defined as an average score of SED undergraduates four years earlier. Scores of new BA graduates are defined above. The components of the inflow of scores to the teacher market talent pool reflect an automatic and continuous time delay. The scores of each inflow component are constrained by conditions that prevailed at a time when those populations entered the system.

Scores flow out of the teacher market pool as follows: (1) scores of teachers hired for classroom teaching positions, (2) scores of people leaving the market to enter graduate school, and (3) scores of people leaving the market to enter other sectors of the economy. The outflow from the teacher market talent pool reflects the earlier-defined premises regarding talent flow. As the teacher demand curve rises, relative to supplies, the most talented in the pool seek that opportunity, and thus average scores of those applying for teaching jobs are higher; when employment opportunities in teaching deteriorate, the scores of those applying are lower, relative to those seeking employment in other sectors.

RELIABILITY OF THE MODEL

The model has been initially tested in two ways: "robustness" testing and output correspondence to historical data. In the first of these tests, the objective is to perturb the model to observe whether the model will operate reasonably over an extreme range of conditions. In successive tests, the elementary-secondary schools are "depopulated" in a one-step function that removes a fraction of the population while the model is in equilibrium mode. In the first test 25 percent of the enrollment is removed, and in the second test the entire population is removed. Model results (see Figures 4.19, 4.20, and 4.21)* show expected adjustments: Applications shift to other fields of study at the college level as the teacher job pool fills with released teachers. Test scores sink as expected, and the model settles to low levels of students in schools of education.

In correspondence testing, the model is run in a growth or decline mode over the period 1960-90 regulated by the demand for teachers. The mode reflects changes in enrollments, teacher turnover, and desired student-teacher ratios. Model-generated data are compared with historical and projected data from other sources. The figures show that model output corresponds reasonably well to historical and projected data prepared by the National Center for Educational Statistics and the College Board. In Figures 4.22 to 4.29 (see Appendix A) the model's output is compared with historical data on teacher demand, supply and demand, school of education graduates (undergraduate and graduate), total supply of new teachers, and test scores.

These tests provide at least some reasonable level of confidence that the model will operate over an extreme range of conditions (even hypothetically improbable ranges), and the model generates output

---

*Figures 4.19-4.29 are shown in Appendix A.

that reasonably simulates actual data regarding demand and supply conditions and test scores documented by other sources.

Forecasting Teacher Supply and Demand

The model runs in Figures 4.22 to 4.24 show increasing teacher demand beginning in 1983 and continuing through 1990. Both the model-generated data and the NCES-projected data show rising demand for total teachers. The demand increases will be due to rising birth-rates in the United States beginning in the mid-1970s and continuing into the 1980s. The projection of enrollments (and thus teacher demand) above grade 6 for the period 1982 to 1990 is relatively fixed, given that the students are already in the system. The documented data show declining enrollments above grade 6 for much of the present decade (NCES 1982). Thus, the rising demand for teachers is primarily a function of increases in enrollments in elementary grades.

The data in Table 4.3 (see Appendix A) are generated from live birth figures provided by the Natality Division, National Center for Health Statistics. That is, enrollment in grades 1 to 6 is calculated as the number of live births 6 to 12 years earlier. Based on these estimates, the demand for additional elementary school teachers to fill vacancies would increase from 30,090 in 1982 to 86,841 in 1987.[19] The supply of new elementary teachers graduating from colleges of education may be insufficient to fill demand. The model and NCES projections show that supply will fall below demand until 1990, when supplies will gradually rise above demand, followed by another cycle of oversupply. These findings are consistent with estimates appearing elsewhere (Pillich 1980; Frankel 1979).

The reversal in the supply-demand condition (surplus to shortage) will be expected to have a gradual positive effect in quality of those preparing (as seen in Figures 4.28 and 4.29). The question for public policy is whether the conditions produced by these long-term cycles are in the public interest. If not, what should be done? We will address that question in the next chapters.

NOTES

1. The assumption here being that the application fraction will increase or decrease as opportunity is perceived to increase or decrease, relative to other fields of college preparation. When opportunity in education increases, and the application fraction rises, more students, as a percentage of applicants to SEDs, with higher test scores will apply.

2. The model does not attempt to account for other factors, although it might be reasonably argued that other factors influence decisions of college freshmen to enter education programs. For example, some fraction of students might pursue teacher education, even though the demand for teachers were zero (hypothetically) on the belief that teacher education is a form of general education, much as the liberal arts. It may also be the case that teacher education would be viewed by some as an appropriate preparation for other occupational roles. Given either of these motivations, it is unlikely that teacher education would receive no applications under any reasonable circumstances of the job market, but it also seems reasonable to conclude that the fraction applying would be small. For these reasons, the fraction applying in the model cannot fall to zero, but it is responsive to job market conditions, averaged over time to reflect delays and modulated so as to reflect the notion that not everyone believes the information or acts rationally even if the information is believed. Clearly, some people will enter teacher preparation under the worst job conditions feeling that they, as opposed to others, will be the ones hired once they graduate.

3. At least anecdotal evidence (in addition to research provided by Thorndike and Hagen, 1960; Pavalko, 1970; Levin, 1970; Vance and Schlechty, 1982) from school officials suggests that the pool of highly talented teachers of five to ten years ago has dried up, leaving, as one official said, "the crumbs" (Teacher Preparation: Problems and Prospects; see also Useem 1982).

4. The relationship is far from precise, however. Colleges may accept and graduate students with the intention of readying those students for professional practice even though the college is not "certified" by professional bodies to do so, nor are its graduates. Nonetheless, that does not prevent the college from recruiting, admitting, and graduating students. The fact that some colleges of education, for instance, are not certified by the NCATE does not prevent those colleges from accepting and graduating students prepared to teach. It will be the case that when professional qualifications are embodied in law, professional qualifications will more closely resemble educational attainment standards, but even then educational institutions may accept and even graduate many students whom faculties believe will fail to meet state certification requirements. On the other hand, colleges' educational attainment standards may, and often do, exceed legal professional qualifications.

5. It may be the case that secondary standards serve in place of primary standards, as in the case of equivalency testing. The primary standard is not abandoned, but rather is substituted for, that is, a test score is equivalent to credits in the decision rule. Primary standards also may be waived. It was not uncommon for students in

the recent past to be admitted to colleges of education at the graduate
level even though they had no prior credits in education at the undergraduate level. Indeed, that was the direct intent of the MAT programs. Primary standards may be waived in considering entrants, but
it will rarely be the case that primary standards are waived or substituted for exiting the system. It will not be the case, except in very unusual circumstances, that both primary and secondary standards will
be waived or substituted for either in entrance or exit flows (the awarding of "honorary" degrees being one of those circumstances, and the
advanced placement of a child prodigy in a college or university being
another).

6. There are exceptions. We all know of the case in which a
student is taken aside and encouraged not to pursue a degree, even
though on the basis of secondary standards the student has not failed
and may, in fact, be highly motivated. Doubts exist as to the student's
ability to master desired skills. On the other hand, some colleges
prize motivation and attitude far more than aptitude, and the cases
are many where a "brain" has been encouraged to leave because of
"improper" attitude. (My guess is that the latter cases are more
likely to characterize the human service colleges, while the former
may more often be found in the arts and sciences colleges.)

7. The presence of the "invisible hand" is clear in the teacher
job market. Teachers' salaries, relative to salaries in general,
are bid down from 1970 to 1980 as a surplus of approximately one
million qualified teachers enters the teacher job market. Precisely
the reverse picture may be observed in the decade just before when
jobs exceeded qualified applicants. The recent testimony before the
House Labor and Education Subcommittee details the present dismal
state of teacher salaries, relative to other occupations (Teacher
Preparation: Problems and Prospects; Frankel 1982; NCES 1982).

8. It is instructive to examine the historical literature on
teacher supply and certification requirements. For example, in the
period 1918 to 1982, there is a sudden shift from perceived teacher
shortages to teacher surpluses (American School Board Journal
1920a; Nations Schools 1930). The arguments began to arise for
stricter admissions and qualifications for teachers. In the period
from 1925 to 1940, the bachelor's degree became a requirement of
most states for teaching at the high school level, and by 1955 at the
elementary level. There was a concurrent shift in certification authority from local districts to states during the long period of teacher
oversupply (1925-40) (see Frazier 1940).

9. The data on education enrollments show a 12-year decline
from 1.118 million (1966) to 781,000 (1978). The dropoff in graduates
from 1972 to 1980 is about 49.7 percent (317,254 to 159,485), but
much of this decline occurred after 1974 (a 22 percent decline in

graduates between 1975 and 1977 alone) when professors of education began to take note of the teacher surplus problem.

10. This may be a case where the criterion of qualifications shifts from attainment considerations to achievement considerations. Now, instead of hiring the Ed. D. from the local state university, we may find institutions hiring only Ph. D. s from the most prestigious private universities.

11. Data reported in testimony before the Committee on Education and Labor, U.S. House of Representatives, show an increase in graduating credits and course work within the professional school for elementary majors at University of Florida, 1969 to 1979 (Teacher Preparation: Problems and Prospects), a condition one would no doubt find elsewhere.

12. Compare Hardin (1968).

13. Because of dynamics present in the system, and thus simulated by the model, graduate enrollments tend to track undergraduate trends, delayed by a time factor. When undergraduate enrollments are declining, following a period of growth, graduate enrollments will be growing temporarily. By the time undergraduate enrollments have bottomed and are rising once again, graduate level enrollments will have peaked and begun to decline. Thus it turns out that pressure on undergraduate admissions due to graduate overcapacity (too many faculty members, not enough students) is maximized as undergraduate enrollments are reaching the bottom of a decline phase and are beginning to grow. Therefore, just when undergraduate selectivity can begin to increase, there will be a counterpressure not to increase selectivity emanating from the graduate level collapse. The same counterpressure can be seen at the graduate level on admissions as growth begins after the slope of the curve of increasing undergraduate asymptotes and begins a downward movement.

14. The effect of a collapsing job market on graduate and undergraduate enrollments in the short term is, therefore, inverse: Graduate enrollments rise and undergraduate enrollments fall. It is assumed that in the long run continued market decline will drive down both levels.

15. An alternative to model formulation would be to keep track of new teacher graduates from SED graduate schools, compared with an initial level, which would in turn affect older teachers' decisions to attend graduate school.

16. It is assumed that new teachers have a higher marginal return on investments in advanced degrees than those higher on the seniority scale and already holding advanced degrees. In addition, mandatory state requirements and attractive wage inducements also account for increasing graduate enrollments among younger teachers.

17. It is assumed that such decisions are often, perhaps most often, made before the fact, that is, students with low test scores will not apply to programs with high test score cutoffs (compare Nolfi et al. 1977).

18. Defined in the model as an average annual verbal and mathematics score of the college-bound test-taking population.

19. This assumes, of course, that enrollments are a strict function of births 6 to 12 years earlier, that 100 percent of those born will enroll in and attend school up through grade 6, and that net in- and outmigration effects are zero. In addition, demand for elementary teachers assumes a constant student-teacher ratio of 20:1 and a constant turnover rate of 6 percent annually.

5
Policy Testing:
Alternatives for Reform

TESTING APPROACH AND PROCEDURES

The approach to and procedures for testing policies in a system dynamics model are discussed elsewhere in detail (Weaver 1982a). But, briefly, these procedures differ in several respects from those used to test the majority of social science models. The difference has to do with modeling purposes.

Policy analysis using a system dynamics model consists of generating a base run that exhibits the particular problematic behavior or behaviors of concern. In the teacher supply, demand, and quality model, that behavior is a decline in academic quality (test scores) that accompanies a decline in the teacher job market. Once a base run is established, the efficacy of policies is tested by determining what impacts each has on the problematic behavior. Effective policies are those that either improve the condition temporarily only to see it worsen again, or worsen the condition for the period in question, or create new problems.

Thus, the question for policy testing is a relative one: How much has the particular policy improved the problematic behavior relative to the base run?

Four types of policies are tested and their results reported in this chapter. Each of the tests simulates broadly discussed, hypothetical intervention proposals aimed at improving the level of talent entering teaching under conditions producing the opposite pressure. Policy test A simulates the establishment of an entrance qualification test as a condition for acceptance into teacher education programs. Policy test B simulates the establishment of teacher examinations as a condition for employment after graduation from a teacher education program. Policy test C simulates the upgrading and lengthening

of teacher certification standards. Policy test D simulates the effect
of successful alternative career programs in schools of education.

These policy tests reflect a long history of remedies discussed
in Chapter 1. For example, Frank G. Davis (1932) of Bucknell concluded during the "first great teacher surplus" that colleges of education ought to police their admissions standards and screen out the intellectually weak. Davis was bold enough to argue that intelligence
quotients were at least one way (but of course not the only way) to determine admittance into teacher preparation. James D. Koerner
(1963), 30 years after Davis, would shock the educational establishment with a blast at the intellectual inferiority of students admitted
to colleges of education. His prescriptions included a radical upgrading of the criteria for admissions using verbal and quantitative
measures of scholastic ability. Although the idea is intuitively appealing, there is little evidence of its being implemented. Indeed,
the picture one gets of the decade just past is the complete abandon-
ment of any standards imposed at the admissions point in teacher
education.

The second policy test, teacher examinations, was also proposed
by Koerner among others and has been recently tried in a number of
states (see Table 5.1 for a list of states now requiring teacher examinations or with such legislation pending). This intervention has wide
appeal, but as we will show later through computer simulation, its
implementation does not produce the results desired. And that is the
case with the third policy test, upgrading and lengthening certification
requirements. There is a very long history of this strategy beginning
in the early years of this century and continuing up to the present (compare Kinney 1964). As we will argue later, the net result is to create
a more involuted system without affecting the root causes of the talent
problem. And, finally, the alternative careers strategy is untested
for the most part (except in modeling terms), but in those few cases
where it has been tested (see Chapter 6), the results are consistent
with model-generated behavior.

The policy tests (in modeling terms) are designed to show the
impact of a policy intervention under conditions in which the model
is perturbed from an equilibrium state by an abrupt decrease in elementary and secondary enrollments. The first model base run, shown
in Figures 5.1 to 5.5, * is used to display the system's adjustment to
a hypothetical decrease of 25 percent in students enrolled in the elementary and secondary schools. The result is a temporary inflation
of the teacher job pool as teachers are released, followed by decreasing applicants to schools of education, adjustments of SED standards

---

*Figures 5.1 to 5.15 are shown in Appendix A.

(lowering), and a negative effect on the quality (test scores) of people
moving through the system. Thereafter, each policy test simulated
in the model is designed to show the impact of an intervention at the
time of the hypothetical decrease in student enrollments, and for the
time period following. The policies are designed intentionally to try
to counteract the tendency (in the base run just described) of the system to sacrifice talent in the face of collapsing enrollments and jobs.

POLICY TEST A: INCREASING SED
ENTRANCE STANDARDS

In policy test A the model simulates a condition in which schools
of education would raise entrance standards to offset declining quality
in the applicant pool. As quality declines below a desired standard,
school of education acceptance fraction (percentage of applicants accepted) is reduced. Figure 5.6 shows that the policy has one of the
effects desired, namely, limiting the loss of talent by refusing acceptance to those below a desired standard (defined in the policy test
as an SAT score equal to the average College Entrance Examination
Board-tested students seeking admission to college).

However, Figure 5.7 shows that the "price" to be paid for such
a policy is a sharp reduction in the enrollments of undergraduate education majors and the firing of large numbers of faculty members,
followed by some recovery and then a second period of overbuilding
and collapse about ten years later. Given the high price of this intervention (at least as viewed by incumbent job holders in the college
system), it seems reasonable to assume that the policy would not be
offered by faculties of education as a solution, nor be received with
enthusiasm if attempts were made to impose it from the outside. If
imposed externally, the policy, at a minimum, would be expected to
stimulate resistance from faculty members and college administrators
on grounds of academic freedom and control of the process of admissions to academic institutions. (The real motivation behind the rhetoric undoubtedly would be self-preservation.) In short, while the
policy would hypothetically produce the desirable objective of conserving talent, it would cause the collapse of many academic institutions. This policy can be expected to join debate on matters that some
would view as having more importance than the desired objective,
and for that reason it may be an important initiative to consider.
However, the time required to produce a consensus, and thus action
from that consensus, may possibly exceed the period in question
(1982-2000).[1]

POLICY TEST B: TESTING NEW
TEACHER APPLICANTS

In policy test B the model simulates a condition in which employment of new teachers would be restricted by examination standards
designed to offset declining quality of new graduates and others in the
teacher market seeking teaching jobs. This policy intervention, as
an approach to conserving talent, appears to have relatively strong
support (outside the profession).[2] The policy test, in modeling terms,
regulates teacher hiring based on the discrepancy between average
scores of those available to be hired and a "desired" score (defined
as an SAT score equal to the mean score of College Board-tested
students seeking admission to colleges). When fewer meet the standard, fewer will be hired.

Figure 5.8 shows that this policy not only fails to limit the erosion of quality but worsens the erosion to a serious extent. The dynamic effects of this policy (as seen in Figures 5.8 to 5.11) are to
(1) reduce the fraction of those in the job pool who could be hired at
any given time, (2) drive up the average class size in schools as school
districts find themselves unable to hire teachers to fill vacancies,
(3) drive down the attractiveness of teaching as an occupational choice
and thus reduce further the quantity and quality of students seeking
entrance to schools of education, and (4) drive down acceptance standards of education in response, thus further reducing the level of
quality in the system.

The effects of this policy are clearly in the category of counterintuitive responses. It seems reasonable to attempt to preserve talent
in teaching by establishing what amounts to teacher examination boards.
But unless this intervention is coupled with a means of offsetting the
dynamic response of schools of education when confronted with further deterioration in the rate of applications, the testing of new
teachers as a single-minded solution to the talent drain will likely
fail. It seems apparent that the "artificial" shortage of qualified
teachers to fill vacancies created by this policy would have a disrup-
tive and potentially unacceptable impact on the teacher labor market.[3]
Imagine the situation in which school districts in California, Colorado,
Georgia, or elsewhere were actually compelled by state law to hire
only from those in the teacher pool with test scores equal to the
average college freshman (a standard that would appear on the surface at least to be reasonable). Under conditions in the model such
a standard would reduce school boards' choices of new teachers to
about one-third of those entering the market and seeking teaching
jobs.[4] Two effects might be expected: serious temporary shortages
of qualified teachers offset only (as shown under hypothetical conditions in the model) by a 50 percent increase in average class size

and an upsurge in competitive wage bidding for those qualified. The first of these effects is unlikely to be politically accepted, and the second is unlikely to be economically feasible, given present taxpayer attitudes (reinforced by legislative caps in California and Massachusetts and other states).

The net result may be examinations for new teachers, but with standards that adjust to the level of talent in the test-taking pool. In short, testing as a condition of employment may become widely implemented, but the failure rate for those tests is unlikely to be high enough (after the initial discovery that the majority would fail unless the standard for passing is lowered) to restrict seriously entry to the teacher force for political and economic reasons. But that is exactly the consequence necessary for the policy to produce the desired objective of preventing further talent drain.

POLICY TEST C: INCREASING CERTIFICATION REQUIREMENTS

In policy test C the model simulates a condition in which schools of education increase requirements for graduation and successful qualification for a teaching certificate. In operational terms, the length of time to complete requirements for the professional certificate in teaching is increased from four to five years. This policy test makes no assumptions about aptitude characteristics of those preparing for teaching careers except as produced by model dynamics (a condition that corresponds to the actual history of this policy effort).

The net effect of policy test C is to delay by one year the system's adjustment to the oversupply of teachers and subsequent quality decline (Figure 5.12). While this strategy has wide support, its effect on the quality problem, to the extent "quality" and "qualification" are understood to have different meanings, is likely to be inconsequential. This is not to say the policy is undesirable. For some it may be very desirable to increase the paper qualifications of those entering the profession. At least as seen in Figure 5.13, policy test C has one very appealing secondary benefit (for those in education faculties), namely, preventing a collapse of enrollments and faculty jobs that would accompany policy test A.

POLICY TEST D: ALTERNATIVE CAREERS FOR EDUCATORS

In policy test D, the model simulates the establishment of graduate and undergraduate programs in schools of education that directly prepare graduates for education and training jobs in the private sector. The intention of this policy is to offset decline in the teacher market by recruiting from and producing graduates with educational skills for teaching outside the school market.

The expected effect of this policy is to reestablish school of education attractiveness and therefore reestablish conditions under which selection standards can be increased. Theoretically, such a policy would have the effect of removing more people from an inflated teacher job market and, in the longer term, of improving the talent flow into teacher education (as an indirect result of improving the supply-demand imbalance in the teaching field) and therefore into public schoolteaching.

In modeling terms, the policy test increases the "employability" of those in the teacher job market seeking alternative careers in the private sector. The net result is to limit the downturn in quality of those preparing for education careers in the short term and, in the longer term, to raise the level of quality above its equilibrium point (Figures 5.14 and 5.15). It should be noted that this policy, like policy C, also has the added attraction (for faculties of education) of preventing the collapse of SED enrollments and faculties, but unlike policy C, it improves the quality problem. In short, policy test D works, in theory, because it meets the self-interests of incumbent job holders while also meeting the objectives of talent conservation.

IMPLICATIONS OF POLICY TESTING

The tendency of the system, as modeled, is to deplete talent, when necessary, in order to protect resources of the system other than talent, that is, jobs of incumbents. Policy interventions that seek to reverse that tendency are possible to imagine but impossible to implement. The primary underlying forces in the system are the individual's preservation of self-interest and the self-perpetuation of institutions. These virtually universal human tendencies are set in motion by conditions in which the conservation of talent means sacrificing jobs, careers, and decades of institutional building. The model simulates the dynamic adjustments incumbents and institutions are forced to make and will make in response to changing opportunity, individual choices, and the flow of talent into areas of opportunity. Only to the extent policy interventions are compatible with these forces, rather than attempting to defeat them, will their prospects of success be enhanced.

The conditions we have documented (and subsequently modeled) are clearly not in the public interest. They are long term and of extreme ranges of magnitude in terms of costs. Consider the costs of producing 1.5 million unneeded teachers in the past decade, to say nothing of the hidden and less direct but more serious cost of depleting the talent in teaching. The hidden costs will eventually affect this society's capacity to prepare and adjust to rapid changes in worldwide economic and political conditions.

From the point of first perturbing the model to its point of "recovery," dynamic adjustments require about 15 to 20 years. The model simulations that reproduce historical and projected time series data show approximately the same periodicity (1970-90). Without intervention the system seems to respond to supply–demand imbalances and subsequent talent flight over a fairly long period of time. Without intervention, the most likely scenario for the future is a continuing boom-bust cycle in the teaching field, tracking demographic cycles of growth and decline, and accompanied by long periods of declining quality. Given that talent loss to the system, which requires approximately two decades to restore fully, is an undesirable component of these cycles, the importance of policy intervention is clear enough. What are the alternatives for reform?

The most direct measure would be the construction of barriers to the teaching field, in a fashion resembling medicine and law (a point made by D. B. Waldo of the Kalamazoo State Normal School in 1919, and repeated by reformers for six decades). High entrance standards to schools of education and high standards for teacher hiring appear at first blush to be the answers. In Koerner's mind, the only problem was to get the education establishment to stop resisting. However, the consequences of these solutions turn out to be dynamically very complex and counterintuitive. The immediate raising of standards at either point (admissions to college or teaching) would demand consensus on what is the appropriate standard for restricting entrance to the teaching profession. But even if that issue is resolved, the political and economic effects of restricting entry on any ground whatsoever would be far reaching—so far reaching that many school boards would be forced into bankruptcy in the effort to compete for qualified candidates; at the very least, the inevitable result would be a much higher bill for the taxpayer. How much higher would depend on how restrictive the entrance qualifications. This appears to be the bottom line. First-year law school graduates in Boston's largest law firms were offered salaries between $30,000 and $40,000 in 1983. As a standard of comparison (albeit a high one), these beginning salaries are more than twice the level of the average experienced schoolteacher in the United States. This example is not offered to show the absurdity of such comparisons, nor to embarrass teachers (or lawyers), but to place some perspective on the problem.

If schools are to compete for the most (and not the least) talented individuals this society's colleges can produce, then they can expect to pay the highest wages such talent can command. Under any but the most utterly unimaginable circumstances, cities and states will not choose to afford, nor be able to afford, a free system of schools that competes for that level of talent. The model does not attempt to simulate these economical and political dynamics simply because of the enormous complexity and unpredictability entailed. However, even a superficial reading of the present political and economic climate suggests that, other things being equal, the doubling of entry wages for teachers, with consequential ripple effects up the seniority ladder, would be highly resisted by the public in every corner of the United States.

Certification changes that lengthen and intensify teacher preparation will be much more politically and economically acceptable but are also more likely to produce weak effects, or indeed, as the case has been, no effects. While certification may influence paper requirements, the root cause of the quality problem rests with the selection of candidates to be trained and with the total system in which professional educators are prepared.

Certification reform (in its most ideal sense) may speak to the teaching competencies for which faculties of education are responsible, but that does not consider where the actual teaching of college-level verbal and quantitative skills takes place. Where it takes place is precisely where James Koerner preferred: in the arts and sciences faculty. The teacher who cannot write effectively, or understand a scientific principle, or explain number sets, or speak convincingly in public presumably has also failed to display such skills earlier under the watchful eyes of professors of English, science, mathematics, and the humanities. If we wish to take seriously the idea that teachers should meet high level academic standards, then it must be recognized that the liberal arts faculty is already responsible for the results we see. At least half or more of the undergraduate preparation of all teachers takes place in the arts and sciences departments.

However, our contention, made earlier, is that the real issue rests with the market-driven attractiveness of the field, not with preparation requirements, irrespective of where those requirements are taught. People attracted to the field (see Chapters 2 and 3) in the bottom third of economic rewards turn out to be persons in the bottom third of scholastic ability. Certification changes will not affect this condition, nor will transferring the training entirely to the liberal arts departments. This condition is a function of the dynamics inherent in all recursive systems. There has been a historic oversupply of some teaching categories (notably those in which graduates have the least occupational training relevance to employers outside teaching in public schools) and a historic undersupply of those most attractive to employers other than school districts, that is, mathematics and technical-scientific fields. Any successful policy intervention must take this phenomenon into account.

Finally, there may be enough public clamor to induce some school boards and some states to adopt teacher testing, but I do not believe the public has the slightest idea what such a policy would mean if it actually restricts hiring on the basis of scholastic aptitude. For these reasons, I conclude that there will be teacher testing, but it is unlikely to result in any significant change in the academic quality of persons in the field precisely because testing, if restrictive, will produce counterpressures that drive the testing standards toward the level of ability of those tested.

If we really wish to deal with the problem of scholastic abilities of those entering the teaching field, then we have to understand more about how the system qua system operates, both in its larger context and over long periods of time. That understanding will lead to a conclusion that the remedies of the past have not worked as a matter of historical record, and, moreover, are cumulatively part of the cause of the problem that we are examining. The alternative careers strategy (discussed in detail in Chapter 6) holds the same desired goal—improved talent in teaching—but it does not ignore the lessons of history or the dynamics of the marketplace.

SHIFT IN THE PROBLEM

Just as the public hears about the full effects of decline (from reports emanating from government and foundations, which always seem to appear eight to ten years after the fact) and colleges are in the final state of dismantling education programs, the boom-bust cycle is shifting. The projected data reported in Chapter 4 show that overall teacher demand will begin to increase around the middle of this decade. Given the time delays built into the system and a depletion of the teacher reserve pool, the most likely scenario for the period 1985-90 is a general shortage of new teachers to fill demand, bearing in mind that the demand increases (and shortages) will be primarily at the lower grade levels. The shift from declining to increasing demand will create a shortage of new teachers for some years, to be followed by still another period of oversupply. The restoration of quality will be gradual, and it will probably take another ten years to reach the level of talent seeking entry to the field in the late 1960s. The restoration of faculties of education will take even longer. The point is that "recovery" will occur with or without the proposed reforms, but an understanding of why the teacher glut and talent drain happened will be lost.

As a separate matter, shortages of mathematics and science teachers are being reported, and have been reported, for several years.[5] Solving the mathematics and science teacher shortage will inevitably require some form of differentiating salary incentives (see reference to salary differential effects on college major choices of students in Cebula and Lopes [1982] and attitudes of those leaving and staying in teaching regarding salary increases as a major career factor in Chapman and Hutcheson [1982]). Where competitive wage bidding results in mathematics and science majors' rejecting teaching as a career, school systems that wish to attract highly qualified mathematics and science teachers will be forced to offer higher salary incentives (Wall Street Journal 1982). The resistance to this solution will likely come from the teaching profession itself (Pipho 1983). Merit pay and other forms of differential compensation, apart from seniority and credentials, have had, to say the least, a less than enthusiastic response from organized teacher groups.[6]

The paradox is that the teaching fields oversupplied now have also been in the past, while others have always been in short supply historically without apparent effect on compensation policies. The science and mathematics teacher shortage has not had the effect of attracting more students into preparation programs or into the job market. It is assumed this is the case, not because a new law of supply and demand is at work, but because demand is being satisfied at the expense of quality. Given the choice of no mathematics or science teacher versus employing a poorly qualified teacher, school districts (like professors) are forced to choose the lesser evil. Given no change in present compensation policies, which fail to recognize competitive bidding differences within teaching fields, the present condition is likely to continue until overall supply-demand conditions force all teachers' salaries higher. But, to the extent Elizabeth Useem's (1982) findings are representative, there may not be a rising level of supplies of mathematics and science teachers occurring with an anticipated shift in the aggregate supply and demand of teachers. If the present growth in the technology industries, with accompanying demand pressure for people with quantitative aptitudes, continues, and if this pressure is acting as a drain on mathematics and science talent in teaching, the longer-term solution will not occur spontaneously with a rebound in teacher hiring. The condition we see now may be expected to worsen until such time as the attractiveness of preparing to be a mathematics or science teacher is competitive with the attractiveness of employment in the private sector.

CONCLUSION: A LONG-TERM STRATEGY

The longer-term solution to the boom-bust cycle in the teaching field, and its detrimental effects on quality, rests in part with a redefinition of the mission of schools of education. We will take this up in more detail in the next chapter, but consider for now the fact that colleges of education have existed primarily, if not entirely, to train teachers and school specialists. If this were not the case, the decline of education colleges would not be a necessary outcome of the decline in job opportunities for teachers. Efforts to regulate this system have not solved the problem. They have made it worse by reinforcing the dictum that if we do not need schoolteachers there is no reason to go into a school of education. That, of course, is preposterous, because the teaching requirements of this society do not begin to be defined by the requirements of the public school systems. Consider the following irony: While the market for schoolteachers shrinks, the major corporations of America are investing billions of dollars in educational activities ranging from employee technical skill development to executive seminars, and that investment has been growing.

What are the competencies needed to teach adults in these corporate settings? Presumably, many of the same skills colleges of education now teach (or should teach): curriculum design and evaluation, media and instructional technology, instructional planning, and problem solving. But if colleges of education wish to enter this market, they will be forced to define a specific corpus of knowledge and skills in teaching, and they will be forced to cooperate with other faculties because no credible program to prepare industry-oriented educators could exist without incorporating other disciplines. For example, education and training specialists in high-technology firms (and in most firms) must have a background in computer programming and business administration well beyond the skill level offered in all but the most unusual school of education. Schools of education have something to offer in the discipline of teaching, but education faculties will have to define much more precisely than they have what teaching is and then actually deliver the goods. Otherwise, unlike those preparing to teach in schools, trainers will not spend their time or money on education courses.

But how will this affect the talent pool for public school teaching? Our initial argument, presented in Chapter 1 and detailed in Chapter 6, suggests that the effect will be positive. The creation of alternatives for education majors, if taken seriously, is a feasible way to reduce (not eliminate) the chronic oversupply of education graduates now being prepared for one educational role—namely, public school teaching. By collectively relieving pressure in the teacher job market, the attractiveness of colleges of education may be increased and reasonable selectivity restored to the field. Colleges of education will not voluntarily cut back the supply of teachers (for now, their only product) through raising standards unless and until new sources of students are developed.

What appears to be inevitable, with or without institutional action by colleges of education, is that states will restrict and lengthen teacher certification requirements in response to pressure to restrict supplies of teachers. That may be a solution some welcome. This strategy does one thing. By extending the length of preparation for future teachers, and by increasing the costs of preparation for students and institutions, it may temporarily delay teacher supply. However, graduates will still end up in the teacher job applicant pool, but after even more intensely investing in preparation for school teaching. The long-term effect is to create more overcapacity, which will worsen the problem. The effort to regulate the quality and quantity of new teacher graduates through extending certification standards simply reinforces the tendency of schools of education to expend energy elaborating and enlarging the very capacities they need least. If schools of education are to attempt to address educational problems outside the public schools, their energies must be redirected. Schools of education have not responded to the growth of learning needs in industry, health care, and social services precisely because faculties of education are heavily entrenched in preparing schoolteachers. The effort required to develop a discipline worthy of the name simply is not compatible with the more political requirements for certifying school personnel.

Legislative and policy advisement bodies considering the problems of recruitment and selection of schoolteachers should reexamine the traditional remedies. Regulatory actions that have the effect of restricting entry to classroom teaching jobs on the basis of test scores, but do not at the same time restrict entrance to schools of education, will lead to a deepening of the very problem those actions are aimed at eliminating. If states are going to take seriously the testing of new teachers, then the schools of education that produce candidates who fail the tests must be accountable. That might mean something like an annual, public report card on the success–fail rates of school of education graduates who take the exams. Schools of education with a successful record would be rewarded presumably by being the choice of students who seek to prepare for teaching careers. Those with a poor record of success would suffer the consequences. But while this might be desirable, it is not a feasible solution to the problem. Regulatory actions of this kind end up costing a great deal in the forms of political conflict and management resources. They focus corrective attention on precisely the wrong dynamics of this problem, that is, imposed restrictions that attempt to substitute government actions for private motives. Such efforts would be better devoted to interventions consistent with an understanding of the dynamics of the problem.

For reasons we will discuss in the next chapter, it is in the public interest for policy bodies to explore and implement effective measures that increase attractiveness of graduates of schools of education to employers other than school districts. One of those measures is the creation of interdisciplinary programs that prepare graduates for educational roles in the private sector. Incentives to encourage schools of education to move in that direction might include (1) funds for retraining or relocating existing faculty members; (2) reallocation of state higher education budgets so that state funding for college favors those which implement effective new career programs; (3) special funds for feasibility and needs assessment activities that incorporate private sector involvement in the study of long-term private sector education and training problems; (4) scholarship aid for new students preparing for nonschool educational jobs; and (5) tax incentives for businesses that identify and support financially college training of presently employed education and training personnel.

In summary, the long-term solution to the quality problem is to reduce the dependency of schools of education on the teacher market. This prescription runs counter to conventional wisdom. We shall see why the conventional wisdom is wrong in Chapter 6.

NOTES

1. Just such a controversy has arisen in two states. In Colorado, the qualification test for entry into student teaching has been challenged by education faculties and students (Education Week 1983). In Alabama, the evaluation of teacher education programs tied to student examinations has produced, first, contentious battling and, second, a policy many think is so compromised that it is unenforceable (Education Week 1983). In California, the examination is administered after completion of college requirements, but colleges are voluntarily permitted to use the examination as a screening device. However, even if students fail, they may be admitted into teacher preparation. Thus, the real issue has not yet been joined in California (Los Angeles Times 1983). The new Texas examination will be administered to students prior to entering teacher education, as planned in 1984. It is not clear what will happen if most fail (Education USA 1983).

2. Nineteen states require teacher examinations (Vlaanderen 1982), and 33 states are reported to have pending legislation to require minimum competency standards for teachers (Teacher Preparation: Problems and Prospects 1982). Table 5.1 reports the states requiring testing of new teachers as compiled by the Education Commission of the States.

3. Evidence on this problem is beginning to appear; the majority of first test takers failed the mathematics part of the Colorado

teachers' examination. Approximately 38 percent failed the spelling and grammar parts of the test. The test used was the California Achievement Test, a test ordinarily given to high school seniors. The passing standard for Colorado's prospective teachers was set at a 75th percentile score on the test. Pressure has arisen to change the standard. See Education Week (1983)

4. See Chapter 2 for a more detailed analysis of the distribution of test scores among college graduates majoring in teacher education.

5. The estimate of a shortage in chemistry and physics, for example, based on NCES and NEA data, extends back at least to 1960 (Chapman 1980).

6. Typical is the reaction of the Maryland State Teachers Association minority report calling the "Final Recommendations of the Commission on Quality Teaching" a "sham." Those recommendations called for differential pay and evaluations of teacher competency (Maryland State Board of Education, October 1982). The reaction of the NEA to the National Commission on Excellence in Education recommendation for merit pay is equally typical: "We've never seen a plan that had balance, fairness and objectivity . . . merit pay hasn't worked yet" (Education Week 1983).

6

Human Resources
and Education

INTRODUCTION

We began in Chapter 1 with a review of the history of teacher
supply, demand, and quality. In Chapter 5 we saw the model-tested
effects of widely proposed policy alternatives. The basic conclusion
is that the boom-bust cycles over the past eight decades are reflections
of a training system with a singular purpose: production of people
for one occupational role, schoolteaching. The efforts to regulate
these cycles have failed because the regulations themselves produce
an ever more involuted system, which is part of the cause of the
problem in the first place. By defining teacher certification in terms
of courses and diplomas awarded by teachers colleges, the primary
means of regulating supplies have been to intensify college requirements during a surplus and to relax them during shortages. The net
result, however, is a bloated system of teacher training institutions,
precariously perched on a market demand that rises and falls with
birthrate.

Each effort to restrict supplies by raising requirements leads
to more capacity building. In the next growth cycle, the system is
inflated by the previous period's embellishments and new certification
requirements. The self-corrections produce a phenomenon whereby
graduates over time are more and more intensely (but no more effectively) trained in a manner making them less and less adaptable
(by virtue of training) to employment outside the occupation of schoolteaching. The institutional capacity to deliver the form of training
expands exponentially during periods of growth. An increase in the
rate of demand for teachers causes an even higher rate of demand
for college faculties in education departments who must train teachers, train undergraduate-level faculty members, and train graduate-

level faculty members. The "defensive" credentialing in the form
of graduate credits, which is part of and indigenous to a system built
upon paper qualifications, has the illusory effect of stimulating more
growth in response to demand when jobs initially become scarce, but
the demand is temporary and the illusion collapses of its own accord.
Graduate schools exhaust the available pool of such candidates, while
the system is adding no new candidates, such as young, uncredentialed
new teachers who would be a primary source of graduate students.
The effect is similar to a ball rolling along and then suddenly falling
off a table. The entire process resembles nothing so much as a chain
letter. All goes well until the chain breaks, as it did in the 1970s,
and each crash of the system is larger than the one before.

While I do not necessarily disagree with James D. Koerner's
extremely unflattering description of the state of teacher education,
or even the intent of his prescriptions, I do not think they would cure
the problem. Koerner was convinced that his recommendations would
not cure the problem either, because the educational establishment
would prevent their implementation. I am convinced that his prescriptions would not cure the problem even if they were carried out to the
letter. His prescriptions ignore the market dynamics, which are the
root cause of the problem. Institutional regulations and controls,
and the subsequent building of capacity described above, are secondary
causes of the problem. They dynamically operate over time to magnify the amplitude of surpluses and shortages in response to market
changes. A transference of this training capacity to the liberal arts
faculties would not eliminate the problem. As the evidence shows
and common sense tells us, the surpluses these faculties produced
in the 1970s, in part due to the collapse of the education market,
were different from the surplus produced by education faculties only
in scale. Given a larger role in teacher training, the surpluses produced by the liberal arts faculties in the 1970s would not have differed
even in scale. The Koerner critique also overlooks the fact that
liberal arts faculties are already responsible for at least half of the
education of teachers.

There is no complete and final solution to the problem simply
because the system of academic labor supply and demand is inherently
recursive. The other components of the college market behave like
the education market. No field is entirely free of boom and bust
cycles. However, I do believe that the extreme conditions we have
seen in teaching can be avoided or lessened.

As its most fundamental level, the process we are talking about
is the "tragedy of the commons." In Garrett Hardin's well-known
thesis (1968), the inherent self-defeating conflict between private interests and the collective good produces a vicious circle in which
commonly held resources are destroyed by efforts of individuals to

maximize private gain. Academic institutions, which produce graduates for the labor market, behave, predictably, in ways that maximize private gain—even if that means, collectively, that they eventually destroy the market for their products. The case in point is education, but other disciplines also provide excellent examples. When teacher training institutions suffered the first downdrift of the students in the early 1970s, they reacted individually in exactly the way Hardin would have predicted and with an equally predictable result. Their efforts to avoid collapse led them to do individually precisely what they should not have done for the good of all: admit and graduate as many students as they could find. Needless to say, one can find identical cases in engineering, sociology, foreign language, journalism, law, biology, and virtually every other field that does not have the means to enforce quotas and behave as a cartel. Medicine may be the exception, but even in medicine, it appears that expansion of medical schools may be having some effect on the closed market of physicians.

The Training Alternative as Policy

In terms of model dynamics, policy test D (see Chapter 5) "solved" the problem of teacher quality by simulating the effects of a policy in which schools of education offer training and credentials for those wishing to become educators, not only of children in the public (and private) schooling system, but also of adults in training situations in business, industry, and other sectors. In this concluding chapter, we will examine the "real" (and not model) world of that policy. In the real world, educators and defenders of such a policy, as a solution of public interest in the supply of qualified teachers, would have to answer to the plausibility, feasibility, public-regardingness, and originality tests applied to any policy proposal. These are not just logical but practical, political requirements of any policy. Does the policy proposal make intuitive sense consistent with the premises underlying the problem it is supposed to solve (the plausibility test)? Is there a likelihood of its implementation given (again) the premises underlying the problem definition (the feasibility test)? Does the solution commend itself to those affected interests other than the institution or interest group that is either the agent and/or direct beneficiary of the policy being proffered (the public-regardingness test)? And how different is this policy proposal from others on the table where premises are challenged by the problem definition underlying the current policy proposal (the originality test)?

Plausibility

Consider again the four policies tested in our model in Chapter
5. And consider again why the other three "failed" to correct the
model's problem run. We have seen (as modeled) that teacher testing,
as a condition of certification awards (and not admission to or graduation from teachers colleges), degrades the teacher job market further and is not plausible even if the model run had been successful
because the "price" exceeds the limits of common sense. Recall that
70 percent of the teacher graduates, in any of the past five years,
tested by a hypothetical national teacher board would have failed,
using average high school aptitude as the standard. School systems
under such conditions would be left with thousands of unfilled teacher
vacancies.

The "price" of imposed entrance standards renders the second
policy unfeasible (and unenforceable) because admissions decisions
by practice and convention, if not by law, are the province of those
who would be forced out of business. Thus, even if the policy produces a model run that solves the problem, it does not meet the real-
world test of plausibility. To imagine it would do so is to imagine a
world devoid of natural instincts of self-preservation.

The third policy, upgrading certification requirements, fails
not only the model test but nearly 100 years of history. As pointed
out above, the effort to regulate the system by controlling certification has caused further degrees of centralization and a more involuted
system that worsens rather than alleviates the problem.

The market strategy (educators as adult trainers) as a policy
test provides a desired model outcome because it leverages a system
suffering from centripetal paralysis. We have addressed already
the "real"-world test of plausibility. The initial argument is made
in Chapter 1, but in brief, the claim—and evidence to support that
claim in Chapter 2—holds that academic institutions will act to conserve talent when the alternative is not extinction. The market
strategy would produce such a condition for education departments
where demography, and only demography, now dictates the opposite
condition. But is the policy feasible? We take up that argument next.

Feasibility

Any policy, such as the alternative policy proposed, that ad-
vertises itself as harnessing rather than trying to change or ignore
the realities of "talent flowing into opportunity" and "individual and
institutional self-preservation" has the burden of showing that there
is in fact the kind of opportunity that can drive individual and institu-

tional behavior in the desired direction. It will have to show, for example, that there is a market demand for the kind of talent that wants to teach but not necessarily in the public (or private) school setting; and that the needs of that market are such that schools of education can meet them by adjusting and reallocating their present capacity (thereby meeting the need for institutional self-preservation without resorting to lower admissions standards).

We will take up the question of opportunity later, but for now I will assert (and later demonstrate) the case that the need is real and increasing. Schools of education have not played a major role in meeting the opportunity that exists, in part because of their involuted character and place in a politically driven system to regulate the flow of credentialed teachers. It does not follow that because they should meet the teaching needs of institutions other than schools they will be able to do so. In the absence of such efforts, however, I see little reason why one of the main problems Koerner identified (lack of a coherent body of knowledge skills) would ever be remedied. There is at present no test of the ability of schools of education to produce a corpus of knowledge. As in the case of utilities, their market (schools) is forced to accept whatever they produce. The capability of schools of education to teach effectively useful pedagogical skills required of adult trainers would be tested in and by the market for such talent. If schools of education have nothing to offer trainers, they can and will go elsewhere (unlike schoolteachers). The discovery that such a practice is the basic requirement of survival, and one without which many schools of education will close, would create the condition (self-preservation) for change. However, simply having the condition for change does not ensure change. But the teacher "depressions" of the past have not motivated such changes because the actual opportunity for testing whether schools of education are good for anything other than training schoolteachers has not been present. Corporate training, on the scale we now see it, is a very recent phenomenon, as recent as the technological industries that have spawned it.

I am also inclined to believe that there is a potentially useful corpus of skills and knowledge that schools of education can define and claim but have not been forced to because of their "protected" status. As long as teachers or would-be teachers have to take whatever schools of education hand out, and as long as schools of education are not compelled to define their curriculum in terms of specific, generic skills but rather in terms of things mysteriously thought to be unique to schoolteachers and only schoolteachers, the conditions are not present to motivate change. I am not asserting that there is a hidden, grand theory of education waiting to be discovered, and that only the conditions have to be right. I am asserting that hidden in the morass of the hundreds of education courses is a limited but useful body of skills and competencies that teachers, whether teachers of children or teachers of adults, need to practice. I am inclined to think the skills colleges of education can contribute are limited (but important), and for this reason any prospect that schools of education will succeed at this strategy will depend upon their ability to utilize faculties outside education. The prototype program described later rests on this premise (that is, the effective training of trainers requires university-wide resources). However, I also see this requirement as a benefit in the long term in prying open education schools.

Finally, the evidence that adult training does not merely give lip service to but utilizes the corpus of skills that education has produced may be found in the programs of instruction offered by business corporations and training/consulting firms. As opposed to the undignified examples Koerner offered of education faculty members failing to display the skills of teaching, trainers seem to take seriously the art and practice of teaching.[1] Such practices can probably be reduced to a reasonably small number of courses and months, not years, of study, but nonetheless, training professionals appear actually to use and rely upon the work of Benjamin Bloom, Jerome Bruner, B. F. Skinner, N. L. Gage, and others who have contributed to the literature on instruction.

Public Regardingness

Thus far, it has been asserted (and will later be shown) that the market solution is based on the existence of a real rather than hypothetical market demand and on a real rather than fanciful assessment of teacher educators' ability (when combined with other faculties) to meet this demand. Those who want to teach but find school-teaching unattractive now have a reason, if the human resource education model (later described as a prototype) is adopted, to enroll in schools of education. Schools of education can attract more students and preserve programs and faculties. Business firms and other employers would have an identifiable pool of talent to draw upon. But where is the public interest in all of this?

Let us go back to the original formulation of the problem. Our whole analysis was triggered by data showing a persistent decline in the academic talent of graduating teacher candidates. After exploring the issues and history of proposed remedies (Chapter 1), analyzing the data and defining the recent problem (Chapters 2 and 3), and testing the representative range of proposed remedies (Chapter 5), we now arrive at a solution that prescribes (somewhat paradoxically) the following: The polity's interest in having an adequate supply of high-quality teachers for its children is best served by an initiative in which schools of education undertake the function (with other faculties) of preparing teachers, not for the young, but for training programs in business and industry. A sense of paradox is further heightened by the fact that talent flows into areas of opportunity, and it is the greater opportunity in industrial training (as opposed to schoolteaching). That makes the proposed policy subject to further disbelief. Where is the public's interest in quality teachers served? Is this not a further disservice?

In order to dissolve this apparent paradox, let us recall the argument in Chapter 1. The current private interest of schools of education in trying to get students when their students are not employable contributes to and worsens the quality problem. The range of policies thus far offered as attempts to police and compel education faculties to behave more nobly than anyone else has failed. The policy proposed here would have (and has had)[2] the desired effect of producing applicants from a different pool of talent than colleges of education have heretofore attracted and thereby creating the conditions under which every teacher applicant, regardless of talent, does not receive an acceptance letter. The net result is fewer but better qualified teacher candidates and an emptying of the flooded teacher market. The latter effect is absolutely necessary to restore faith in the occupation of teaching as a career choice, and it is fundamentally necessary to attract talented college-bound students who want to enter a profession not swamped with mediocre job seekers. The long-term effect would be to accomplish what teacher-testing advocates claim they desire—much higher caliber candidates—but will not attain even if, and precisely if, their policy were fully implemented nationwide.

Originality

A review of the history of the teacher quality problem leads one to the conclusion that the finest minds of three generations are of one mind: The quality problem stems from teacher training institutions being inferior and students who attend not knowing the difference. The cure is to be found in entry regulations, salary, certification and testing, and academic training. Proposed remedies fall into the following categories:

Category 1: Higher rewards produce better quality, or "you get what you pay for." This is the classic NEA position.

Category 2: More quality control produces more quality (where quality is defined as qualifications). That is, have stricter and higher professional standards through tougher admissions, certification, and entrance into employment regulations policies A, B, and C tested in the model in Chapter 5). The "theory" is that quality means qualified, and qualified is certified—the circular nature of which says the more of the latter, the better the former.

Category 3: Increase the quality of the product by improving or substituting the production process, that is, the Koerner formula. His thesis was that teachers were (and presumably are) paid what they deserve based on the training they receive (nonacademic) and the talent they have.

The Koerner solution is not only generic and representative but crosses over into the other remedies; for example, part of the reform is to impose policing of the profession (Category 2), and part of his salary argument (they get what they deserve) joins with and debates the Category 1 remedies.

In examining our proposed policy, we discover elements of the desired goals of each of the above remedies, but the means of achieving those desired goals acknowledge and entail the dynamic forces of private interests, opportunities, and flows of talent to opportunities. I do not ignore but in fact assume as a given that market dynamics are the determinants of political and economically driven responses of institutions and individuals.

But the alternative proposal, in historical perspective, is Koerner-like in its interest in defining (or redefining) the corpus of knowledge and skills that teachers (of children and adults) are required to practice and required to master before practice. The proposed strategy ultimately solves the quality problem by screening (out of individuals' choices and institutions' conserving of talent) intellectually weak candidates and thereby improving the choices schools have among candidates, as well as the salaries teachers are justified in claiming. But seeking higher salaries, in the absence of opportunities for job seekers, is a misunderstanding of economics. When employers have ample choices among equally qualified teachers, even if the quality is extremely high, the wage offerings will not be high. Demand relative to supply is the determinant. To bring salaries up in teaching, the labor market must cooperate. In order for the labor market to cooperate, the supply of teachers must be adaptive to changes in demand.

Moreover, I agree with Koerner that the educational interests of the polity will be disinclined to pay more for a product if quality (or at least one measure of quality) is perceived as declining. However, unlike Koerner, I emphasize that the polity also has independent fiscal constraints. The educational system is not a "moral economy" in which rewards are based on norms of "just deserts," but rather, has basic aspects of any labor market. And, as in all markets, the fiscal interests of the polity will cause it to bid down salary levels whenever supply (of labor) exceeds demand, irrespective of any private (for example, Koerner's thesis that, in 1963, teachers got paid what they deserved) or public evaluation of desert. Consequently, the proposed strategy drives salaries up by creating a shortage (or re-balancing of supply and demand), which in turn is created by increased selectivity in the selection of "raw material" in the production process (higher admissions standards congruent with Category 2 remedies) in a way that does not dictate that schools of education commit insti-tutional suicide.

The distinguishing feature of the market strategy, and hence its response to the "originality" test, is that it manipulates (rather than ignores or passively responds to or attempts fruitlessly to defeat) the "invisible hand" of the labor market. The strategy does so in ways that do not expect would-be teachers and teacher educators to forgo the "pursuit of happiness" (and financial security and self-preserva-tion) that our system of choices and resource allocations grants and legitimates to all other professionals. The educational system has managed to produce four major teacher boom-bust cycles in this cen-tury, each worse than the last one and each accompanied by even more intensive efforts to regulate the problem with no lasting effect.

And, finally, the proposed strategy, consistent with Category 3 (improved or substitute production of skills), pushes toward a rede-fined, more specific curriculum emphasizing skills and knowledge essential in teaching that must be taught not just by education facul-ties but in conjunction with faculties across the university. It assumes that the market will be relatively brutal in testing schools of education because the market for trainers is not dependent upon supplies from a single, politically controlled system of preparing institutions (as is the case of schoolteaching).

Prying Open the System

If there were no schoolteaching jobs, would there be a reason for education colleges to exist? The answer is probably no, as things now stand. The cynical reply by some would be that there is even less reason for colleges of education to exist when teachers are in great demand. I reject this argument because it leads nowhere in a practical sense and, worse, leads to a condition in which teachers would be trained by liberal arts faculties who are equally capable of tragedy-of-commons behavior and are equally culpable in producing the level of talent we now see entering teaching. But my reply and the cynic's reply draw us to a similar conclusion: Schools of educa-tion represent a closed, inward-turned system, and the closeness with which they are married to the fortunes of the teacher market is all the evidence one needs to prove the point.

Consider what happens when employment opportunities in the schools rise or fall. There is an almost perfect, but time-delayed, correlation with expansion or contraction of applications, of enrollments and faculties in schools of education. The conventional wisdom among students is that if there are few schoolteaching jobs, there is little reason to attend a college of education. Is this an adequate test of the proposition that without teaching jobs there is no reason for schools of education to exist? It certainly is not an adequate test because students could (and should) be mistaken. But at least a cursory review of catalogs of education schools suggests that students probably are not mistaken. An examination of the education literature reveals an overwhelming preoccupation with education as an institutionalized schooling process and with the "craft-wisdom" peculiar to that process. For example, the Encyclopedia of Educational Research, 4th edition (1969), contains 1,552 pages of material on educational research.* There is a six-page discussion of adult education. The clear impression is that formal inquiry (at least up to 1969) in the field of education is concerned with activities that occur in the schooling system. The term training and development, for instance, is not defined in the 1969 edition at all. The fifth edition of the Encyclopedia of Educational Research in four volumes (1982) is 2,126 pages long, but like the earlier version makes no reference to training and development or human resource development. There is a reference to industrial training with five pages devoted to the topic (864-870). Adult education is covered in four pages (83-87).

Such a view of education is undesirable, even as a matter of scholarship. It tends to limit those interested in educational inquiry to an interest only in the features of the schooling system. It also tends to reinforce the generally held view that schooling and education are synonymous. It is unfortunately the case that in virtually every country in the world when one is asked "Where were you educated?", the common reply will be some particular school or schools. Thus, it should surprise no one that education is taken to be virtually synonymous with credentialed, certified completion of a given level of schooling, and that scholars in schools of education are preoccupied with issues having to do with schools, teachers, children, and credentials.

This definition of educational inquiry would not begin to exhaust the totality of educational scholarship. It obviously omits studies of highly formal education in business, industry, public services, and the military and a vast array of educational activities and learning arrangements outside even these institutions.[3] But that is the point. The schooling system as the defined field of inquiry does not begin to exhaust the limits of any society's total interests or investments in education. By ignoring this fact, we end up with an a priori defini-

tion of our discipline that excludes vast areas of the subject we wish
to study. It arbitrarily delimits the body of concepts, theories, and
expressions of education that should be of interest to scholars in the
field. Moreover, it leads to a curriculum inflated with idiosyncratic
definitions of educational practices peculiar to the schooling system,
which cover entire semesters or even years of study.

This is my principled argument: The failure to be interested
in the whole of education is a failure of scholarship, and that failure
in part explains why the education curriculum has become irrelevant
even to those studying to be teachers. It circumscribes our capacity
to understand. The disutility of this narrow view is to disengage
schools of education from service to the larger needs of society because the curriculum they have invented is not testable in a free market of ideas or practice. The curriculum of education is whatever
education professors say it is, and the practice setting (public schools),
which denies much of that curriculum's relevance, is stuck with the
results. Little wonder that few, outside the profession or even inside, have much faith that schools of education offer anything of substance. They are organized in such a way as to deny that education
might consist of a generic discipline embodying skills and knowledge
of value to the practice of teaching regardless of the setting. There is
a distinct occupational uniformity to the manner in which schools of
education are organized. For each major occupational role in the
schooling system, there will be a department (or faculty specialist)
consisting of faculty members who themselves once served in the
occupational role in the schooling system (Kuuskraa et al. 1978). It
would be unusual to find a contrary case. This is the testament of a
system that defines "teaching" as "the occupation of teachers." It is
here that we discover the real meaning of the "miseducation of American teachers." Teaching, if it is to be a recognized discipline, consists not of a "station" (duties and roles) but of activities that transcend any one occupational setting.

To quote a passage from Thomas F. Green's book The Activities of Teaching:

> To understand the idea of teaching we need to grasp the
> nature of knowing, believing, thinking, learning, ex-
> plaining, judging, wondering, defining, demonstrating,
> and so forth. Each of these activities has its place in
> teaching. Still, not even collectively do they consti-
> tute all that we mean by "teaching" and certainly they
> do not exhaust what we mean by "education."
> The essential point I want to make is that in the activi-
> ties of teaching, considered collectively, we may dis-
> cover the model of a process whereby people might test

their capacity to face the truth and enhance their ability
to change their minds, and in such a process men might
learn not only to change their minds in respect to what
they believe is true but also to change their minds in
respect to what they decide to do. The activities of
teaching are the activities of deliberation and inquiry.

We ought not to suppose that the education of a people
is something that can be relegated to a set of institutions that we call schools. I do not mean simply that
the entire environment is itself a part of education and
that schoolmen should take that into account. I mean
that we can expect specific consequences to arise from
the way society arranges activities unconnected with
schools. (pp. 215-16)

There would appear to be no logical or theoretical reason for
the present organization and mission of colleges of education. There
may be other reasons. The protection of professional interests may
be one of them. This would have nothing to do with educational inquiry as Green defines it, but everything to do with the educational
system as a political entity through which power, authority, and resources are distributed. In this sense, the organization of colleges
of education reflects quite accurately their function in a system of
formal education, namely, that of controlling entry to professional
practice of schoolteaching.

Should colleges of education abandon this function? Probably
not, because that would simply mean some other institution would take
their place. Indeed, the system of schooling itself is quite appropriate as an area of specialized inquiry, but the manner in which
schools of education are organized makes it the only area of inquiry.

The "Feasibility" Test Revisited: The
Need for Adult Training

Changes in society that ignore political boundaries of states and
countries are producing a demand for teaching outside the schooling
system that will be satisfied with or without notice by colleges of
education. These changes have to do with the long-term accumulation
of educational resources, a capacity to teach, within institutions other
than schools or colleges. There is a self-reinforcing dynamic at
work in both the developed and developing countries that produces a
centrifugal force: The higher the stock of accumulating educational
resources, the greater the pressure to accumulate still more. There
is both a private individual component and an institutional component
of this dynamic.

Some years ago, Peter Drucker (1968) and Ivar Berg (1970) noticed that a rising level of formal educational attainment among workers produced its own demand for job restructuring and new job creation that takes advantage of the higher levels. The transformation of jobs created in response to that pressure calls for still more educated workers. What they did not notice is that educational attainment itself produces another dynamic pressure. The source of this pressure is the individual's perceived relative educational and, thus, occupational advantage. When everybody's education level rises, and the coefficient of variation in education decreases, there is an erosion of relative, individual benefit—a form of "education inflation." This causes the quest for still more education in each generation. Thus, we find that a worker in the United States with a high school diploma in 1940 had a two-year advantage in schooling over the average worker. Today, the worker with only a high school diploma finds himself two years below the average education level of his fellow worker (Weaver 1982a).

There is an increasing demand for formal education worldwide and that, in turn, is causing a transformation of the nature of work and workers' attitudes and expectations about work. The management function is changing dramatically and education as a management function is part of the change. When these factors are combined with the tendency in every economy in the world toward increased capitalization per worker, and rising labor costs, the total demand for nongovernmental educational investment is accelerating.

We cannot hope to understand education as an area of inquiry unless we accept the scale of these changes and realize the vast scale of institutional resources outside schools. The budgets of large multinational corporations exceed the size of those of many small countries. The total corporate education budget in the United States exceeds many state education budgets. But of equal importance to the size of these corporations is the blurring of functions among institutions. Universities in the United States have become breeders of new industries— the most recent examples being genetic engineering firms spawned by Harvard University and Massachusetts Institute of Technology. But industries like Wang, Westinghouse, and Control Data have become breeders of new formal institutions of learning, taking on all the functions of colleges, including granting of degrees. For example, Arthur D. Little, a multinational research and development firm, offers a master's of business administration.

Business in the United States has long disregarded the false impression that teaching was a protected domain of the schools and colleges. In addition to those examples cited, some of the biggest companies in the United States have entered, at one time or another, the direct education business. IBM, Xerox, RCA, Litton, General Elec-

tric, Westinghouse, and Raytheon, to name a few, have been in the
business of producing teaching materials and have even contracted
to operate public schools and colleges (successfully or unsuccessfully).
For example, Litton designed and largely ran a community college
just outside Detroit.

But the most enduring change, one that has outlasted the initial
infusion of federal dollars into education and the whetting of these
mammoth corporate appetites, is the permanent establishment within
these giant corporations of an education function to serve the corporation's own learning needs.[4] As this function evolves, it becomes
increasingly difficult to distinguish corporate education activities
from any other form of education.

The key to understanding this context is to understand that the
private sector as a whole is increasingly engaged in the direct production and marketing of knowledge. This means the creation and
exchange of hundreds of millions of pieces of information, quite literally the design and selling of education. Consider the language of the
modern corporation. In Vernon Buehler and Krishna Shetty's book,
Productivity Improvement, one finds numerous examples of language
familiar to any educator. At Hughes Aircraft, one of the important
ingredients of a successful productivity improvement campaign was
called "the principle of teaching," which stated in effect that performance improves when employees are properly taught and that teaching
is a major function of management. Corning Glass has applied the
theory of "learning curves" to analyze productivity problems. Training was an essential part of the efforts of most of the companies cited
by Buehler and Shetty as case examples of how to effectively improve
productivity.

It seems reasonable to conclude that education and its perceived
relationship to productivity in the private sector are among the most
important areas of inquiry for educational researchers in this decade
and well beyond. The perceived importance of industrial training to
economic development alone makes this a topic of vast importance to
corporations, although this by no means ensures that it will be of any
perceived importance to colleges of education as they are presently
organized.

Scope of Training and Development

Until recently, there has been no agreed-upon figure of the
total size and scope of internal corporate investments in education
for employees and customers in the United States. Stanley Moses
(1970) estimated in the late 1960s that the total investment in education
by business, government, military, and other nonschool organizations

exceeded that of the elementary, secondary, and postsecondary education systems combined. That would have placed the amount of money spent on education, outside the formal schooling system, at roughly $113 billion. That figure would appear to be high by several magnitudes, but it is somewhat unchallengable because it includes virtually every human activity outside the schoolhouse walls.

Training reported in October 1982 its first national survey of training in the United States in nongovernment organizations with 50 or more employees. The sample consisted of 991 organizational responses of 10,500 receiving questionnaires, with response rates ranging between 3.7 percent and 15.9 percent of various industry categories.

Of the organizations responding to the survey, 57.7 percent employed one or more trainers and 55.1 percent employed full-time head office based trainers. Almost 20 percent reported no full-time professional trainers. Training estimates from the survey that the total number of full-time professional training and development personnel in American corporations is approximately 212,000. In addition, approximately 33,000 federal training personnel (civilian federal trainers, U.S. Postal Service, and U.S. Navy) are listed as full-time professionals, bringing the total to 245,000. This figure would be equal to about 12 percent of all public school teachers in the United States in 1982 (2,000,080 as reported by NCES in 1978). If the total number of training and development personnel included those with some responsibility for training, the figure would be about 786,000, or roughly 40 percent of the size of the public school teacher force. Since no precise baseline is available for longitudinal comparison, it is not possible to estimate growth rates.

Of the organizations sampled by Training, the most frequently provided area of training was in supervisory skills (a finding consistent with interview results reported later in the Boston metropolitan area). The five most frequently provided training areas in the Training survey were:[5]

		Percent
1.	Supervisory skills	77.1
2.	New employee orientation	71.2
3.	Management skills and development	67.3
4.	Communication skills training (reading, writing, listening, and so forth)	58.2
5.	Technical skills/knowledge updating	58.2

What is not clear from the data is how the training effort is divided in terms of employee populations participating, hours devoted to the training by area, or the total budget devoted to each area. The division of effort would undoubtedly differ by industrial sector and type of product. For example, customer education appears 26th of 27 categories of training with only 17 percent of the surveyed organizations providing such training. While this may be representative of corporations in general, the percentage of computer manufacturers providing customer education would be very much higher.

From the organizations sampled, the following training budgets (not actual expenditures) are estimated by Training for U.S. corporations:[6]

Hardware (audiovisual and computer technologies)	$ 702,566,000
Off-shelf (prepackaged materials—books, manuals, films, and so forth)	680,006,000
Custom design (materials designed for specific needs)	541,349,000
Outside services (vendor training)	1,031,777,000
Total	$2,955,698,000

Not clear from these budget estimates is whether tuition and materials reimbursement for university or college courses is a minor or major cost of training. Training reports the 1980 U.S. government figure (U.S. Office of Personnel Management) for tuition, books, and fees for training of government employees to be $79,866,971. This figure would appear to suggest that college, university, and other outside training costs involving tuition are quite large. Training gives a rough estimate of $81.5 million in corporate employee spending on university and college training.

Also not clear from these budget estimates is the size of indirect costs of training, including travel, lodging, and other logistical costs of moving participants to training sites and perhaps the even greater cost of lost productivity that occurs in off-the-job training. One estimate is that the first category of costs is roughly a third of the training cost (Training, p. 48). We can find no estimate of the second category. Excluding either of these indirect costs, training and development in the private sector is a $3 billion plus business, if the survey is correct.

It is important to realize that these findings not only have implications for education for organizations outside the schools but also inside the schools. There is a dynamic or reciprocal relationship. The first and obvious impact is on the school curriculum. For example, it is within the capacity of business corporations in the United States to provide highly sophisticated training and education for technicians, using expensive equipment and teaching materials that are immediately applicable to job requirements. The existence of this capacity is already rendering the original concept of vocational education obsolete. It has not eliminated the need for vocational education, but it is forcing a rethinking of the purpose and direction of vocational schooling—at both the secondary and postsecondary levels.

It is inevitable that discontinuities will exist between what industry requires in the form of individuals' knowledge and skills and what the schooling system can provide. The likely result is more corporate investment in its own learning needs and more absorption of what the schooling system once provided. To the extent schools and colleges fail to deliver on what remains, there will be further erosion of their position in the total arrangement of education (Adams and Christie 1983).

To cite one concrete example, the failure of colleges of education (with certain exceptions, of course) to provide methods courses for industrial educators, that is, training the trainers, in a form perceived to be relevant and cost-effective has resulted in many of the largest corporations in Massachusetts and elsewhere providing their own in-house courses on teaching methodology. Some of these corporations have hired educational faculty members for this purpose. These former college faculty members now teach courses on learning theory, models of instruction, evaluation, and educational media in the corporate classroom to training personnel.

This trend is likely to continue, and for the reasons Peter Drucker (1968) stated 15 years ago: "The threshold of education needed for effective impact on a country's ability to grow and develop rapidly is clearly much higher today than it was a hundred years ago [or even ten years ago]" (p. 335). The giant corporations of today's world simply will not rely on the formal system of education to deliver knowledge and skills perceived to be vital to growth.

As another kind of example of the impact of corporate educational development on the schooling system, consider the relationship of recent years between companies in Massachusetts, Texas, and California, particularly, and the public schools, community colleges, and colleges and universities these firms are directly assisting. Several large computer firms have contributed computers and software to local schools and colleges for direct use in teaching and research. One of the recent examples in Massachusetts is Wang, which announced that it was donating $3 million worth of computers and software to the Massachusetts higher education system. Digital Equipment Corporation has "on loan" to the Boston city schools not only equipment and software, but education specialists of the company to assist in the design and implementation of vocational education. [7] Hewlett Packard in California is still another example (see Useem 1982).

The institutions outside the schooling system now have educational resources to spare. They are now the advanced providers of teaching and learning resources—monopolizing what the schools and colleges were once solely responsible for. The process has come full cycle. The only question educators seem to be raising is, Why don't these corporations give more?

What Do Educators in Corporations Do?

In order to test the proposition that a set of skills and knowledge can be discovered and defined as relevant to the practice setting in which adult training takes place, we have examined the recent survey literature produced by those actually in the business of training adults. In addition, we have conducted our own survey of trainers and training managers in the New England area (primarily, Massachusetts). Note that our approach is not to ask professors of education what they think the body of skills and knowledge should be. Rather, our starting point was to ask trainers what skills and knowledge they actually use in their work. We wanted to know what they do as trainers. It turns out what they do varies very little, in a generic sense, from what any effective teacher does in the act of teaching.

One of the more recent efforts to survey the field of industrial training and education was conducted by Patrick Pinto and James Walker (1978) under the aegis of the American Society for Training and Development (ASTD). Questionnaires were sent to 13,000 U.S. members of ASTD and to 1,027 counterparts outside the United States. About 20 percent (2,790) of the questionnaires were returned. Briefly summarized below are the most frequently cited professional activities of trainers.

1. Needs assessment and diagnosis of learning needs—constructing questionnaires, conducting interviews, evaluating programs
2. Program design—designing content and methods, evaluating results, selecting and developing materials
3. Managing internal and external learning resources—hiring, supervising, evaluating instructors/resource persons and outside vendors
4. Classroom instruction—teaching, operating audiovisual equipment, leading discussions, revising materials based on feedback
5. Individual development and educational counseling—counseling individuals regarding career development needs
6. Organizational development—team building, role playing, simulation, laboratory training
7. Managing training function—preparing budgets, organizing, staffing, projecting needs, supervising

In order to augment the Pinto and Walker survey, a series of interviews was conducted in the Boston metropolitan area during the spring of 1981, in part to prepare a new program in the School of Education at Boston University, the Human Resource Education Program now in its second year of operation. The results of the interviews are reported below.

The interviews were carried out in two phases: (1) initial interviews with managers of education in 15 organizations in the Boston area to study the functions of education in these private settings, as perceived by managers; and (2) second-level interviews with education specialists in selected firms (set up as a result of the initial interviews with managers) to specify education competencies. Follow-up interviews were conducted with education specialists in six firms.

The field interviews were not intended to meet "sampling" criteria. The initial contacts were identified through a nomination process that began with contacting corporate managers of education in six business firms in the Boston metropolitan area. Each person was asked to identify four key corporate educators in the area, that is, people active in the American Society for Training and Development, consulting, and teaching. Follow-up contacts were made with nominees. There was a deliberate focus on high-technology firms and large banks in the area. Owing to their rapid growth, labor intensiveness, and types of products and services, these firms demand sizable investments in education. The results of the interviews support this initial "bias." The 15 organizations in which interviews were conducted (13 nongovernment, two government) employ a large number of full-time educators.

Although, collectively, more than 100 hours of interviews were conducted with some two dozen educational managers in 15 organizations and selected consultants and specialists, the precise scope of corporate education in this region's firms remains somewhat of a mystery. First, exact information is considered by firms to be proprietary. Second, with few exceptions, the general finding was that no one person in these companies knew exactly and precisely how much time, effort, and money were being devoted to education. Third, these firms represent high-growth enterprises, and within them education is rapidly expanding and in a state of flux. Fourth, typically divisional arrangements separate various educational functions such as organizational development, personnel management, customer education, manufacturing education, and so forth, and reporting channels often lead to different managers and vice-presidents.

Given time and resource limitations, it simply was not feasible to study thoroughly and in depth every aspect of education, even in the limited number of firms contacted. The initial impression was that most of the education investment being made by these firms had to do with skills and knowledge of entry-level employees and customer education. But the fact that most of the trainers in the 13 nongovernment corporations work on problems at lower organizational levels and in customer education suggests the enormous importance top management places on such educational needs.

Any estimate of the number of corporate educators in the region would be highly speculative. Even estimating the number of educators in the 15 organizations surveyed is tentative for the reasons cited. Based on interviews with selected, but not all, education managers of the organizations, we estimate that there were at the time approximately 2,500 full-time professional educators in the 15 organizations.

The backgrounds of educators in these firms varied, from no formal college preparation to Ph. D. s in education. It is not possible to even guess at the exact mix of backgrounds for all educators in the 15 organizations. However, of the 28 managers of education, specialists, and consultants interviewed, 17 had schoolteaching backgrounds before joining the firms, or were prepared to teach, or were working on degrees in education. The others had mastered the skills of teaching on the job and through other formal and informal means.

The primary driving force behind educational growth in these companies seems to be a combination of managerial attitude, economic changes, accelerated growth of the sectors represented by these firms, the nature of their products, and demography (findings consistent with Training's survey). The attitudinal factor seems to have its roots in the perception that education is related to productivity, and if productivity is not rising, or declines, and that is caused by inadequate investments in education, then more education is better. This may be a temporary attitude of top management, but it seemed to the educators interviewed to be permanent. However, for now, one of the "ripe" areas of research for interested academics and their students would be the connection between education and productivity. Cost-benefit analysis of corporate training investments is a topic requiring the combined skills of education, business, and labor economics professors and an example of why human resource development cannot be the sole province of a school of education. The peculiarity of growth in these sectors (as compared, for instance, with steel and automobiles in other regions of the country) adds to the perceived importance of education. Rapid employment of new personnel and rapid obsolescence of skills in technology-driven firms create a built-in demand for skill upgrading and new skill development. This is likely to be the case as long as these firms grow and create new products. (Growth has been slowed by the recent recession but layoffs in the region's high technology firms have been rare.)

These companies are outstripping the availability of talent in the area, creating at present a labor crunch, and in the future a serious, if not disastrous, condition. The competition for talent, at great expense, causes pressure to retain, upgrade, and "keep happy" the firm's workers. Replacing them is expensive, means starting over with additional educational investments, and losing those invest- ments already made.

Finally, all of the firms are aware that the 18-to-24-year-old population in the United States will be shrinking for the next two decades, exacerbating the above-mentioned problems. In short, the underlying forces causing education to be expanded in importance and size in these firms are perceived as being likely to continue for the foreseeable future.

All of these firms make investments in basic employee skill building and orientation, but these efforts seem smaller than expected and are often tasks for part-time teachers and vendors. All of the firms make investments in formal degree pursuits of employees (al- though no one we interviewed in any of the firms seemed to know ex- actly how much money was being spent to reimburse employees for college courses). These issues (basic skills and college programs) were not as important (to those interviewed) as the following:

1. Training of trainers: All of these firms make investments in the teaching of adult education skills to members of their own edu- cation staff. Several firms have developed or are developing custom- ized workshop materials for this purpose. Most of these firms send educators to outside workshops for skill building and to universities where short-term intensive courses are offered. A vast army of con- sultants and vendor groups ministers to these needs in this region. Nonetheless, there is a real opportunity for the faculties of education. But it will be a challenge. Faculty members will have to deliver if they expect to compete in the training-of-trainers market.

2. Self-instruction: Perhaps the single most common educa- tional trend discovered in the interviews is the current rush among these firms to develop self-instructional systems. The driving force seems to be the rising costs of moving people and removing them from jobs to be trained. One company estimates that it now costs $2,500 per person per week to bring people to its training center and that about a third of that cost is travel and lodging. Other firms cited similar reasons for the rapid movement toward self-instruction. Most of the people interviewed were interested in computer-managed instruction, but the bulk of the present packages consist of programmed instruc- tion (pencil-paper), video, slides, and film. Computer-managed in- struction appears to be in its infancy, even in the firms that have "in- vented" computers.

3. Evaluation research: Formal evaluation of learning results (as a rigorous "science") seemed to be absent in most firms. Vir- tually everyone seemed to rely on relatively simple rater-evaluation

forms. Systematic classroom testing and follow-up analysis of on-the-job effectiveness in using competencies taught in training programs seemed to be rare, although most agreed it might be a good idea. Evaluation research constitutes another area of opportunity for schools of education.

4. Problem solving: Problem solving was the single most frequently cited competency needed in the delivery of educational services in these firms. Many, if not all, of the demands for training in these firms seem to end up calling for educators to be problem solvers and to teach others how to analyze problems systematically. Of the needed short-term intensive workshops for training personnel, as suggested by education managers, workshops in problem analysis were the most frequently cited. This is a prime area of opportunity for schools of education but still another example of the need to engage faculty members in other colleges in the design and teaching of the subject matter.

THE DEVELOPMENT OF HUMAN RESOURCES

The term human resource development, or HRD, is widely bantered about in business circles, but it does have one consistent use: employee development where development is explicitly tied to productivity and profit (Nadler 1980). What is the interest of a school of education in human resource development?

While the faculty of any school of education may conceivably have an interest in the total spectrum of functions represented by human resource development, any school's mission in regard to human resource development will focus on education (but not education as schools of education now define it in their curriculum). As a school of education, there is justifiable, direct, and legitimate interest, in principle, in human resource development when human resource development is understood to be concerned with any of the following: instruction and instructional processes; learning and theories of learning; designing learning materials and instructional systems for delivering such materials (including media and technologies); planning instructional programs (including needs assessments to determine learning needs); analysis of instructional problems and organizational problems requiring educational interventions; directing, supervising, and evaluating instructional programs; and guidance, counseling, and evaluation of employees' individual educational plans. I argue that this is true in principle simply because these constitute (or should constitute) the essential interests of any school of education. These areas of interest—instruction and learning—are the ingredients of teaching qua teaching. In a generic sense, they would not distinguish what adult educators do from what kindergarten teachers do. But that is exactly the point, and that is exactly why they constitute or should constitute the essential interests of any school of education.

This justification, however, does not satisfy the earlier argument regarding interdisciplinary studies. It simply makes the case that schools of education have a legitimate role to play in producing training personnel. The requirements of the practice setting would exceed the offerings of education schools even if they are able to define and teach a corpus of knowledge having to do with instruction and learning. The industrial trainer must have professional preparation in organizational development, management science, business economics, and management information systems. The broader HRD function, in addition to these competency areas, encompasses personnel, recruitment, labor relations, business operations, and finance. To prepare adequately graduates for positions in any specialization within HRD will require schools of education to define what they, and they alone, may claim as specialized knowledge, and to place students with management, economics, finance, law, computer science, psychology, and other faculties trained in the disciplines to teach the additional subjects. In addition to our own program at Boston University, a review of programs at George Washington University, the University of Texas at Austin, and the University of Pittsburgh suggests that at least those universities recognize this fact.

By selecting out of the total spectrum of HRD functions those that ought to be of central interest to schools of education, we substitute a new term, human resource education. Such a term carries not merely a putative claim. Human resources and education should be, if they are not, the sine qua non of all schools of education. Even if these are not the central interest of education colleges, they are the central interest of most modern organizations outside the schooling system.

A Prototype Human Resource Education (HRE) Program

Given that schools of education ought to be engaged in the preparation of training and development personnel, what should be the organizing principle and what skills and knowledge should graduates acquire? The competencies listed below were derived from the literature, our interviews conducted in the Boston area firms, and faculty discussions. They are intended to guide the design of curriculum and, as in the case of all curricular guides, are likely to change as definitions of the field of practice change. (The prototype human resource education program briefly outlined here has been implemented at Boston University School of Education under the direction of this author.)

The central focus of the prototype HRE program is that of preparing the graduate, qua professional trainer, as problem solver. Each of the specialized aspects of the program would constitute skills, knowledge, and experience that revolve around the nucleus of problem solving in organizational settings. In order to be effective as a problem solver, the teacher (or trainer) must have a basic grounding in the understanding of organizational structures and dynamics, the processes of formal problem analysis, and the formulation and testing of strategies for carrying out interventions. The effective trainer must also be able to design and manage educational projects. These skills will not, and cannot, be solely the products of education professors. Educationists may have something to offer, but the product must be the result of interdisciplinary studies.

The content logic would move from understanding structural dynamics to communication processes as the underlying foundations of a prototype program. It is consistent with field theory to suggest that individuals perceive objects in their environments against a defined field, but those objects become significant components of stimuli only in context of the field. It would follow, therefore, that context be the beginning point in a program of studies, and that focus on specifics follow. The specialized program of studies in instructional systems design would follow, after a grounding in organization, problem solving, and consultation. This seems to be one of the most serious deficiencies of education school curriculum—an extraordinarily variegated assembly of subspecializations in search of a nucleus.

Computer science is integral to the development of instructional skills, based on (1) our contention (and that of trainers interviewed) that the formal discipline required in computer programming, and some of the generic skills, such as flowcharting, are essential in instructional systems design; and (2) the obvious contention that such skills are necessary for trainers in technological companies, and in most other firms as well (see Training 1982). Computer science is yet another example of the necessity for engaging faculties other than education in the teaching of teachers. (One shudders at the thought of schools of education simply adding to their bloated course inventories a "computers-in-education" course, or "computer literacy" taught, not by those trained in the discipline but by education professors with a casual interest in the topic.)

Our prototype program's organizational structure is displayed in the next section as a sequence of competency strands. The sequence is deliberate and it would be expected that students progress through the sequence in the order prescribed. The prototype program is structured around five competency strands: strand 1: formal problem solving and planning, strand 2: organizational behavior, strand 3: needs assessment and job/performance appraisal, strand 4:

instructional systems design, strand 5: educational program management.

Strand 1: Formal Problem Solving and Planning

The effective human resources (HR) educator will demonstrate that he or she is knowledgeable in formal planning operations. In so doing, the HR educator will study and define educational problem contexts, understand the psychology of problem solving, define action plans, and analyze trade-offs. Competencies will include:

a. Understands and applies tools and concepts in analyzing problem contexts (matrix techniques and dynamic modeling concepts)
b. Identifies appropriate intervention points in problem contexts, specifies courses of action and strategies
c. Analyzes trade-offs and key decision points in proposing alternatives
d. Develops and writes clear, concise project plans, including problem statement, action, alternatives, and costs and benefits
e. Uses trend data and projections to anticipate changing-environment contexts as these affect educational plans

Strand 2: Organizational Behavior

The effective HR educator will demonstrate that he or she is knowledgeable in understanding organizational behavior, interpersonal relations, business practices, systems, and policies required to conduct educational programs for employees. In so doing the HR educator will work with managers and specialists to analyze information systems, organizational structures and dynamics, and role and power issues. Competencies will include:

a. Understands and can apply system dynamics concepts to analyze organizational problems requiring educational interventions
b. Understands and can apply psychological/sociological concepts of organizational behavior to analyze and solve organizational problems requiring educational interventions
c. Understands the social psychology of problem solving and can apply it in concepts to analyze and solve organizational problems requiring educational interventions
d. Understands how to identify and negotiate access to key resource persons in organizations necessary for problem solving
e. Understands and applies social-psychological concepts of human motivation, human relations, and performance appraisal as these relate to design of effective educational programs
f. Shows flexibility in dealing with client's needs, problems, and goals

g. Understands expectations and limitations of learning needs of clients
h. Understands the social psychology of group behavior and can apply its concepts in facilitating effective meetings and negotiations with clients.
i. Understands how to match human resources with instructional goals and tasks
j. Effectively assesses and counsels individual employees in setting career and education goals
k. Listens to and communicates effectively with persons located at different levels of the organization

Strand 3: Needs Assessment and Job/Performance Appraisal

The effective HR educator will demonstrate that he or she is knowledgeable in conducting needs assessments, job analysis, job modeling, and product analysis as these are connected to designing instructional programs. In so doing, the HR educator will work with managers to assess job performance, analyze discrepancies, assess products, and recommend educational interventions. Competencies will include:

a. Analyzes job requirements, interviews employees effectively to determine job-related competencies, responsibilities, tasks
b. Observes master performers/average performers to determine performance problems
c. Identifies key points of educational intervention to improve job performance
d. Experiences, by doing, what employees are expected to do in job performance
e. Analyzes manuals/documents to understand effectively the educational requirements for new users of products and services
f. Designs training packages to teach new users of products and services

Strand 4: Instructional Systems Design

The effective HR educator will demonstrate that he or she is knowledgeable in the concepts and theories of adult learning psychology, design and evaluation of instructional systems, and research and statistics. In so doing, the HR educator will base instructional programs on needs assessment data and on product or job analysis, will clearly define learning objectives, and will design effective delivery systems using appropriate media and technologies. Competencies will include:

a. Understands and applies concepts and theories of adult learning psychology in the development of instructional programs

b. Understands and applies appropriate tools and concepts in defining learning steps, criterion behaviors, test items

c. Understands and applies appropriate tools and concepts in sequencing learning activities and matches learning activities with job or product analysis

d. Understands and applies appropriate tools and concepts in writing scripts, specifying visuals, graphics, and other appropriate media

e. Understands and applies appropriate tools and concepts in designing self-instructional systems (flowcharting, branching, testing, and so forth.

f. Understands and applies appropriate tools and concepts in designing computer-managed instruction and computer-assisted instruction

g. Understands and applies appropriate tools and concepts in designing and using video and instructional television

h. Understands and applies appropriate tools and concepts in designing instructional facilities

i. Understands and applies appropriate tools and concepts in evaluating classroom learning results, instructional effectiveness, and on-the-job application of classroom learning

j. Understands and applies appropriate research and statistical tools and concepts

k. Understands and applies basic tools and concepts of computer programming

Strand 5: Educational Program Management

The effective HR educator will demonstrate that he or she is knowledgeable in the administration and direction of educational programs in profit organizations. In so doing, the HR educator will set goals, establish priorities, allocate resources, and facilitate instructional responses in response to client needs. Competencies will include:

a. Manages external resources (contracts with outside vendors, external training programs, collaboration with colleges, universities, institutes, and so forth.

b. Prepares budgets and plans for educational programs and projects

c. Writes proposals for programs and projects (problem action plan, costs)

d. Supervises and evaluates instructors and courses

e. Negotiates with clients, sets expectations, "contracts" for educational interventions

f. Analyzes needs, understands systems (human, information resources)

g. Anticipates and plans for long-range organizational education needs

This prototype program (qua competency strands) is reflected in several HRD programs already in operation. In addition to the Boston University program of studies in human resource education, 18 programs were reported at the ASTD Second Invitational Conference on the Academic Preparation of TD/HRD Practitioners.[8] The majority of these programs are housed in colleges of education but most require interdisciplinary studies. They appear to have evolved from three basic areas of traditional educational studies: adult/career education, human relations training, and instructional technology (the constituencies and emphasis in the programs more or less reflect these three perspectives). But, collectively, they encompass the cores of competencies outlined above.

The process of developing these initial programs is far from complete. An in-depth analysis of these efforts may result in still another Koerner-like attack on educationists. However, these programs do differ from traditional school of education programs in several important respects: (1) they are based upon and tested against the open practice setting into which graduates market their skills and knowledge, absent the monopolistic protections of traditional teacher programs; (2) they are interdisciplinary, if not by choice, by the requirements imposed by the market; and (3) they represent, for better or worse, efforts to define a specific subspecialty in education that is necessary (but not sufficient) for their graduates to master.

CONCLUSION

I have been perhaps overly harsh on schools of education. It should be emphasized that several schools of education have already begun the task outlined above. And it may be argued that a focus upon schools of education is misplaced, that reforming the occupational practice of schoolteaching is the more cogent remedy for the teacher quality problem. I certainly agree with those who wish to undertake a reform of schoolteaching. Given the learning results schools have produced over the past two decades, one is drawn to the importance of the reforms now offered by the National Commission on Excellence in Education and other groups.[9] Given the findings in Chapter 3, there is a case to be made for changing the nature of schoolteaching as an occupation, which currently acts to drive out the most academically talented, while retaining the least. However, I remain convinced of my earlier contention: The solution of the teacher quality problem does not rest with regulations and institutional controls of the kind these reform efforts imply. Given my view of the problem (one that manifests primarily from the dynamic interplay of talent, choices, and opportunity, and only secondarily from institutional responses), the solution must account for dynamics that transcend efforts to regulate through qualifications tests or reforms of schoolteaching. Moreover, by focusing solely upon the occupation of teaching in public schools, the preparing institutions (as they are now organized), and the regulatory controls of certification and licensure, those who wish to pry open the system will fail because the necessary condition is not present. That condition is an open market in which the product is testable. No matter what we do to reform schools, schoolteaching, or the preparation of schoolteachers, the system remains a closed system.

My prescription, which flies in the face of conventional wisdom, is to deliberately manipulate the existing system toward a condition in which its products are testable. By doing so, I believe that the quality of those who enter public school teaching will rise, because preparing institutions can (and I believe will) act to conserve rather than sacrifice talent under conditions that expand their markets (hence their attractiveness). I believe the alternative proposal carries the added, and necessary, benefit of forcing schools of education to define (and reduce) their curriculum in education. I do not believe this will happen, despite the best intentions of reform-minded educators, as long as the focus of reform is solely on schools and schoolteaching. Indeed, it would be expected, given the history of these reforms, that the problem will fade in the short term (owing to market forces that will drive up demand for teachers) and worsen in the long term owing to the residual effects of the reform actions themselves (assuming they are implemented).

There is a prima facie case to be made for the reform of colleges of education. I have chosen not to ignore the conventional wisdom regarding the means to achieve that reform; rather, I have chosen to demonstrate why I think the conventional wisdom is wrong.

The focus of attention is, however, teacher educators, and that is precisely where it has to be. It is logically impossible to argue that training institutions are not part of the cause of the problem of teacher quality, just as it is impossible to argue they are the entire cause. One could argue that my analysis identifies demography as the cause, if one needs to put the finger of blame somewhere. Thus, it could be said that demographically driven teacher demand ends up producing a talent pool with which teacher educators are stuck. Indeed, such an argument would be consistent with my analysis. By the same logic, one could also argue that schoolteacher employers are stuck with the products of schools of education. While consistent, such arguments are incomplete and wholly fruitless. Both teacher educators and school employers have choices. To grasp fully the nature of this analysis, one has to understand that we are talking about a dynamic process in which talent, choice of persons seeking opportunity, and institutional responses (driven by the choices of talent conservation and self-preservation) interact to produce a problem state. While I agree that improving conditions of teaching and schoolteacher training are important, they will not solve this problem. I do believe that the reform of schools of education is a necessary solution to the problem, but along lines proposed (and not traditional lines proposed by nearly every educator concerned with the problem). That is the key. My goal is not different from that of other reformists. But the means to accomplish that goal are radically different. My target is also the same, but my strategy for reshaping schools of education is entirely different. The present (and past) reform efforts would (if successful) make schools of education into superior training grounds for schoolteachers. It is precisely this logic that fails, for the reasons discussed, of its own accord. The strategy must be to make schools of education into superior training grounds for educators (whether educators of children or adults).

The suppliers of teachers must be the target simply because the system, for over a century, recognizes no other supplier of qualified entrants to schoolteaching. To think this system will vanish, and that schoolteaching will be opened up to anyone, regardless of paper qualifications (even if we recognize the inherent deficiencies in such qualifications), is to misunderstand the basic arguments that produced the system in the first place: The conduct of a compulsory, tax-supported system of free schools for educating all citizens cannot be entrusted to just anyone irrespective of preparation or tests of fitness. This basic argument, which has stood the test of time for more than a century in education, also applies to most professions in most societies. But by all accounts, it applies to every society that provides free public schools. To imagine that we can somehow make the occupation of teaching attractive to the very talented it now loses, independent of the dynamics of the problem we have discussed, is foolhardy.

The strategy I have chosen is not to further regulate or propose new requirements for this system (a system already overregulated and suffering from a century of tinkering). That will not work in the long run. The strategy is to rely on market conditions to redirect the mission of schools of education. While the final choices for action rest with schools of education, it was proposed in Chapter 5 that government can and should play a role in the process through financial inducements that encourage and complement the strategy. The allocation of higher education budget resources ought to reflect choices of schools of education either to remain insular or to join in the larger task of manpower development in the remainder of this century.

NOTES

1. One of the ways to test this proposition is to examine the books and materials trainers use in their professional work. One such example is Thomas Gilbert's Human Competence (New York: McGraw-Hill, 1978). More familiar to educationists, but actually used by trainers, would be such works as Benjamin Bloom et al., Taxonomy of Educational Objectives, Handbook I: Cognitive Domain (New York: Longmans, Green 1965); Robert Mager, Preparing Instructional Objectives (Palo Alto, Calif.: Fearon Publishers 1968); and Robert M. Gagné, The Conditions of Learning (New York: Holt, Rinehart, and Winston, 1965). Granted, these last texts are dated, but the important point is that while they are widely talked about in education courses, education courses rarely are designed or taught in a manner reflecting their contents. From my observation of trainers and training programs in the private sector, the ideas are put into practice.

2. The experience thus far at Boston University School of Education suggests that a sizable number of applicants exists for graduate training in human resource development and that the general level of intellectual ability of candidates (as measured by the Miller Analogies Test and evidence from transcripts) is equal to or higher than in many cases the best education students who would not otherwise (without a training program) have applied to this school of education. In short, the human resource education program at Boston University has initially demonstrated that a market does exist for an interdisciplinary studies program in training and development at the graduate level in this region. The same may be said of the HRD program at George Washington University, in operation since the late 1940s but rapidly expanding since the mid-1960s. In addition, programs in training and development exist in a number of schools of education (see American Society for Training and Development 1981, 1983). Reprinted with permission of the publisher (see note 4 below).

3. In a book by English authors (The Future of Teacher Education), Maurice Craft (1971) presents a proposal to broaden teacher education to include human services such as social work. Others have written on this same idea, and there are existing programs. However, the momentum of human services education has been slowed by a cutback in government spending. Edward Ducharme and Robert Nash of the University of Vermont are recognized leaders in this field.

4. Training (1982) reports that within 197,506 nongovernment organizations with 50 or more employees, more than 212,000 full-time educators provide training and development services for 61.2 percent of the work force, or 33 million workers (p. 21).

5. Excerpted with permission from the October 1982 issue of Training, the Magazine of Human Resources Development. Copyright

1982, Lakewood Publications, 731 Hennepin Ave., Minneapolis, MN 55403 (612) 333-0471). All rights reserved.

6. Ibid.

7. Digital Equipment Corporation has also announced that it will give $1.6 million in computer hardware and software to Boston University, the University's largest single gift and the company's largest single donation.

8. See ASTD (1981, 1983) for a description of academic programs offered by schools of education in training and development. The 1983 edition of the ASTD Directory of Academic Programs lists 58 training and development programs in the United States and Canada awarding education degrees.

9. The findings of the Commission on Excellence in Education (created by Secretary Terrel Bell) have been widely reported (A Nation at Risk: The Imperative for Educational Reform). See Boston Globe, May 1, 1983. The National Endowment for the Humanities (NEH) is sponsoring its own long-term study of educational quality problems. See reports, for example, of studies undertaken by the Institute for Policy Studies, Vanderbilt University, under NEH sponsorship: "Educational Excellence Network."

Appendix A:
Tables and Figures

TABLE 2.1

SAT Mathematics and SAT Verbal Means for College-Bound Seniors Selecting Education and Arts/Sciences Areas as First Choice College Majors, 1972-79

	1972/73	1973/74	1974/75	1975/76	1976/77	1977/78	1978/79	1979/80
SATV								
Business	409	406	406	413	402	401	400	399
Art	440	432	435	438	412	408	404	402
Biological Science	493	488	481	483	475	475	472	469
English	500	496	488	489	504	504	505	507
Foreign Language	491	483	481	485	481	476	475	472
Mathematics	481	479	463	472	464	464	459	455
Music	465	462	448	452	445	439	437	436
Philosophy	479	476	469	478	467	466	465	460
Physical Science	505	503	501	506	500	499	498	495
Social Science	476	463	465	464	456	457	455	456
Engineering	480	465	450	452	448	448	445	444
Education	418	417	405	405	400	396	392	389
National	445	444	434	431	429	429	427	424
SATM								
Business	463	457	461	471	453	447	447	446
Art	451	441	445	443	425	422	421	419
Biological Science	533	528	525	530	515	511	507	506
English	481	473	465	469	478	476	478	481
Foreign Language	498	494	486	487	483	477	476	475
Mathematics	595	584	580	594	588	585	580	577
Music	487	479	464	468	463	456	456	455
Philosophy	500	489	484	495	487	481	482	477
Physical Science	570	568	565	572	572	566	561	560
Social Science	490	477	476	475	474	472	472	473
Engineering	548	554	541	550	546	540	536	535
Education	449	448	434	431	426	422	420	418
National	481	480	472	472	470	468	467	466

Source: College Entrance Examination Board, National College-Bound Seniors, Sub-Career Fields, Intended Areas of Study. First Choice. 1972-79.

TABLE 2.2

ACT English and Mathematics Scores for High School Sample by Planned
College Major, 1970-75
(10 percent national sample)

| Planned College Major | Mean Score by Year | | | | | | N |
	1970	1971	1972	1973	1974	1975	
Education fields							
English	18.6	18.4	18.1	18.1	17.8	17.6	18,626
Mathematics	18.5	18.0	18.0	17.3	16.3	16.1	18,625
Elementary education							
English	18.0	17.4	17.4	17.9	17.4	17.1	6,808
Mathematics	17.1	16.3	16.7	16.2	15.0	14.5	6,808
Secondary education							
English	18.5	18.4	18.4	18.9	18.2	18.3	2,583
Mathematics	18.7	18.9	18.8	18.1	17.4	16.5	2,582
Business administration							
English	16.3	16.6	16.5	16.1	15.9	15.5	8,150
Mathematics	17.8	18.3	18.1	16.6	16.1	15.7	8,148
Nursing							
English	18.4	18.1	17.6	`17.4	17.2	16.8	10,649
Mathematics	17.7	17.0	16.7	15.8	15.1	15.2	10,645
Sociology							
English	18.0	18.3	17.9	17.7	16.8	17.5	2,204
Mathematics	17.3	18.0	16.7	16.2	14.4	14.8	2,204
Engineering fields							
English	17.9	18.1	18.3	17.6	18.0	18.0	10,698
Mathematics	23.3	23.9	23.9	22.0	22.9	22.7	10,697
Chemical engineer							
English	26.0	22.5	21.3	19.8	20.8	20.5	592
Mathematics	27.1	30.6	28.4	26.0	26.5	26.2	592
Aeronautical engineer							
English	17.6	18.0	18.1	17.9	18.1	18.4	1,465
Mathematics	23.3	22.3	23.0	21.9	22.4	25.5	1,465
Premedicine							
English	20.7	20.5	20.0	20.0	20.1	20.0	6,250
Mathematics	24.0	24.5	23.4	23.4	22.9	22.4	6,250
Biology							
English	20.2	19.6	20.0	18.6	18.7	18.8	2,705
Mathematics	22.6	22.7	22.8	20.2	19.6	20.1	2,705
Physics							
English	22.2	21.5	21.7	22.4	22.6	21.4	662
Mathematics	29.1	28.3	29.0	29.5	28.0	28.8	662
National mean							
English	18.0	17.9	18.1	17.9	17.7	17.5	
Mathematics	19.1	18.8	19.1	18.3	17.6	17.5	

Source: The American College Testing Program, Reports prepared
July 26, 1977, and December 12, 1977.

TABLE 2.3

National Sample, ACT Class Profile Report for Enrolled Freshmen,
1975/76: English and Mathematics Scores in 19 Major Fields of Study
(10 percent sample)

Planned College Major	ACT M			ACT E		
	X̄	SD	N	X̄	SD	N
Education	16.3	7.4	5,229	17.4	5.4	5,229
Agriculture	18.1	7.1	1,809	16.8	5.0	1,899
Architecture	19.5	7.4	801	17.4	5.0	801
Biological sciences	21.3	7.0	1,301	19.4	4.9	1,301
Business and commerce	17.0	7.4	6,235	17.0	5.0	6,235
Communications	17.5	7.1	988	17.8	7.1	988
Computers and information	19.8	8.0	810	17.1	5.4	328
Engineering fields	22.9	7.1	2,490	18.0	5.2	2,490
Fine and applied arts	17.0	7.2	2,336	18.7	5.2	2,336
Foreign languages	19.6	7.2	279	20.6	5.3	279
Health professions	18.6	7.6	7,283	18.4	5.0	7,283
Home economics	16.4	7.3	658	18.0	4.9	658
Letters	18.9	7.0	632	20.0	5.3	632
Mathematics	27.4	5.1	436	20.8	4.9	436
Physical sciences	24.3	6.7	626	20.2	4.7	626
Community services	15.2	7.2	1,406	16.5	5.4	1,406
Social sciences	18.5	7.4	3,195	18.9	5.1	3,195
Trade, industry, technology	16.5	7.3	935	14.9	4.9	935
General studies	17.8	7.4	576	18.6	4.8	576
National sample	17.9	7.7	45,222	17.6	5.3	45,222

Source: American College Testing Program, College Student
Profiles: Norms for the ACT Assessment, 1976/77 ed.

TABLE 2.4

National Sample, ACT Class Profile Report for Enrolled Freshmen
1977/78: English and Mathematics Scores in 19 Major Fields of Study
(10 percent sample)

Planned College Major	ACT M			ACT E		
	$\overline{X}$	SD	N	$\overline{X}$	SD	N
Education	15.9	7.3	4,932	17.5	5.3	4,932
Agriculture	17.4	7.2	2,086	16.9	5.0	2,086
Architecture	19.4	7.3	983	17.5	5.0	983
Biological sciences	20.8	7.2	1,308	19.6	4.9	1,308
Business and commerce	16.7	7.5	7,309	17.0	5.0	7,309
Communications	17.0	7.3	1,253	19.2	5.3	1,253
Computers and information	19.1	8.4	969	17.2	5.5	969
Engineering fields	22.8	7.2	2,993	18.1	5.3	2,993
Fine and applied arts	16.5	7.4	2,238	18.6	5.2	2,238
Foreign languages	19.0	6.8	222	20.9	4.8	222
Health professions	18.2	7.6	7,634	18.3	5.0	7,634
Home economics	14.7	7.1	649	16.9	5.2	649
Letters	18.0	7.4	597	19.8	5.3	597
Mathematics	26.8	5.3	393	20.6	4.8	393
Physical sciences	24.1	6.5	745	20.3	5.1	745
Community services	15.0	7.1	1,397	16.6	5.1	1,397
Social sciences	18.6	7.5	3,084	19.3	5.0	3,084
Trade, industry, technology	16.6	7.1	1,056	15.2	4.9	1,056
General studies	18.5	7.4	792	19.0	5.0	792
National sample	17.6	7.8	47,614	17.7	5.3	47,614

Source: American College Testing Program, College Student
Profiles: Norms for the ACT Assessment, 1978/79 ed.

TABLE 2.5

ACTE and ACTM Scores of College Seniors by Field of Study, 1976

Field	Mean	Standard Deviation	N
ACT English			
	20.4832	4.5872	(173,296)
Agriculture and home economics	18.2418	4.5986	(4,977)
Business	19.9984	4.5724	(22,980)
Office Clerical	19.7438	1.6178	(1,700)
Computer	18.3845	3.1968	(1,228)
Education	19.5869	4.1535	(29,341)
Engineering	22.5578	2.6769	(7,337)
Vocational-technical	10.0000	0.0000	(301)
Humanities-arts	22.8414	3.6458	(13,868)
Health related	21.8585	3.7339	(8,354)
Public service	16.7081	3.9049	(1,803)
Physical sciences and mathematics	23.3270	3.8848	(5,227)
Social science	20.7651	4.2757	(20,868)
Biology	22.1188	4.5678	(6,780)
Professional	22.1326	3.9464	(10,483)
Other	20.7819	2.9045	(3,416)
Undecided	23.3003	3.0536	(484)
Missing	19.0617	5.2782	(34,150)

Total cases = 502,687
Missing cases = 329,392 or 65.5 percent

Field	Mean	Standard Deviation	N
ACT Mathematics			
	22.5702	6.8789	(173,531)
Agriculture and home economics	20.0391	6.0387	(4,977)
Business	24.7628	5.9609	(22,980)
Office clerical	16.4338	4.9806	(1,700)
Computer	26.1813	5.6480	(1,228)
Education	20.0004	6.1550	(29,451)
Engineering	28.3702	4.3254	(7,337)
Vocational-technical	17.0000	0.0000	(301)
Humanities-arts	23.2045	6.0685	(14,118)
Health related	23.0588	6.4600	(8,354)
Public service	17.2952	5.3435	(1,803)
Physcial sciences and mathematics	28.2922	5.3742	(5,227)
Social science	21.0685	6.5020	(20,868)
Biology	27.2122	5.3827	(6,780)
Professional	25.7720	5.2781	(10,483)
Other	21.9690	5.4379	(3,416)
Undecided	25.9652	7.2444	(484)
Missing	20.6973	7.6341	(34,026)

Total cases = 502,687
Missing cases = 329,156 or 65.5 percent

Source: National Longitudinal Study, May 1, 1978.

TABLE 2.6

SATM and SATV Scores of College Seniors by Field of Study, 1976

Field	Mean	Standard Deviation	N
SAT Mathematics			
	527.1122	108.1065	(334,892)
Agriculture and home economics	515.7805	91.0730	(3,546)
Business	529.6116	90.3155	(39,590)
Office clerical	408.5083	57.6524	(1,296)
Computer	582.9105	72.2620	(3,406)
Education	475.8848	95.7827	(50,524)
Engineering	624.6569	89.4338	(12,021)
Vocational-technical	501.7814	116.6677	(864)
Humanities-arts	528.3408	96.1730	(33,321)
Health related	513.0300	91.7767	(18,557)
Public service	498.2004	105.5481	(4,209)
Physical sciences and mathematics	631.0436	94.5307	(14,140)
Social science	532.3298	104.2261	(49,522)
Biology	573.3045	112.7788	(18,380)
Professional	550.5878	109.2926	(15,214)
Other	498.6239	107.8514	(6,936)
Undecided	526.7357	64.3147	(1,257)
Missing	510.1777	112.1877	(62,108)

Total cases   = 502,707
Missing cases = 167,815 or 33.4 percent

Field	Mean	Standard Deviation	N
SAT Verbal			
	491.2732	105.9264	(335,876)
Agriculture and home economics	472.0700	84.4113	(3,546)
Business	476.7067	94.7734	(39,590)
Office clerical	339.6273	71.0316	(1,296)
Computer	460.6417	89.5100	(3,406)
Education	445.4050	95.9800	(50,878)
Engineering	524.0096	104.0270	(12,021)
Vocational-technical	432.2041	193.2452	(864)
Humanities-arts	534.3666	99.0534	(33,321)
Health related	498.0776	79.8529	(18,557)
Public service	464.3112	80.3026	(4,209)
Physical science and mathematics	548.7494	109.3708	(14,250)
Social science	509.1446	106.3391	(49,937)
Biology	540.2169	110.2486	(18,380)
Professional	517.7707	96.8162	(15,214)
Other	480.5949	111.8850	(6,936)
Undecided	491.4542	91.9172	(1,257)
Missing	467.9293	103.6412	(62,214)

Total cases   = 502,707
Missing cases = 166,831 or 33.2 percent

Source: National Longitudinal Study, May 1, 1978

TABLE 2.7

SATV and SATM Scores of Graduating College Seniors Majoring in Education Employed or Not Employed as Teachers, 1976/77

Employed as Teacher	Mean	Standard Deviation	N
SAT Mathematics			
Yes	475.8843	97.7840	(50,524)
No	473.7529	85.3945	(23,696)
	477.7668	104.0670	(26,828)
Total cases = 79,080			
Missing cases = 28,556 or 36.1 percent			
SAT Verbal			
Yes	471.1382	96.0289	(246)
No	471.3793	85.7488	(116)
	470.9231	104.6844	(130)
Total cases = 406			
Missing cases = 160 or 39.4 percent			

Source: National Longitudinal Study, May 1, 1978.

TABLE 2.8

NLS Vocabulary Test Scores of College Seniors by Field of Study,
1976

Field	Mean	Standard Deviation	N
	57.5910	9.0591	(481,855)
Agriculture and home economics	54.1751	7.6934	(8,969)
Business	56.0546	9.0253	(54,756)
Office clerical	49.3882	8.0170	(2,510)
Computer	57.8140	5.4512	(4,296)
Education	55.2463	8.6161	(16,660)
Engineering	58.6916	8.7738	(15,717)
Vocational-technical	58.7673	9.1674	(1,133)
Humanities-arts	61.9814	8.1873	(42,867)
Health related	59.5165	7.6008	(22,669)
Public service	53.9759	9.1165	(6,037)
Physical sciences and mathematics	60.3290	8.3020	(17,247)
Social science	59.5118	8.5164	(66,977)
Biology	60.4320	8.4436	(21,163)
Professional	59.8279	8.0302	(23,388)
Other	59.2438	8.0395	(9,045)
Undecided	58.2213	8.9266	(1,401)
Missing	55.5476	9.5965	(107,020)

Total cases   = 502,712

Missing cases = 20,857 or 4.1 percent

Source: National Longitudinal Study, May 1, 1978.

TABLE 2.9

NLS Mathematics Scores of College Seniors by Field of Study, 1976

Field	Mean	Standard Deviation	N
	58.0750	7.6636	(481,855)
Agriculture and home economics	57.2624	6.5216	(8,969)
Business	59.8465	6.6031	(54,756)
Office clerical	49.9569	8.4303	(2,510)
Computer	61.6065	3.8212	(4,296)
Education	55.8567	7.3902	(16,660)
Engineering	63.9832	3.3007	(15,717)
Vocational-technical	59.2364	6.4596	(1,133)
Humanities-arts	58.6049	6.8059	(42,867)
Health related	59.4186	5.6960	(22,669)
Public service	54.0602	8.9277	(6,037)
Physical sciences and mathematics	63.5291	3.9118	(17,247)
Social science	58.6488	7.0316	(66,977)
Biology	62.1330	4.7544	(21,163)
Professional	60.8877	6.0423	(23,388)
Other	57.5387	7.4198	(9,045)
Undecided	59.0567	3.4299	(1,401)
Missing	55.1010	9.0514	(107,020)

Total cases = 502,712

Missing cases = 20,857 or 4.1 percent

Source: National Longitudinal Study, May 1, 1978.

TABLE 2.10

NLS Reading Comprehension Scores of College Seniors by Field of Study, 1976

Field	Mean	Standard Deviation	N
	57.0168	8.1598	(481,855)
Agriculture and home economics	54.3237	8.0504	(8,969)
Business	56.5204	7.3906	(54,756)
Office clerical	45.6448	8.0944	(2,510)
Computer	55.4981	4.8923	(4,296)
Education	54.9324	8.4871	(76,660)
Engineering	58.3007	7.2390	(15,717)
Vocational-technical	57.9378	6.8986	(1,133)
Humanities-arts	60.0701	7.2536	(42,867)
Health related	59.2206	6.7959	(22,669)
Public service	55.2876	6.3207	(6,037)
Physical sciences and mathematics	61.0945	7.4819	(17,247)
Social science	58.4985	7.5045	(66,977)
Biology	59.8536	7.0589	(21,163)
Professional	59.1778	6.1343	(23,388)
Other	57.2584	9.2206	(9,045)
Undecided	58.6998	4.9385	(1,401)
Missing	54.8664	8.8142	(107,020)

Total cases = 502,712

Missing cases = 20,857 or 4.1 percent

Source: National Longitudinal Study, May 1, 1978.

TABLE 2.11

NLS Composite Test Scores of College Seniors by Field of Study,
1976

Field	Mean	Standard Deviation	N
	228.4848	24.9339	(481,855)
Agriculture and home economics	219.6006	22.3864	(8,969)
Business	228.7950	21.7743	(54,756)
Office clerical	193.9880	25.0399	(2,510)
Computer	233.8053	13.0094	(4,296)
Education	221.7675	24.2692	(76,660)
Engineering	238.3680	18.1826	(15,717)
Vocational-technical	234.1111	19.2441	(1,133)
Humanities-arts	237.8241	20.7303	(42,867)
Health related	235.6697	17.0096	(22,669)
Public service	217.4200	23.4711	(6,037)
Physical sciences and mathematics	243.5067	19.2493	(17,247)
Social science	232.2663	23.6654	(66,977)
Biology	240.3161	19.4005	(21,163)
Professional	237.5642	17.6446	(23,388)
Other	228.5215	25.5004	(9,045)
Undecided	231.7576	20.8486	(1,401)
Missing	219.1700	28.7704	(107,020)

Total cases = 502,712

Missing cases = 20,857 or 4.1 percent

Source: National Longitudinal Study, May 1, 1978.

TABLE 2.12

National Teacher Examination Test Scores, 1969-75

Year	$\overline{X}$	Standard Deviation	N
1969	577	96	93,000
1970	581	103	70,000
1971	573	104	101,000
1972	570	105	103,000
1973	576	105	82,000
1974	566	102	78,000
1975	561	109	70,000

Source: Educational Testing Service, Personal communication, Norman Wexler.

TABLE 2.13

Selected Fields of Study as Indicated by College-Bound Seniors in
High School

Selected Fields	Percentage				
of Study	1972	1973	1974	1975	1976
Agriculture	2.0	2.0	2.0	2.4	2.6
Architecture/ environment	2.0	2.0	2.0	2.0	1.9
Biological science	14.0	12.0	13.0	8.0	4.8
Business and commerce	9.0	10.0	10.0	11.5	12.6
Communications	2.0	2.0	2.0	2.7	2.9
Computer	—	—	—	1.6	1.9
Education	11.0	10.0	8.0	9.1	8.7
Engineering	6.0	6.0	5.0	6.7	8.4
English	4.0	4.0	3.0	2.4	1.9
Ethnic studies	0.0	0.0	0.0	0.1	0.1
Foreign language	2.0	2.0	2.0	1.4	1.2
Forestry	—	—	—	1.2	1.6
Geology	—	—	—	0.0	0.0
Health and medicine	6.0	10.0	10.0	14.9	17.9
History	—	—	2.0	1.4	1.6
Home economics	2.0	2.0	2.0	1.0	0.1
Library science	—	—	—	0.1	0.0
Mathematics	4.0	3.0	3.0	2.4	2.2
Military science	—	—	—	0.6	1.8
Nursing	3.0	3.0	3.0	2.2	2.0
Philosophy	1.0	1.0	1.0	0.7	0.8
Physical science	4.0	4.0	4.0	2.8	3.8
Psychology	—	—	3.0	3.6	2.0
Social science	17.0	15.0	10.0	7.7	6.9
Theater arts	—	—	—	1.0	0.6
Trade vocational	2.0	3.0	2.0	1.4	1.0
Other	—	—	—	1.7	2.7
Undecided	5.0	7.0	9.0	6.5	5.0
Total sample (N)	548,323	767,903	816,590	812,883	776,065

Source: College Entrance Examination Board, 1972-76.

TABLE 2.14

A Comparison of 1972 and 1976 SATV and SATM Scores for College-Bound Seniors and College Graduates by Selected Fields of Study

College Major	1972 College-Bound, Scores (mean)		1976 College Graduates, NLS, Scores (mean)	
	SATV	SATM	SATV	SATM
Business	409	463	476	529
Education	418	449	445	475
Engineering	460	548	524	624
Social science	476	490	509	532
Physical science	505	570	548[a]	631[a]
Agriculture	427	471	472[b]	515[b]
Health	419	444	498	513
Vocational	400	450	432	501
Biology	440	451	540	573
Mathematics	481	595	548[a]	631[a]

[a]Mathematics and physics combined.
[b]Combines agriculture and home economics.

Sources: College Entrance Examination Board, On Further Examination, app., table 7; National College-Bound Seniors, 1972–73; and National Longitudinal Study, May 1978.

176

TABLE 2.15

A Comparison of Enrolled Freshmen Class Profiles (1970 and 1975) with Previous Year's
Applicant Pool, ACT English and Mathematics Scores; and a Comparison of 1970 and 1975
Enrolled Freshmen Class Profiles, ACT English and Mathematics Scores, by Selected
Majors
(10 percent national sample)

Planned College Major	College-Bound, 1969		Enrolled Freshmen, 1970		College-Bound, 1974		Enrolled Freshmen, 1975	
	$\overline{X}$	N	$\overline{X}$	N	$\overline{X}$	N	$\overline{X}$	N
Elementary education								
English	18.5	4,542	19.4	2,950	17.4	949	17.2	689
Mathematics	17.8	4,542	19.0	2,950	15.0	949	15.3	689
Secondary education								
English	19.1	2,165	20.0	1,568	18.2	191	18.2	112
Mathematics	19.6	2,165	20.7	1,568	17.4	191	17.7	112
Nursing, RN								
English	18.1	2,763	19.2	1,523	17.2	1,991	17.5	1,291
Mathematics	17.4	2,762	18.5	1,523	15.1	1,991	15.6	1,291
Sociology								
English	18.3	1,014	19.0	523	16.8	323	16.7	233
Mathematics	17.6	1,014	18.4	523	14.4	323	14.9	233
Business administration*								
English	16.2	3,462	16.9	1,989	15.9	1,183	15.8	901
Mathematics	18.0	3,462	18.9	1,989	16.1	1,183	15.9	901
Premedicine								
English	20.1	1,202	21.0	756	20.1	1,203	20.0	741
Mathematics	23.5	1,202	24.4	756	22.9	1,203	23.2	741
Prelaw								
English	18.4	1,572	19.0	1,027	19.2	1,109	18.8	714
Mathematics	20.6	1,572	21.5	1,027	20.0	1,109	20.0	714
Psychology								
English	19.5	1,734	20.1	986	18.9	926	19.2	526
Mathematics	19.5	1,734	20.2	986	17.6	926	17.6	526
Biology								
English	19.9	1,018	20.4	702	18.7	340	19.1	228
Mathematics	22.1	1,018	23.1	702	19.6	340	20.9	228
Aeronautical engineering								
English	18.5	534	19.3	322	18.1	301	18.1	156
Mathematics	23.8	534	24.6	322	22.4	301	22.5	156
Chemical engineering								
English	20.4	252	21.3	175	20.8	130	21.0	77
Mathematics	27.1	252	27.7	175	26.5	130	27.2	77
Physics								
English	21.5	259	21.9	199	22.6	116	21.2	81
Mathematics	28.1	259	28.4	199	28.0	116	27.8	81

*The sample size decline, contrary to actual percentages choosing business adminis-
tration as a field, suggests an aberration in the data, perhaps caused by a change in the
types of categories students could select in the general field of business and commerce.
See ACT College Student Profiles 1972, 1976.

Source: Weaver 1978.

TABLE 2.16

Comparison of Acceptances and Score Declines by Intended Field of Study

Planned College Major	Acceptance Ratio, 1969 to 1970	Acceptance Ratio, 1974 to 1975	1975 ACT Mean Scores as a Ratio of 1970 Mean Scores	
			ACT E	ACT M
Elementary education	.649	.726	.886	.805
Secondary education	.724	.586	.910	.855
Nursing, RN	.551	.648	.911	.843
Sociology	.515	.721	.878	.809
Business administration	.574	.761	.934	.841
Premedicine	.628	.615	.952	.950
Prelaw	.652	.643	.989	.930
Psychology	.568	.568	.955	.871
Biology	.689	.670	.936	.904
Aeronautical engineering	.602	.518	.937	.914
Chemical engineering	.694	.582	.985	.981
Physics	.768	.698	.968	.978

Note: Freshman admittances expressed as ratio of previous year's applicant pool.

Source: American College Testing Program, National Sample.

178

TABLE 2.17

Comparison of Test Scores and Enrollments for Ten Teacher Programs,
1970 and 1975

		1970		1976	
		SATV/M	Enrollment	SATV/M	Enrollment
1.	SED. university based (I)	52/53	602	47/49	175
2.	SED. university based (II)	51/54	215	47/49	175
3.	Teachers college A— elementary education	42/48	333	39/41	28
4.	Teachers college B— elementary education	50/56	380	42/45	84
5.	Teachers college C— elementary education	47/50	208	42/45	31
6.	Teachers college D— elementary education	49/52	244	44/48	39
7.	Teachers college E— elementary education	46/48	169	43/46	19
8.	Teachers college F— elementary education	49/52	282	40/43	77
9.	Teachers college G— elementary education	50/52	164	43/46	8
10.	Teachers college H— elementary education	45/47	160	41/42	29

TABLE 2.18

Ratio of Acceptances to Applications, and SAT Scores in Two Schools of
Education, 1969-75

Year	(I)			(II)		
	Ratio	SATV	SATM	Ratio	SATV*	SATM*
1969	.532	534	551	.398	517	539
1970	.614	526	530	.290	518	541
1971	.833	488	510	.414	539	556
1972	.729	485	510	.581	511	538
1973	.832	450	476	.508	494	505
1974	.917	449	459	.743	488	526
1975	.709	470	494	.548	471	498

*Median scores.

TABLE 2.19

Three Academic Divisions within One University, Comparison of Ratio of Acceptances, Applications, Enrollments, and Test Scores

	(1) Applications to Acceptances	(2) Applications to 1968 Total	(3) Net Annual Change in Applications	(4) Net Annual Change in Enrollments	(5) Enrollments in Ratio of 1968 Total	(6) Acceptances as Ratio to 1968	(7) SATV	(8) SATM
SED								
1968	.526	1.000	—	—	—	—	532	540
1969	.532	1.124	—	—	—	—	534	551
1970	.614	1.208	-.074	.089	1.091	1.091	526	530
1971	.833	0.946	-.277	-.084	1.006	1.006	488	510
1972	.729	0.838	-.128	-.199	0.839	0.839	485	510
1973	.853	0.461	-.818	-.486	0.564	0.564*	450	476
1974	.917	0.328	-.404	-.209	0.446	0.446	449	459
1975	.709	0.301	-.088	-.125	0.390	0.390	470	494
Engineering								
1968	.603	1.000	—	—	—	—	559	636
1969	.425	1.153	.153	-.060	0.942	0.813	545	655
1970	.527	1.153	.000	-.106	0.842	1.007	573	654
1971	.795	0.612	-.469	-.033	0.871	0.806	542	590
1972	.666	0.532	-.150	-.848	0.471	0.507	507	595
1973	.907	0.445	-.194	.696	0.800*	0.670	510	615
1974	.871	0.874	.961	.946	1.557	1.261	490	571
1975	.775	1.216	.391	.909	1.414	1.562	481	571
Allied health								
1968	.632	1.000	—	—	—	—	524	535
1969	.714	1.021	.021	.085	1.085	1.153	505	545
1970	.773	1.097	-.074	.078	1.170	1.340	527	536
1971	.830	0.962	-.140	.058	1.239	1.262	490	519
1972	.717	1.343	.396	.110	1.376	1.524	505	527
1973	.887	1.706	.269	.341	1.846	2.393	482	513
1974	.763	1.244	.371	.317	1.401	1.501	485	513
1975	.548	1.521	.222	.044	1.341	1.318	504	534

*Key Year: Acceptances began to fall more slowly than applications (for both education and engineering).

TABLE 2.20

A Within-University Comparison of Applications, Acceptances, and Test Scores

Academic Department	Applications		Acceptances		Ratio		SATV Applicants		SATV Acceptances		SATM Applicants		SATM Acceptances	
	1973	1980	1973	1980	1973	1980	1973	1980	1973	1980	1973	1980	1973	1980
Agriculture	413	303	222	203	.538	.670	486	484	514	498	536	523	563	539
Fine arts	480	722	258	302	.444	.341	527	513	551	539	536	516	554	536
Languages	150	156	114	73	.760	.468	536	513	553	540	555	526	569	541
Social sciences	1,088	1,291	578	526	.531	.407	525	514	550	550	552	539	573	571
Arts and sciences	1,180	1,455	734	643	.622	.445	526	505	546	528	574	550	591	570
Education	679	558	306	298	.708	.726	472	460	487	474	519	494	535	511
Business administration	408	922	145	275	.355	.298	468	474	490	505	542	542	570	573
Engineering	393	735	315	471	.802	.641	500	496	512	512	595	602	610	620
Mathematics, computer science, statistics	61	304	57	162	.934	.533	514	486	517	497	637	595	636	613
Home economics	244	169	131	121	.537	.716	467	450	499	467	507	490	543	512
Natural resources	282	434	107	199	.379	.459	489	491	518	524	542	528	567	559
Nursing	418	266	179	147	.428	.553	490	466	511	490	516	505	537	528
Allied health (2)	242	113	78	79	.322	.699	458	428	452	451	491	477	488	498
Allied health (4)	430	436	143	139	.333	.319	495	479	516	500	543	527	575	545
Total	7,772	9,009	4,406	4,455	.567	.495	507	494	530	514	553	544	576	566

181

TABLE 2.21

Ratio of Acceptances to Applications, and SAT Scores in Three Engineering Schools, 1969–75

Year	(1)			(2)			(3)		
	Ratio	SATV	SATM	Ratio	SATV*	SATM*	Ratio	SATV	SATM
1969	.425	545	655	.517	513	621	.881	522	634
1970	.527	573	654	.567	516	602	.904	519	626
1971	.795	542	590	.594	530	630	.901	519	626
1972	.666	507	595	.734	494	613	.954	514	615
1973	.907	570	615	.789	511	622	.957	505	611
1974	.871	490	571	.728	517	609	.943	500	609
1975	.775	481	571	.691	500	601	.944	496	606

*Median test scores.

TABLE 4.1

National Supply/Demand Estimates in Elementary Education in the United States, 1970-90

Year	(A) Previous Year's Enrollment[a]	(B) Present Year's Enrollment[b]	(C) Net Enrollment Change (B - A)	(D) Percent of Teachers in Subject Area[c]	(E) Average Student-Teacher Ratio, Previous Year[d]	(F) Average Student-Teacher Ratio, Present[e]	(G) Teachers Needed, Previous Year (A - E*D)	(H) Total Teacher TOR[f]
1970	27,455,000	27,501,000	46,000	1	24.80	24.39	1,107,056	.0810
1971	27,501,000	27,688,000	187,000	1	24.39	24.94	1,127,552	.0788
1972	27,688,000	27,323,000	-365,000	1	24.94	23.98	1,110,184	.0766
1973	27,323,000	26,435,000	-888,000	1	23.98	22.94	1,139,408	.0744
1974	26,435,000	26,382,000	-53,000	1	22.94	22.62	1,152,354	.0722
1975	26,382,000	25,640,000	-742,000	1	22.62	21.74	1,166,313	.0700
1976	25,640,000	25,430,000	-210,000	1	21.74	21.93	1,179,393	.0678
1977	25,430,000	24,954,000	-476,000	1	21.93	21.05	1,159,599	.0656
1978	24,954,000	25,017,000	63,000	1	21.05	21.01	1,185,463	.0634
1979	25,017,000	24,851,000	-166,000	1	21.01	20.92	1,190,719	.0612
1980	24,851,000	24,287,000	-564,000	1	20.92	20.66	1,187,906	.0590
1981	24,287,000	23,955,000	-332,000	1	20.66	20.45	1,175,557	.0590
1982	23,955,000	23,686,000	-269,000	1	20.45	20.28	1,171,394	.0590
1983	23,686,000	23,506,000	-180,000	1	20.28	20.00	1,167,949	.0590
1984	23,506,000	23,513,000	7,000	1	20.00	20.08	1,175,300	.0590
1985	23,513,000	23,738,000	225,000	1	20.08	19.80	1,170,966	.0590
1986	23,738,000	24,236,000	498,000	1	19.80	19.57	1,198,889	.0590
1987	24,236,000	24,860,000	624,000	1	19.57	19.34	1,238,426	.0590
1988	13,860,000	25,598,000	738,000	1	19.34	19.12	1,285,419	.0590
1989	25,589,000	26,305,000	716,000	1	19.23	19.12	1,338,337	.0590
1990	26,305,000	27,022,000	717,000	1	19.12	18.94	1,388,860	.0590

(continued)

183

TABLE 4.1 (continued)

Year	(I) Additional Teachers owing to TOR, Previous Year $(G * H)$	(J) Additional Teachers owing to Net Enrollment Change $(C \div F * D)$	(K) Additional Teachers owing to Student-Teacher Ratio Change $[(A \div F * D) - G]$	(L) Total Demand for New Teachers $(I + J + K)$	(M) Reentering Rate for Classroom Teachers[g]	(N) Demand Filled by Reentering Teachers $(G * M)$	(O) Demand Filled by New Graduates $(L - N)$	(P) Supply New Graduates (total)[h]
1970	89,672	1,886	18,599	110,156	.0320	35,426	74,730	98,278
1971	88,851	7,499	-24,762	71,588	.0308	34,729	36,859	103,402
1972	85,040	-15,221	44,405	114,225	.0296	32,861	81,363	111,817
1973	84,772	-38,717	51,875	97,930	.0284	32,359	65,571	108,942
1974	83,200	-2,343	16,073	96,930	.0272	31,344	65,586	92,900
1975	81,642	-34,132	47,259	94,769	.0260	30,324	64,445	91,400
1976	79,963	-9,576	-10,209	60,178	.0248	29,249	30,929	87,100
1977	76,070	-22,610	48,326	101,786	.0236	27,367	74,419	78,000
1978	75,158	-2,999	2,347	80,504	.0224	26,554	53,950	73,400
1979	72,872	-7,935	5,094	70,031	.0212	25,243	44,788	66,400
1980	70,086	-27,298	14,882	57,671	.0200	23,758	33,913	60,525
1981	69,358	-16,235	12,078	65,201	.0200	23,511	41,690	55,751
1982	69,112	-13,262	9,588	65,438	.0200	23,428	42,011	51,000
1983	68,909	-9,000	16,351	76,260	.0200	23,359	52,901	46,849
1984	69,343	349	-4,701	64,990	.0200	23,506	41,484	42,826
1985	69,087	11,363	16,440	96,890	.0200	23,419	73,471	39,230
1986	70,734	25,448	14,123	110,305	.0200	23,978	86,327	35,972
1987	73,067	32,261	14,575	119,903	.0200	24,769	95,134	32,953
1988	75,840	38,597	14,759	129,196	.0200	25,708	103,488	30,197
1989	78,962	37,805	12,762	129,529	.0200	26,767	102,762	27,658
1990	81,943	38,216	13,197	133,356	.0200	27,777	105,579	25,342

(continued)

184

TABLE 4.1 (continued)

Year	(Q) Total Supply of New Graduates Relative to Demand (P ÷ O)	(R) Demand for New Graduates Relative to Supply of New Graduates (O ÷ P)	(S) Total Demand Relative to Supply of New Graduates (L ÷ P)	(T) Supply of New Graduates Relative to Total Demand (P ÷ L)	(U) Graduates Adjusted for Job Seeking (P * .692)	(V) Adjusted Supply Relative to Demand for New Graduates (U ÷ O)	(W) Demand for New Graduates Relative to Adjusted Supply (O ÷ U)
1970	1.32	0.76	1.12	0.89	81,767	1.09	0.91
1971	2.81	0.36	0.69	1.44	86,030	2.33	0.43
1972	1.37	0.73	1.02	0.98	93,032	1.14	0.87
1973	1.66	0.60	0.90	1.11	90,640	1.38	0.72
1974	1.42	0.71	1.04	0.96	77,293	1.18	0.85
1975	1.42	0.71	1.04	0.96	76,045	1.18	0.85
1976	2.82	0.36	0.69	1.45	72,467	2.34	0.43
1977	1.05	0.95	1.30	0.77	64,896	0.87	1.15
1978	1.36	0.74	1.10	0.91	61,069	1.13	0.88
1979	1.48	0.67	1.05	0.95	55,245	1.23	0.81
1980	1.78	0.56	0.95	1.05	50,357	1.48	0.67
1981	1.43	0.75	1.17	0.86	46,385	1.11	0.90
1982	1.21	0.82	1.28	0.78	42,432	1.01	0.99
1983	0.89	1.13	1.63	0.61	38,978	0.74	1.36
1984	1.03	0.97	1.52	0.66	35,631	0.86	1.16
1985	0.53	1.87	2.47	0.40	32,640	0.44	2.25
1986	0.42	2.40	3.07	0.33	29,928	0.35	2.88
1987	0.35	2.89	3.64	0.27	27,417	0.29	3.47
1988	0.29	3.43	4.28	0.23	25,124	0.24	4.12
1989	0.27	3.72	4.68	0.21	23,012	0.22	4.47
1990	0.24	4.17	5.26	0.19	21,085	0.20	5.01

aNCES (1990–80), table 7, col. 5, Public Elementary Schools.
bNCES (1990–91), table 7, col. 5, Public Elementary Schools.
cNCES (1980), table 50.
dNCES (1990–91), table 18.

eNCES (1990–91), table 18.
fNEA (1970–80).
gNEA (1970–80).

hNEA (1970–80). Figures for 1970, 1971, 1972, 1973, and 1974 are calculated from table values under column 2 ("Estimated Supply of Beginning Teachers").
Column values, as reported by NEA, are adjusted by 69.2 percent. Job-seeking figures are not total supply figures. After 1974, figures reported are total supply as reported by NEA for 1975, 1976, 1977, 1978, 1979, and 1980 in column 2.

TABLE 4.2

National Supply/Demand Estimates in Secondary Teaching Fields in the United States, 1970-90

Year	(A) Previous Year's Enrollment[a]	(B) Present Year's Enrollment[b]	(C) Net Enrollment Change (B - A)	(D) Percent of Teachers in Subject Area[c]	(E) Average Student-Teacher Ratio, Previous Year[d]	(F) Average Student-Teacher Ratio, Present[e]	(G) Teachers Needed, Previous Year (A ÷ E*D)	(H) Total Teacher TOR[f]
1970	18,163,000	18,408,000	245,000	1	20.00	19.84	908,150	.0860
1971	18,408,000	18,393,000	-15,000	1	19.84	19.32	927,823	.0833
1972	18,393,000	18,421,000	28,000	1	19.32	19.12	952,091	.0806
1973	18,421,000	18,995,000	574,000	1	19.12	19.27	963,441	.0779
1974	18,995,000	18,671,000	-324,000	1	19.27	18.69	985,729	.0752
1975	18,671,000	19,151,000	480,000	1	18.69	18.83	998,983	.0725
1976	19,151,000	18,887,000	-264,000	1	18.83	18.52	1,017,047	.0698
1977	18,887,000	18,623,000	-264,000	1	18.52	18.18	1,019,816	.0671
1978	18,623,000	17,534,000	-1,089,000	1	18.18	17.27	1,024,265	.0644
1979	17,534,000	16,728,000	-806,000	1	17.27	16.84	1,015,219	.0617
1980	16,728,000	16,708,000	-20,000	1	16.84	16.92	993,643	.0590
1981	16,708,000	16,234,000	-474,000	1	16.92	17.12	987,443	.0590
1982	16,234,000	15,858,000	-376,000	1	17.12	17.04	948,066	.0590
1983	15,858,000	15,659,000	-199,000	1	17.04	16.92	930,865	.0590
1984	15,659,000	15,526,000	-133,000	1	16.92	16.75	925,447	.0590
1985	15,526,000	15,428,000	-98,000	1	16.75	16.61	926,902	.0590
1986	15,428,000	15,220,000	-208,000	1	16.61	16.45	928,766	.0590
1987	15,220,000	14,944,000	-276,000	1	16.45	16.31	925,376	.0590
1988	14,944,000	14,569,000	-375,000	1	16.31	16.18	916,067	.0590
1989	14,569,000	14,300,000	-269,000	1	16.18	16.08	900,364	.0590
1990	14,300,000	14,245,000	-55,000	1	16.08	15.95	889,460	.0590

(continued)

186

TABLE 4.2 (continued)

Year	(I) Additional Teachers owing to TOR, Previous Year (G * H)	(J) Additional Teachers owing to Net Enrollment Change (C ÷ F * D)	(K) Additional Teachers owing to Student-Teacher Ratio Change [(A ÷ F * D) - G]	(L) Total Demand for New Teachers (I + J + K)	(M) Reentering Rate for Classroom Teachers[g]	(N) Demand Filled by Re-entering Teachers (G * M)	(O) Demand Filled by New Graduates (L - N)	(P) Supply of New Graduates (total)[h]
1970	78,101	12,348	7,265	97,714	.0300	27,245	70,470	167,802
1971	77,288	-776	24,972	101,484	.0287	26,629	74,855	176,237
1972	76,733	1,464	9,958	88,155	.0274	26,085	62,070	182,715
1973	75,052	29,787	-7,500	97,340	.0261	25,146	72,194	165,639
1974	74,127	-17,335	30,590	87,381	.0248	24,446	62,935	167,839
1975	72,426	25,491	-7,427	90,490	.0235	23,476	67,014	144,931
1976	70,990	-14,256	17,107	73,841	.0222	22,578	51,262	121,580
1977	68,430	-14,520	18,969	72,878	.0209	21,314	51,564	119,432
1978	65,963	-63,053	54,007	56,916	.0196	20,076	36,841	102,079
1979	62,639	-47,876	26,301	41,064	.0183	18,579	22,485	93,100
1980	58,625	-1,182	-5,018	52,425	.0170	16,892	35,533	81,625
1981	58,259	-27,682	-11,696	18,882	.0170	16,787	2,095	72,886
1982	55,936	-22,071	4,870	38,735	.0170	16,117	22,618	65,871
1983	54,921	-11,761	6,343	49,503	.0170	15,825	33,679	58,496
1984	54,601	-7,940	9,395	56,057	.0170	15,733	40,324	52,336
1985	54,687	-5,900	7,763	56,551	.0170	15,757	40,793	46,644
1986	54,797	-12,646	9,257	51,408	.0170	15,789	35,619	41,706
1987	54,597	-16,919	7,610	45,288	.0170	15,731	29,557	37,301
1988	54,048	-23,175	7,472	38,345	.0170	15,573	22,772	33,291
1989	53,121	-16,732	5,828	42,217	.0170	15,306	26,911	29,742
1990	52,478	-3,449	7,150	56,180	.0170	15,121	41,059	26,563

(continued)

TABLE 4.2 (continued)

Year	(Q) Total Supply of New Graduates Relative to Demand (P ÷ O)	(R) Demand for New Graduates Relative to Supply (O ÷ P)	(S) Total Demand Relative to Supply of New Graduates (L ÷ P)	(T) Supply of New Graduates Relative to Total Demand (P ÷ L)	(U) Supply of New Graduates Adjusted for Job Seeking (P * .692)	(V) Adjusted Supply Relative to Demand for New Graduates (U ÷ O)	(W) Demand for New Graduates Relative to Adjusted Supply (O ÷ U)
1970	2.38	0.42	0.58	1.72	116,119	1.65	0.61
1971	2.35	0.42	0.58	1.74	121,956	1.63	0.61
1972	2.94	0.34	0.48	2.07	126,439	2.04	0.49
1973	2.29	0.44	0.59	1.70	114,622	1.59	0.63
1974	2.67	0.37	0.52	1.92	116,145	1.85	0.54
1975	2.16	0.46	0.62	1.60	100,292	1.50	0.67
1976	2.37	0.42	0.61	1.65	84,133	1.64	0.61
1977	2.32	0.43	0.61	1.64	82,647	1.60	0.62
1978	2.77	0.36	0.56	1.79	70,639	1.92	0.52
1979	4.14	0.24	0.44	2.27	64,425	2.87	0.35
1980	2.30	0.44	0.64	1.56	56,485	1.59	0.63
1981	34.78	0.03	0.26	3.86	50,437	24.07	0.04
1982	2.91	0.34	0.59	1.70	45,583	2.02	0.50
1983	1.74	0.58	0.85	1.18	40,479	1.20	0.83
1984	1.30	0.77	1.07	0.93	36,217	0.90	1.11
1985	1.14	0.87	1.21	0.82	32,278	0.79	1.26
1986	1.17	0.85	1.23	0.81	28,861	0.81	1.23
1987	1.26	0.79	1.21	0.82	25,812	0.87	1.15
1988	1.46	0.68	1.15	0.87	23,037	1.01	0.99
1989	1.11	0.90	1.42	0.70	20,581	0.76	1.31
1990	0.65	1.55	2.11	0.47	18,382	0.45	2.23

aNCES (1990–91), table 7, col. 6, Public Elementary Schools.
bNCES (1990–91), table 7, col. 6, Public Elementary Schools
cNCES (1980), table 50.
dNCES (1990–91), table 18.

eNCES (1990–91), table 18.
fNEA (1970–80).
gNEA (1970–80).

hNEA (1970–80). Figures for 1970, 1971, 1972, 1973, and 1974 are calculated from table values under column 2 ("Estimated Supply of Beginning Teachers").
Column values, as reported by the NEA, are adjusted by 69.2 percent. Job-seeking rates are not total supply figures. After 1974, figures reported are total
supply as reported by the NEA for 1975, 1976, 1977, 1978, 1979, and 1980 in column 2.

TABLE 4.3

An Estimate of Elementary Schoolteacher Demand Based on Birthrates, 1981–87

Year	(1) Estimated Enrollment Grades 1–6[a]	(2) Net Change in Enrollment	(3) Total Teachers Needed[b]	(4) Additional Teachers Needed owing to Enrollment Change	(5) Additional Teachers Needed owing to Turnover[c]	(6) Total Additional Teachers Needed to Fill Vacancies[d]
1981	19,986,888	—	—	—	—	—
1982	19,423,290	-563,598	971,165	-28,180	58,270	30,090
1983	19,193,952	-229,338	959,698	-11,467	57,582	46,115
1984	19,268,820	74,868	963,441	3,744	57,806	61,550
1985	19,626,253	357,433	981,313	17,872	58,879	76,751
1986	20,064,295	438,042	1,003,215	21,902	60,193	82,095
1987	20,567,087	502,802	1,028,354	25,140	61,701	86,841

[a]Calculated from live births 6 to 12 years earlier (National Center for Health Statistics).
[b]Calculated by dividing estimated enrollment by 20.
[c]Turnover estimated to be 6 percent.
[d]Column 4 plus column 5.

TABLE 5.31

A Compilation and Comparison of States that Require a Test for Certification

State Developed	Authority	Year Adopted	Year Effective	Type of Test	Areas to Be Tested	Test Required of
Alabama	SBE	1980	1981	State developed	Professional and teaching field content	Applicants for initial teaching certificate
Arizona	Legislature Secs. 15-235 and 236 of Education Code	1980	1980	State developed	Reading, grammar, and mathematics	Applicants for basic or standard certificate
Arkansas	Legislature H.B. 475	1979	1980 extended by legislature to 1983	NTE	The commons and area examinations	Applicants for initial certification and those seeking certification in additional areas
California	Legislature A.B. 757	1981	1983	State developed or adopted	Basic skills in reading, writing, and mathematics	Applicants for initial teacher certificate and instructional aides
Colorado	Legislature	1981	1983	State developed	Basic skills in oral and written communication and mathematics	Applicants for teacher education sequence and out-of-state teachers applying for certificates
Connecticut	SBE	1982	1985	To be selected or developed	Professional knowledge and subject matter area	Applicants for initial teacher certification
Florida	Legislature CB/SB 549	1978	1980	State developed	Grammar and sentence structure, listening, reading comprehension, mathematics, student development, and others as adopted by SBE	Applicants for initial teaching certificate
Georgia	SBE	1975	1978	State developed	Subject matter areas	Applicants for initial teaching certificates and also librar-

...ians, media, counselors, and administrators

State	Authority			Test	Content	Applies to
Louisiana	Legislature	1977	1979	NTE	Commons plus subject areas	Applicants for initial teaching certificates
Mississippi	Legislature	1972	1972	NTE	Commons plus subject matter areas	Applicants for initial teaching certificate
New Mexico	SBE	1981	1983	State developed	General education, communication skills, methods and practices, and content specialization	Applicants for initial teaching certificate
New York	Regents	1980	1984	State developed	Communications and computational skills, pedagogical knowledge, and subject matter content	Applicants for initial teaching and administration licenses
North Carolina	SBE	1979	1981	State developed	Liberal arts preparation and subject matter areas	Applicants for professional sequence and initial certification
Oklahoma	Legislature H.B. 1706	1980	1982	State developed	Subject matter area (curriculum examination)	Applicants for a teaching license; certification follows entry-level year
South Carolina	Legislature S.528	1979	1982	NTE and state developed	Subject matter areas (NTE) and basic skills (state developed)	Applicants for initial teaching certificates
Tennessee	SBE	1980	1981	NTE	Commons	Applicants for initial teaching certificates
Texas	Legislature S.B. 50	1981	1985	State developed	Basic skills and subject matter area	Applicants for initial teaching certificates
Virginia	Legislature H 1723	1980	1980	NTE	Professional skills and subject matter areas	Applicants for initial teaching certificate
West Virginia	SBE	1961	1964	NTE	Commons and subject matter areas	Applicants for initial teaching certificate

Source: School Products News 21 (October 1982): 27. Originally compiled by Russ Vlaanderen, director, Education Commission of the States.

FIGURE 4.2

Supply of New Science Teachers Relative to Positions for New
Graduates, Log. 1970-90

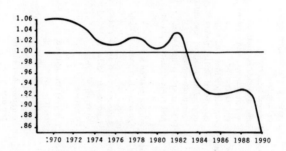

FIGURE 4.3

Supply of New Mathematics Teachers Relative to Positions for
New Graduates, Log. 1970-90

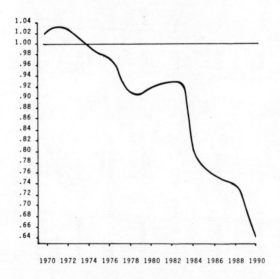

FIGURE 4.4

Supply of New English Teachers Relative to Positions for New Graduates, Log. 1970-90

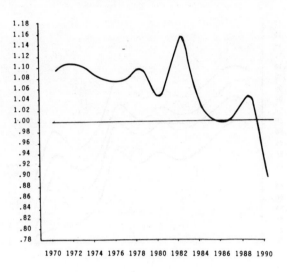

FIGURE 4.5

Supply of New Social Science Teachers Relative to Positions for New Graduates, Log. 1970-90

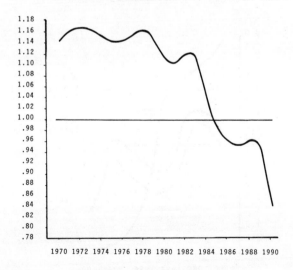

FIGURE 4.6

Supplies of New General Science, Biology, Chemistry, and Physics
Teachers Relative to Positions for New Graduates, Log. 1970-90

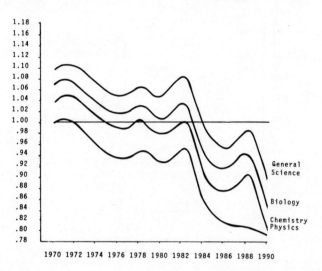

FIGURE 4.7

Adjusted Turnover Rate Required to Fill Vacancies in Physics,
Mathematics, and Elementary Education, 1980-90

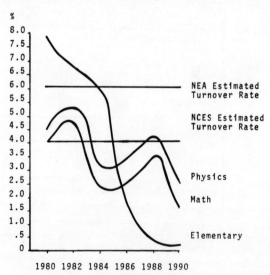

FIGURE 4.8

Adjusted Reentry Rate Required to Fill Vacancies in Mathematics,
Physics, and Elementary Education, 1980–90

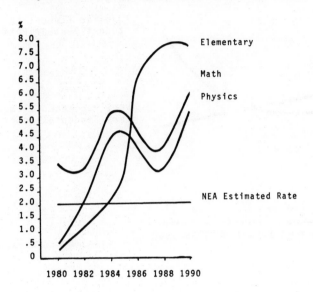

FIGURE 4.9

Adjusted Student-Teacher Ratio Required to Fill Vacancies in
Physics and Mathematics, 1980–90

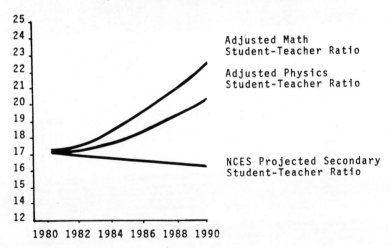

FIGURE 4.10

Adjusted Student-Teacher Ratio Required to Fill Vacancies in Elementary Education, 1980-90

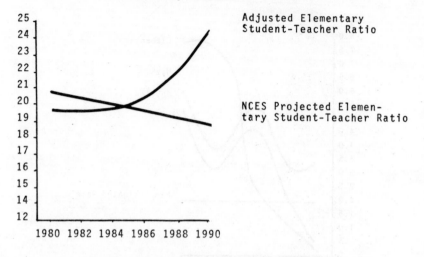

FIGURE 4.19

Depopulated Model Test: School System Variables

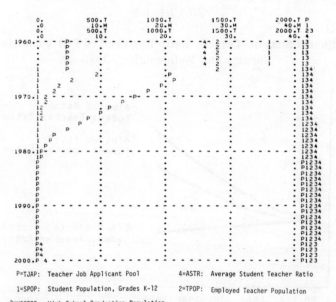

P=TJAP: Teacher Job Applicant Pool   4=ASTR: Average Student Teacher Ratio

1=SPOP: Student Population, Grades K-12   2=TPOP: Employed Teacher Population

3=HSGPOP: High School Graduation Population

FIGURE 4.20

Depopulated Model Test: School of Education Variables

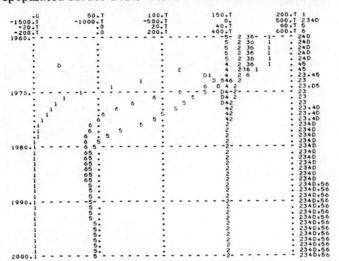

1=RACSED: Acceptance Into Schools of Education
2=RESED: Graduation from Schools of Education (BA Majors in ed.)
3=RGRAD: BA Majors in ed. plus minimally qualified graduates
4=THR: Teacher Hire Rate

D=DESTHR: Desired Teacher Hire Rate
5=SEDFAC: SED Faculty
6=SEDSE: SED Enrollments

FIGURE 4.21

Depopulated Model Test: SAT Co-flow Variables

1=SATEP: SAT's of SED Applicants
2=SAXTE: SAT's of SED Graduates
H=NTSAT: SAT's of New Teachers
T=SATSE: SAT's of SED Acceptances

*=SAT: SAT Constant
C=STJAP: SAT's of Those in Teacher Job Pool
A=NACT: SAT's of Those Entering Alternative Careers

197

FIGURE 4.22

Correspondence Test: Documented and Model Generated Teacher Demand

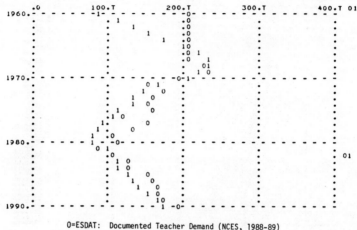

O=ESDAT: Documented Teacher Demand (NCES, 1988-89)
1=DESTHR: Model Generated Teacher Demand

FIGURE 4.23

Correspondence Test: Model Generated Teacher Supply and Demand

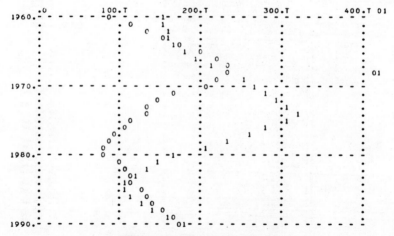

O=DESTHR: Model Generated Teacher Demand
1=SNTG: Model Generated Teacher Supply

FIGURE 4.24

Correspondence Test: Documented Teacher Supply and Demand

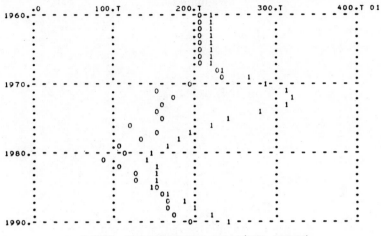

0=ESDAT: Documented Teacher Demand (NCES, 1988-89)
1=ESNTG: Documented Teacher Supply (NCES, 1988-89)

FIGURE 4.25

Documented and Model Generated Education Graduates
(undergraduates)

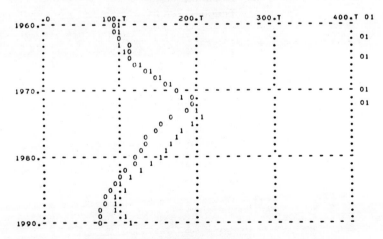

0=BSSED: Documented Education Graduates (NCES, 1988-89)
1=RESED: Model Generated Educated Graduates

FIGURE 4.26

Correspondence Test: Documented and Model Generated Graduates
(graduate SED)

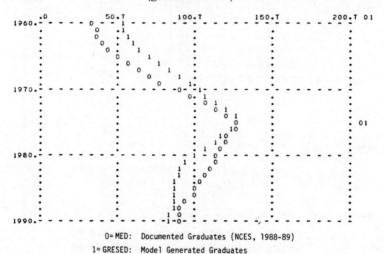

O= MED: Documented Graduates (NCES, 1988-89)
1= GRESED: Model Generated Graduates

FIGURE 4.27

Correspondence Test: Documented and Model Generated New
Teacher Supply

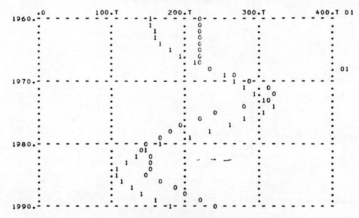

O= ESNTG: Documented New Teacher Supply (NCES, 1988-89)
1= SNTG: Model Generated New Teacher Graduates

FIGURE 4.28

Correspondence Test: Documented and Model Generated SATs (verbal)

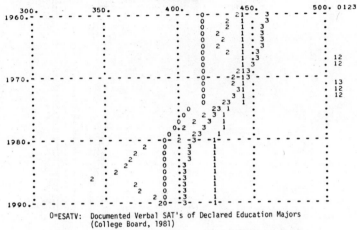

0=ESATV: Documented Verbal SAT's of Declared Education Majors (College Board, 1981)

1=NSATV: Documented Verbal SAT's of Total Test Takers (College Board, 1981)

2=SATEP: Model Generated SAT's of SED Applicants

3=RSAT: Model Generated SAT's of Arts & Sciences Applicants

FIGURE 4.29

Correspondence Test: Documented and Model Generated SATs (mathematics)

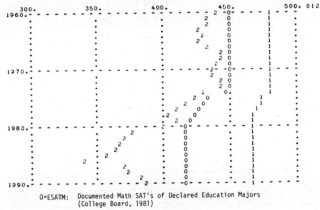

0=ESATM: Documented Math SAT's of Declared Education Majors (College Board, 1981)

1=NSATM: Documented Math SAT's of Total Test Takers (College Board, 1981)

2=SATEP: Model Generated SAT's of SED Applicants

201

FIGURE 5.1

Base Run from Equilibrium: Test Scores

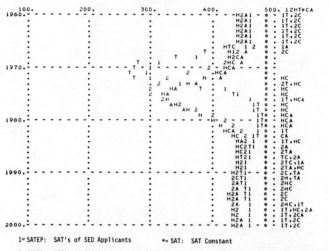

1= SATEP:	SAT's of SED Applicants
2= SAXTE:	SAT's of SED Graduates
H= NTSAT:	SAT's of New Teachers
T= SATSE:	SAT's of SED Acceptances

*= SAT:	SAT Constant
C= STJAP:	SAT's of Those in Teacher Job Pool
A =NACT:	SAT's of Those Entering Alternative Careers

FIGURE 5.2

Base Run from Equilibrium: School of Education Variables

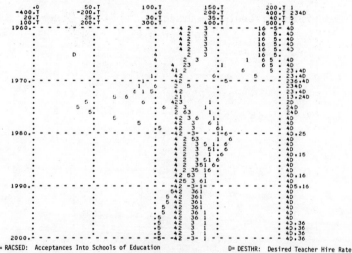

1= RACSED:	Acceptances Into Schools of Education
2= RESED:	Graduation From Schools of Education (BA Majors in ed.)
3= RGRAD:	BA Majors in ed. Plus Minimally Qualified Graduates
4= THR:	Teacher Hire Rate

D= DESTHR:	Desired Teacher Hire Rate
5= SEDFAC:	SED Faculty
6= SEDSE:	SED Enrollments

FIGURE 5.3

Base Run from Equilibrium: Graduate Schools of Education

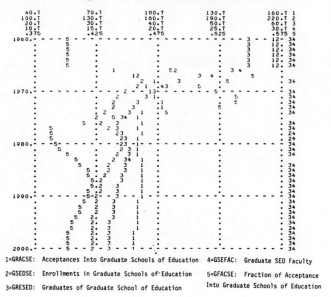

1=GRACSE: Acceptances Into Graduate Schools of Education   4=GSEFAC: Graduate SED Faculty

2=GSEDSE: Enrollments in Graduate Schools of Education   5=GFACSE: Fraction of Acceptance

3=GRESED: Graduates of Graduate School of Education   Into Graduate Schools of Education

FIGURE 5.4

Base Run from Equilibrium: Teacher Market

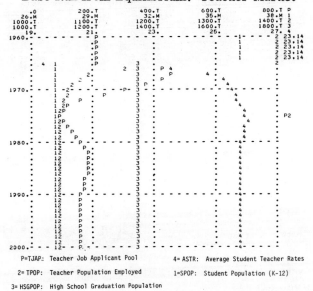

P=TJAP: Teacher Job Applicant Pool   4= ASTR: Average Student Teacher Rates

2= TPOP: Teacher Population Employed   1=SPOP: Student Population (K-12)

3= HSGPOP: High School Graduation Population

203

FIGURE 5.5

Base Run from Equilibrium: Admissions Variables

1= FCBSED: Fraction of College Bound Seniors Applying to SED's   4= CBSED: College Bound Seniors in SED Applicant Pool

2= FACSED: Fraction of Applicants Accepted by SED's   5= GFACSE: Fraction of Acceptances Into Graduate Schools

3= FXCT: Fraction of Those in Teacher Job Pool Hired as Teachers

FIGURE 5.6

Policy Test A: SED Entrance Qualification Test
(test score results)

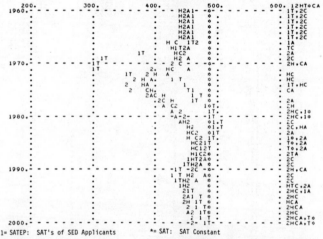

1= SATEP: SAT's of SED Applicants   *= SAT: SAT Constant

2= SAXTE: SAT's of SED Graduates   C= STJAP: SAT's of Those in Teacher Job Pool

H= NTSAT: SAT's of New Teachers   A= NACT: SAT's of Those Entering Alternative Careers

T= SATSE: SAT's of SED Acceptances

FIGURE 5.7

Policy Test A: SED Entrance Qualification Test (SED results)

1= RACSED: Acceptances Into Schools of Education   D=DESTHR: Desired Teacher Hire Rate

2= RESED: Graduation From Schools of Education (BA Majors in ed.) 5=SEDFAC: SED Faculty

3= RGRAD: BA Majors in ed. Plus Minimally Qualified Graduates   6= SEDSE: SED Enrollments

4=THR: Teacher Hire Rate

FIGURE 5.8

Policy Test B: New Teacher Examinations as a Condition of Employment

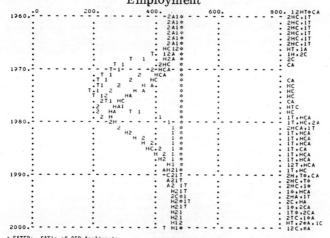

1=SATEP: SAT's of SED Applicants   *=SAT: SAT Constant

2=SAXTE: SAT's of SED Graduates   C=STJAP: SAT's of Those in Teacher Job Pool

H=NTSAT: SAT's of New Teachers   A=NACT: SAT's of Those Entering Alternative Careers

T=SATSE: SAT's of SED Acceptances

FIGURE 5.9

Policy Test B: New Teacher Examinations as a Condition of Employment

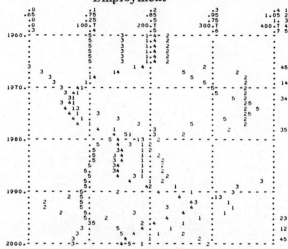

1= FCBSED: Fraction of College Bound Seniors Applying to SED's   4= CBSED: College Bound Seniors in SED Applicant Pool

2= FACSED: Fraction of Applicants Accepted by SED's   5= GFACSE: Fraction of Acceptance Into Graduate Schools

3= FXCT: Fraction of Those in Teacher Job Pool Hired as Teachers

FIGURE 5.10

Policy Test B: New Teacher Examinations as a Condition of Employment

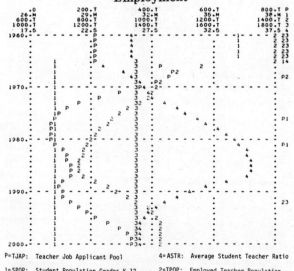

P=TJAP: Teacher Job Applicant Pool   4= ASTR: Average Student Teacher Ratio

1= SPOP: Student Population Grades K-12   2=TPOP: Employed Teacher Population

3= HSGPOP: High School Graduation Population

FIGURE 5.11

Policy Test B: New Teacher Examinations as a Condition of Employment

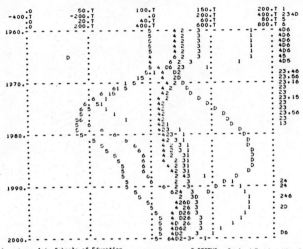

1=RACSED: Acceptance Into Schools of Education   D=DESTHR: Desired Teacher Hire Rate

2= RESED: Graduation From Schools of Education (BA Majors in ed.)   5=SEDFAC: SED Faculty

3= RGRAD: BA Majors in ed. Plus Minimally Qualified Graduates   6=SEDSE: SED Enrollments

4=THR: Teacher Hire Rate

FIGURE 5.12

Policy Test C: Increasing Teacher Certification Requirements

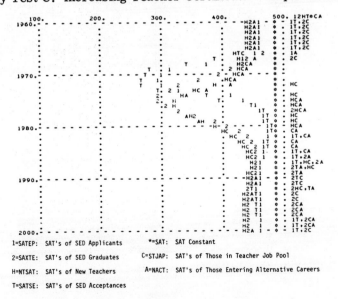

1=SATEP: SAT's of SED Applicants   *=SAT: SAT Constant

2=SAXTE: SAT's of SED Graduates   C=STJAP: SAT's of Those in Teacher Job Pool

H=NTSAT: SAT's of New Teachers   A=NACT: SAT's of Those Entering Alternative Careers

T=SATSE: SAT's of SED Acceptances

207

FIGURE 5.13

Policy Test C: Increasing Teacher Certification Requirements

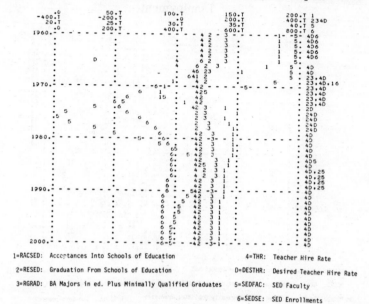

1=RACSED: Acceptances Into Schools of Education   4=THR: Teacher Hire Rate

2=RESED: Graduation From Schools of Education   D=DESTHR: Desired Teacher Hire Rate

3=RGRAD: BA Majors in ed. Plus Minimally Qualified Graduates   5=SEDFAC: SED Faculty

6=SEDSE: SED Enrollments

FIGURE 5.14

Policy Test D: Alternative Career Preparation for Educators

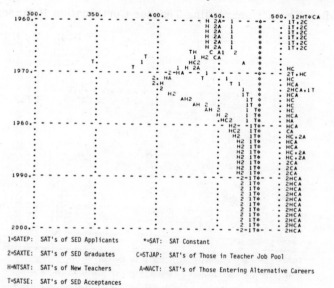

1=SATEP: SAT's of SED Applicants   *=SAT: SAT Constant

2=SAXTE: SAT's of SED Graduates   C=STJAP: SAT's of Those in Teacher Job Pool

H=NTSAT: SAT's of New Teachers   A=NACT: SAT's of Those Entering Alternative Careers

T=SATSE: SAT's of SED Acceptances

FIGURE 5.15

Policy Test D: Alternative Career Preparation for Educators

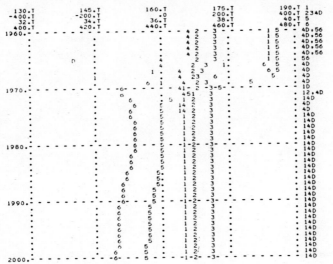

1=RACSED: Acceptances Into Schools of Education   D=DESTHR: Desired Teacher Hire Rate

2=RESED: Graduation From Schools of Education   5=SEDFAC: SED Faculty

3=RGRAD: BA Majors in ed. Plus Minimally Qualified 6=SEDSE: SED Enrollments

4=THR: Teacher Hire Rate

Appendix B:
Teacher Supply, Demand, and Quality Model

```
NOTE      TEACHER SUPPLY - DEMAND MODEL (GSDTSAT6) RUN MODE
NOTE      AUGUST 1982
*
NOTE      STUDENTS IN  SCHOOLS OF EDUCATION--UNDERGRADUATE LEVEL
*
L SEDSE.K=SEDSE.J+DT*(RACSED.JK-RESED.JK-RSDOR.JK)
N SEDSE=SEDSEN
C SEDSEN=474.17E3
*
*
R RACSED.KL=IPOPHG.K*FHSGCB*FCBSED.K*FACSED.K
A IPOPHG.K=SW70*DLINF3(HSGPOP.K,TGRAD)+SW75*TLB.K
C SW70=1
C SW75=0
C TGRAD=6
A HSGPOP.K=(SPOP.K*FHSG.K)
A FHSG.K=FHSGI
C FHSGI=.0497
A TLB.K=TABHL(TTLB,TIME.K,1960,1990,2)
T TTLB=1633000/1685000/2015000/2334000/2402000/2596000/
X 2706000/2771000/2844000/2832000/2764000/2637000/2380000/
X 2299000/2410000/2144000/
C FHSGCB=.6
A FCBSED.K=TABHL(TFCBSED,RAFXCT.K,.15,.65,.05)
T TFCBSED=.05,.08,.10,.16,.18,.2,.22,.2457,.27,.32,.36
A RAFXCT.K=SMOOTH(FXCT.K,STFXCT)
C STFXCT=6
*
*
A FACSED.K=MIN(ACSE.K*ESEDC.K*SW30.K*EDESGF.K,1)
A EDESGF.K=TABHL(TEDESF,DESGFC.K/GSEFAC.K,.5,1.5,.25)
T TEDESF=1.4,1.2,1,1,1
A ACSE.K=TABHL(TACSE,FCBSED.K,.15,.65,.1)
T TACSE=.9,.85,.65,.5,.4,.32
A ESEDC.K=TABHL(TESEDC,RECAP.K,.5,1.5,.25)
T TESEDC=1.35,1.3,1,.9,.85
A SW30.K=CLIP(EPOLTA.K,1,TIME.K,TPOLTA)
C TPOLTA=2050
A EPOLTA.K=TABHL(TEPOLTA,DISAT.K,0,2,.2)
T TEPOLTA=0,.1,.1,.12,.15,1,1,1,1,1,1
A DISAT.K=SATEP.K/CSAT
C CSAT=485
A CBHSG.K=IPOPHG.K*FHSGCB
*
*
```

213

```
R  RESED.KL=(1-(SDOR*DFXCT.K))*(BASED.K)
A  BASED.K=DLINF3(RACSED.JK,TGSED.K)
A  TGSED.K=TGSEDN+SW100*SW40.K
C  TGSEDN=4
C  SW100=0
A  SW40.K=CLIP(EPOLTC.K,1,TIME.K,TPOLTC)
C  TPOLTC=2050
A  EPOLTC.K=ATSEDC
C  ATSEDC=1.5
A  CBSED.K=CBHSG.K*FCBSED.K
*
*
S  SNTG.K=RESED.JK*MGRAD*EASED.K
R  RSDOR.KL=RESED.JK*SDOR+DOR*SEDSE.K*DFXCT.K
C  DOR=.062104
C  SDOR=.4
A  DFXCT.K=TABHL(TDFXCT,RDFXCT.K,.05,.35,.05)
T  TDFXCT=1.24,1.25,1.235,1.215,1,1,1
A  RDFXCT.K=SMOOTH(FXCT.K,TSMDFXCT)
C  TSMDFXCT=1.5
*
NOTE STUDENTS IN SCHOOLS OF EDUCATION--GRADUATE LEVEL
*
*
*
*
L  GSEDSE.K=GSEDSE.JK+DT*(GRACSE.JK+GXTJAP.JK+LSTEF.JK+MATP.JK
X  -GRESED.JK-GRSDOR.JK)
N  GSEDSE=GSEDSEN
C  GSEDSEN=217.88E3
R  GRACSE.KL=(((TPOP.K*FTGRS.K)/PTGS)+RESED.JK*FREGS.K
X     +((DRATHR.K*FGTHR.K)/PTGS)+FXAG.K)*GFACSE.K
R  MATP.KL=DLINF3(DMATP.K,TDMAT)
A  DMATP.K=((ARTSS.K-RACSED.JK)*FMATP.K*GFACSE.K)
A  ARTSS.K=IPOPHG.K*FHSGCB
A  FMATP.K=NFMAT*METJM.K
A  METJM.K=TABHL(TMETJM,FXCT.K,0,.9,.3)
T  TMETJM=.4,1,3,4
C  TDMAT=4
C  NFMAT=.015
R  GRESED.KL=RGSEDSE.K/GATSED
A  RGSEDSE.K=SMOOTH(GSEDSE.K,TSGSED)
C  TSGSED=2
C  GATSED=4
R  GRSDOR.KL=GSEDSE.K*(GSDOR*EFTH.K)
C  GSDOR=.55
A  EFTH.K=TABHL(TEFTH,RAFXCT.K,0,.9,.3)
T  TEFTH=1.2,1.15,.9,.75
A  FTGRS.K=NFTGRS*ETJM.K*EMAT.K
A  EMAT.K=TABHL(TEMAT,THR.JK/ITHR,0,2,.5)
```

214

```
C  ITHR=84E3
T  TEMAT=1,1,2,2.5,3
C  NFTGRS=.18
A  ETJM.K=TABHL(TETJM,RAFXCT.K,0,.9,.3)
T  TETJM=1,2,2.4,1
A  FREGS.K=NFNTGS*ETJM.K
C  NFNTGS=.05
A  DRATHR.K=DLINF3(RATHR.K,TDRTHR)
C  TDRTHR=2
A  FGTHR.K=NFGTH*ETJM.K*EMAT.K
C  NFGTH=.18
A  FTJGRS.K=NFTJG*ETJM.K
C  NFTJG=.06
A  FXAG.K=NFXAG*RXAJ.JK*SW80*EPOLTD
C  NFXAG=.001
C  PTGS=3
C  SW80=0
R  LSTEF.KL=RATPOP.K*NFPCT*ECTM.K*EFAP.K*GFACSE.K
C  NFPCT=.15
A  ECTM.K=TABHL(TECTM,TFDISC.K,.5,1.5,.25)
T  TECTM=.25,.5,1,1.5,2
A  TFDISC.K=(DESFAC.K+DESGFC.K)/(SEDFAC.K+GSEFAC.K)
A  EFAP.K=TABHL(TEFAP,LAGSEFN/LAGSEF.K,0,2,.5)
T  TEFAP=1.3,1.2,1,.85,.65
A  GFACSE.K=GFACSEN*ESEDC.K*EGCAP.K
C  GFACSEN=.4
A  EGCAP.K=TABHL(TEGCAP,GCAP.K,.5,1.5,.25)
T  TEGCAP=1.9,1.8,1,.98,.95
A  GCAP.K=DESGFC.K/GSEFAC.K
*
*
*
*
NOTE FACULTY IN SCHOOLS OF EDUCATION--UNDERGRADUATE LEVEL
*
*
L  SEDFAC.K=SEDFAC.J+DT*(FHFR.JK-FTOR.JK)
N  SEDFAC=SEDSEN/DSFR
*
*
R  FHFR.KL=RAFTOR.K+(DISCF.K/HFAT.K)
A  RAFTOR.K=SMOOTH(FTOR.K,STFTOR)
C  STFTOR=2
A  DISCF.K=DESFAC.K-SEDFAC.K
A  DESFAC.K=RASEDS.K/DSFR
A  RASEDS.K=SMOOTH(SEDSE.K,STSEDS)
C  STSEDS=1
C  DSFR=12
A  HFAT.K=TABHL(THFAT,DISCF.K/DESFAC.K,-.5,.5,.25)
T  THFAT=4,1.5,1,1,1.5
```

```
A  RECAP.K=DESFAC.K/SEDFAC.K
*
*
R  FTOR.KL=FFTOR*ERIF.K*SEDFAC.K
C  FFTOR=.05
A  ERIF.K=TABHL(TERIF,DISCF.K/DESFAC.K,-.8,0,.4)
T  TERIF=1.2,1.1,1
*
*
*
*
NOTE FACULTY IN SCHOOLS OF EDUCATION--GRADUATE LEVEL
*
*
*
*
L  GSEFAC.K=GSEFAC.JK+DT*(GFHFR.JK-GFTO.JK)
N  GSEFAC=GSEDSEN/DGSFR
C  DGSFR=8
R  GFHFR.KL=RAGFTO.K+(DISGCF.K/HFAT.K)
A  RAGFTO.K=SMOOTH(GFTO.K,STFTOR)
A  DISGCF.K=DESGFC.K-GSEFAC.K
A  DESGFC.K=RASEDG.K/DGSFR
A  RASEDG.K=SMOOTH(GSEDSE.K,TSGSE)
C  TSGSE=1
R  GFTO.KL=GFFTO*ERIFG.K*GSEFAC.K
C  GFFTO=.05
A  ERIFG.K=TABHL(TERIFG,DISGCF.K/DESGFC.K,-.8,0,.4)
T     TERIFG=1.2,1.1,1
*
*
L  LGRESE.K=LGRESE.JK+DT*(GRESED.JK-GFXAG.JK-GTPOP.JK
X  -GLSTEF.JK-GTJAP.JK-GMATP.JK)
N  LGRESE=LGRESEN
C  LGRESEN=41.081E3
R  GFXAG.KL=DLINF3(FXAG.K,TGFXAG)*GFACSE.K*(1-GSDOR*EFTH.K)
C  TGFXAG=2
R  GTPOP.KL=DTHPOP.K+DRTHR.K*(1-GSDOR*EFTH.K)
R  GLSTEF.KL=GASEF.K*(1-GSDOR*EFTH.K)
A  GASEF.K=DLINF3(LSTEF.JK,GATSED)
R  GTJAP.KL=MAX(RGTJAP.K,0)
A  RGTJAP.K=GRESED.JK-GTPOP.JK-GLSTEF.JK-GFXAG.JK
X  -GMATP.JK
R  GMATP.KL=DGMATP.K*(1-GSDOR*EFTH.K)
A  DGMATP.K=DLINF3(DMATP.K,TGDMAT)
C  TGDMAT=6
*
*
*
L  LAGSEF.K=LAGSEF.JK+DT*(GLSTEF.JK-FSEHR.JK-DUMP.JK)
```

NOTE TEACHER HIRING AND FIRING
*
R THR.KL=MAX(DESTHR.K,0)*FTHR.K
A DESTHR.K=(DISCT.K*FTHAT.K)+RATTOR.K
A FTHAT.K=TABHL(TFTHAT,DISCT.K/DESTCH.K,-.1,.1,.1)
T TFTHAT=1,1,1
A FTHR.K=TABHL(TFTHR,FRHR.K,0,1,.25)*SW35.K
T TFTHR=1,1,1,.67,0
A SW35.K=CLIP(EPOLTB.K,1,TIME.K,TPOLTB)
C TPOLTB=2050
A EPOLTB.K=TABHL(TEPOLTB,DISACT.K,0,2,.2)
T TEPOLTB=0,.1,.1,.12,.15,1,1,1,1,1,1
A DISACT.K=RANTSAT.K/THSAT

A RANTSAT.K=SMOOTH(NTSAT.JK,SNTSAT)
N RANTSAT=441.19
C   SNTSAT=1
C THSAT=485

A FRHR.K=RATHR.K/TJAP.K
A RATHR.K=SMOOTH(THR.JK,STHR)
N RATHR=84E3
C STHR=2
A RATTOR.K=SMOOTH(TTOR.JK,STTOR)
C STTOR=2
A DISCT.K=DESTCH.K-TPOP.K
A DESTCH.K=MAX(SPOP.K/STR.K,.0001)
A STR.K=(SPOPN/TPOPN)*CSTR.K
A CSTR.K=CLIP(TCSTR.K,1,TIME.K,STRT)
A TCSTR.K=TABHL(TTCSTR,TIME.K,1960,2000,2)
T TTCSTR=1,1,1,.98,.94,.90,.88,.86,.86,.86,
X .87,.84,.81,.78,.79,.80,.82,.90,.94,.92,.88
C STRT=2050
A SPOP.K=SPOPN+SW5*STEP(FSPOP*SPOPN,STT5)+(SW59*SW60.K)
X +(SW63*SW64.K)-(36.2E6*SW61)
C SW63=1
A SW64.K=CLIP(EDEM.K,1,TIME.K,STDEM)
C STDEM=2050
A EDEM.K=TABHL(TEDEM,TIME.K,1982,1990,2)
T TEDEM=-19E3/-562E3/-1.263E6/-1.263E6/-1.263E6
C SW59=0
C SW61=0
A SW60.K=TABHL(TDEM,TIME.K,1960,1990,2)
T   TDEM=36.2E6,38.653E6,41.206E6,43.472E6,44.944E6,45.909E6,45.744E6
X 45.053E6,44.316E6,42.550E6,40.984E6,39.544E6,39.039E6,39.456E6,
X 40.158E6,41.267E6
C SPOPN=36.2E6
C SW5=1
C FSPOP=-1.0
C STT5=1965
S ASTR.K=SPOP.K/TPOP.K

```
N  LAGSEF=LAGSEFN
C  LAGSEFN=8.8288E3
R  FSEHR.KL=FHFR.JK+GFHFR.JK
R  DUMP.KL=MAX(RDUMP.K,0)/TDUMP
A  RDUMP.K=GLSTEF.JK-FSEHR.JK
C  TDUMP=1
*
NOTE TEACHER JOB APPLICANT POOL
*
*
L  TJAP.K=TJAP.J+DT*(RGRAD.JK+REENT.JK+GTJAP.JK+GMATP.JK
X  -GXTJAP.JK-RXAJ.JK-THR.JK+TRIF.JK)
N  TJAP=TJAPN
C  TJAPN=217.90E3
*
R  GXTJAP.KL=TJAP.K*FTJGRS.K*GFACSE.K
*
R  RGRAD.KL=MGRAD*EASED.K*FRESED.K
A  FRESED.K=(1-FREGS.K*GFACSE.K)*RESED.JK
A  EASED.K=TABHL(TEASED,FCBSED.K,.1,.5,.1)
T  TEASED=.67,1,1,1,1
C  MGRAD=1.56
R  REENT.KL=(RATPOP.K*FREENT.K)/TDTRP
C  TDTRP=2
L  RATPOP.K=RATPOP.J+DT*(TTOR.JK-TRPX.JK-REENT.JK-LSTEF.JK)
N  RATPOP=RATPOPN
C  RATPOPN=150.00E3
R  TRPX.KL=(1-FREENT.K)*RATPOP.K/TXRAT
C  TXRAT=2
A  FREENT.K=FREENTN*RETJM.K
A  RETJM.K=TABHL(TRETJM,RAFXCT.K,0,1,.25)
T  TRETJM=.8,1,1,1,3
C  FREENTN=.29
*
*
R  RXAJ.KL=(TJAP.K*FXAJ.K)/(TXAJ*EJPS.K*SW50.K)
C  TXAJ=1.12
A  EJPS.K=TABHL(TEJPS,TJAP.K/TJAPN,0,2,.25)
T  TEJPS=.85/.9/1/1/1/1.4/1.8/2/2.5
A  SW50.K=CLIP(EPOLTD,1,TIME.K,TPOLD)
C  TPOLD=2050
C  EPOLTD=.5
A  FXAJ.K=NFXAJ*EFXCT.K
C  NFXAJ=.4
A  EFXCT.K=TABHL(TEFXCT,RAFXCT.K,0,.9,.3)
T  TEFXCT=1.5,1.5,.9,.2
A  FXCT.K=THR.JK/TJAP.K
*
*
*
```

```
*
*
*
R  TRIF.KL=-MIN(DESRIF.K,0)*FTRIF.K
A  DESRIF.K=(DISCT.K*FRT.K)+RATTOR.K
A  FRT.K=TABHL(TFRT,DISCT.K/DESTCH.K,-.5,0,.1)
T  TFRT=1,1,1,1,1,1
A  FTRIF.K=TABLE(TFTRIF,FRIT.K,0,1,.25)
T  TFTRIF=1,1,1,.67,0
A  FRIT.K=RATRIF.K/TPOP.K
A  RATRIF.K=SMOOTH(TRIF.JK,STRIF)
N  RATRIF=0
C  STRIF=2
*
*
*  TEACHER POPULATION
*
*
L  TPOP.K=TPOP.J+DT*(THR.JK-TTOR.JK-TRIF.JK)
N  TPOP=SW3*(SPOPN/STR)+SW4*TPOPN
C  TPOPN=1.4E6
C  SW3=0
C  SW4=1
*
*
*
*
R  TTOR.KL=TPOP.K*(FTTOR*SW99.K*EDISCT.K)
C  FTTOR=.06
A  SW99.K=CLIP(ITTOR,1,TIME.K,TITTOR)
C  ITTOR=1.25
C  TITTOR=2050
A  EDISCT.K=TABHL(TEDISCT,DISCT.K/DESTCH.K,-.8,0,.4)
T  TEDISCT=3,2.5,1
*
*
*
*
NOTE   CO FLOW SAT IN COLLEGE BOUND POPULATION
*
*
L  SATCBS.K=SATCBS.J+(DT)*(ICBST.JK-CBST.JK-SEDSAT.JK)
N  SATCBS=SATCBN
C  SATCBN=539.750E6
R  ICBST.KL=CBHSG.K*SAT.K
A  SAT.K=SATN*SW20+ISAT.K*SW21
C  SATN=485
A  ISAT.K=TABHL(TSAT,TIME.K,1960,2000,5)
T  TSAT=485,484,474,455,435,425,415,410,410
C  SW20=1
C  SW21=0
```

219

```
A RSAT.K=SAT.K*FCSAT.K
A FCSAT.K=TABHL(TFCSAT,FCBSED.K,.05,.4,.05)
T TFCSAT=1.045,1.04,1.03,1.01,1.005,1.005,1.0005,1.0005
R CBST.KL=(1-FCBSED.K)*CBHSG.K*RSAT.K
R SEDSAT.KL=ICBST.JK-CBST.JK
A SATEP.K=SEDSAT.JK/CBSED.K

A SATGCP.K=CBST.JK/((1-FCBSED.K)*CBHSG.K)
S SATNECP.K=ICBST.JK/CBHSG.K
*
NOTE   CO FLOW SAT IN SCHOOL OF EDUCATION TALENT POOL
*
L SEDTP.K=SEDTP.J+(DT)*(SEDSAT.JK-ISATUS.JK-FXTP.JK)
N SEDTP=SEDTPN
C SEDTPN=81.7E6
R ISATUS.KL=ASTEUS.K*RACSED.JK
A ASTEUS.K=ASTAF.K*EACF.K
A ASTAF.K=SATEP.K
R FXTP.KL=SEDSAT.JK-ISATUS.JK
A EACF.K=TABHL(TEACF,FACSED.K,.8,1,.02)
T TEACF=1.02,1.02,1.015,1.01,1,.98,.96,.94,.92,.9,.9,
A SATSE.K=ASTEUS.K
*
*
NOTE   CO FLOW SAT IN SCHOOLS OF EDUCATION
*
*
*
L SATUSE.K=SATUSE.J+(DT)*(ISATUS.JK-GSATUS.JK-DSATUS.JK)
N SATUSE=SATUSI
C SATUSI=162.267E6
R GSATUS.KL=FRESED.K*(ASTXUS.K*ETM.K)
A ASTXUS.K=DLINF3(SATSE.K,TSATSE)
C TSATSE=4
A ETM.K=TABHL(TETM,FXCT.K,.3,1,.1)
T TETM=.96,.97,.98,1,1,1.01,1.02,1.02
R DSATUS.KL=ISATUS.JK-GSATUS.JK
S ASESAT.K=SATUSE.K/SEDSE.K
S SAXTE.K=(GSATUS.JK+GESATUS.K)/(RESED.JK)
A GESATUS.K=(FREGS.K*GFACSE.K*RESED.JK)*(ASTXUS.K*ETM.K)
*
*
*
NOTE CO FLOW SAT IN TEACHER JOB APPLICANT POOL
*
L SATJP.K=SATJP.J+(DT)*((GSATUS.JK*FGRAD*EASED.J)+SATRVS.JK+GTJAP.
X *ASTXUS.J+GMATP.JK*SATATS.J-CTSAT.JK-ACSAT.JK-GXTJAP.JK*ASTXUS.
N SATJP=SATJPN
C SATJPN=97.176E6
C FGRAD=1.56
```

```
R  SATRVS.KL=(RACTSAT.K)*(REENT.JK+TRIF.JK)
A  RACTSAT.K=SMOOTH(NTSAT.JK,TSM)
C  TSM=5
A  SATATS.K=DLINF3(SATGCP.K,TDSATA)
C  TDSATA=6
R  CTSAT.KL=(STJAP.K*ETHRST.K)*THR.JK
A  ETHRST.K=TABHL(TETHRST,FXCT.K,0,.9,.1)
T  TETHRST=.97,.975,.98,.985,.99,1,1,1.005,1.015,1.02
R  ACSAT.KL=((2-(ETHRST.K))*STJAP.K)*RXAJ.JK
A  NTSAT.K=STJAP.K*ETHRST.K
A  NACT.K=ACSAT.JK/RXAJ.JK
A  STJAP.K=SATJP.K/TJAP.K
A  DTHPOP.K=((((TPOP.K*FTGRS.K)/PTGS)*GFACSE.K)/GATSED)
A  DRTHR.K=((((DRATHR.K*FGTHR.K)/PTGS)*GFACSE.K)/GATSED)
X  *(1-GSDOR)
S  DTJAP.K=TJAP.K*FTJGRS.K*GSDOR
*
*
*
NOTE SUPPLEMENTARY TABLES
*
*
*
NOTE TABLES FOR SED GRADUATES
*
*
S  BSSED.K=TABHL(TBSSED,TIME.K,1960,1988,1)
T  TBSSED=91187/95983/100909/110559/116529/115173/117482/
X  132087/148554/161904/176571/191172/194210/185181/
X  166969/154758/143658/136079/133620/129130/121470/117140/
X  108130/100940/93390/88840/81950/77270/73530
*
*
S  MED.K=TABHL(TMED,TIME.K,1960,1988,1)
*
*
NOTE TABLES FOR TEACHER SUPPLY AND DEMAND
*
*
S  ESNTG.K=TABHL(TESNTG,TIME.K,1967,1990,1)
T  TESNTG=220000/233000/264000/284000/314000/317000/313000/279000/
X  238000/222000/194000/181000/163000/144000/141000/154000/
X  153000/153000/149000/169000/187000/203000/220000/238000
*
*
*
S  ESDAT.K=TABHL(TESDAT,TIME.K,1967,1990,1)
T  TESDAT=209000/229000/233000/192000/152000/174000/161000/
X  155000/162000/122000/154000/130000/107000/113000/86000/
X  107000/127000/124000/156000/163000/168000/169000/174000/
```

```
X 192000
T TMED=33658/35728/37276/40376/43323/49905/55155/62927/
X 70231/78275/88716/97880/105242/112252/119778/127948/
X 126375/118582/119000/117020/113910/111870/108820/105030/
X 102120/100350/98390/93110/89460/
NOTE CONTROL STATEMENTS
*
C DT=.1
C PRTPER=0
C PLTPER=1
N TIME=TIMEN
C TIMEN=1960
C LENGTH=2000
PLOT SATEP=1,SAXTE=2,NTSAT=H,SATSE=T,SAT=*,STJAP=C,NACT=A
PLOT RACSED=1/RESED=2,RGRAD=3,THR=4,DESTHR=D/SEDFAC=5/SEDSE=6/
PLOT GRACSE=1/GSEDSE=2/GRESED=3/GSEFAC=4/GFACSE=5/
PLOT TJAP=P/SPOP=1/TPOP=2/HSGPOP=3/ASTR=4/
PLOT FCBSED=1/FACSED=2/FXCT=3/CBSED=4/GFACSE=5/
PLOT LGRESE,DTJAP,SATNECP,ASESAT,SEDTP,SATCBS/
PRINT TJAP,GSEDSE,SEDSE,LGRESE,RATPOP,LAGSEF,SATJP,RANTSAT
PRINT RXAJ,FXAJ,TXAJ,EJPS
PRINT REENT,GXTJAP
PRINT TJAP,RGRAD.REENT,GTJAP,GMATP.GXTJAP,RXAJ,THR,TRIF
PRINT LGRESE,SATJP,RATPOP,RXAJ,FXCT,TJAP,SEDSE,GSEDSE,GRACSE,GRES
PRINT SATGCP,DTJAP,SATCBS,SATNECP,DTHPOP,ASESAT,SEDTP,DRTHR/
PRINT TRPX,LSTEF,FRESED,RGRAD,THR,GRSDOR,GFACSE,RATPOP,MATP
PRINT SATEP,SAXTE,NTSAT,SATSE,SAT,STJAP,NACT
PRINT FCBSED,FACSED,FXCT,CBSED,GFACSE
RUN
NOTE POLICY TESTS
C TPOLTA=1965
RUN POLICY TEST A
C TPOLTB=1965
RUN POLICY TEST B
C TPOLTC=1965
C SW100=1
RUN POLICY TEST C
C TPOLD=1965
C SW80=1
RUN POLICY TEST D
```

Appendix C:
Model Definitions

LIST OF VARIABLES

SYMBOL	T	WHR-CMP	DEFINITION
ACSAT	R	164	EFFECT OF AVAILABLE ALTERNATIVE JOBS ON SAT SCORES OF TEACHERS MOVING OUT OF TJAP TO ACCEPT ALTERNATIVE JOBS (DIMENSIONLESS) <164>
ACSE	A	11	TABLE FUNCTION SHOWING EFFECT OF ACCEPTANCE FRACTION DUE TO FRACTION OF COLLEGE BOUND STUDENTS APPLYING TO SED <11>
ARTSS	A	31	ARTS AND SCIENCES MAJORS APPLYING TO UNDERGRADUATE COLLEGES (PEOPLE) <31>
ASESAT	S	155	AVERAGE SAT SCORE OF ALL STUDENTS IN UNDERGRADUATE SED (SCORE/PEOPLE/YEARS) <155>
ASTAF	A	146	AN AVERAGE SCORE OF STUDENTS ENTERING UNDERGRADUATE APPLICANT POOL (SCORE/PEOPLE/YEARS) <146>
ASTEUS	A	145	AN AVERAGE SCORE OF STUDENTS ACCEPTED BY SED (UNDERGRAD) (SCORE/PEOPLE/YEARS) <145>
ASTR	S	121	AVERAGE STUDENT-TEACHER RATIO (K-12) (YEARS) <121>
ASTXUS	A	152	AN AVERAGE SAT SCORE OF ENTERING FRESHMEN IN SED (SCORE/PEOPLE/YEARS) <152>
ATSEDC	C	21.1	ADDED TIME FOR SED TO CERTIFY NEW TEACHER CANDIDATES (YEARS) <21>
BASED	A	18	DELAY FUNCTION PRODUCING SED BACCALAUREATE GRADUATES FROM THOSE STUDENTS ENTERING SED 4 YEARS EARLIER (YEARS) <18>
BSSED	S	172	BACHELORS DEGREES AWARDED TO EDUCATION MAJORS (PEOPLE/YEARS) <172>
CBHSG	A	16	COLLEGE BOUND HIGH SCHOOL GRADUATES (PEOPLE) <16>
CBSED	A	22	COLLEGE BOUND HIGH SCHOOL GRADUATES APPLYING TO SED (PEOPLE) <22>
CBST	R	138	OUTFLOW OF SCORES FROM POOL FOR STUDENTS APPLYING TO ARTS AND SCIENCE COLLEGES (SCORES/YEAR) <138>
CSAT	C	15.1	SAT STANDARD FOR STUDENTS APPLYING TO SED (YEARS) <15>
CSTR	A	115	CHANGE IN STUDENT-TEACHER RATIO REFLECTING TRENDS (YEARS) <115>
CTSAT	R	162	TOTAL SAT SCORES OF TEACHERS MOVING OUT OF TJAP INTO CLASSROOM TEACHING JOBS (SCORES/PEOPLE/YEAR) <162>
DESFAC	A	57	DESIRED NUMBER OF FACULTY (UNDERGRAD) (DIMENSIONLESS) <57>
DESGFC	A	68	DESIRED GRADUATE SED FACULTY (DIMENSIONLESS) <68>
DESRIF	A	123	DESIRED TEACHER REDUCTION IN FORCE (DIMENSIONLESS) <123>
DESTCH	A	113	DESIRED STUDENT/TEACHER RATIO (DIMENSIONLESS) <113>
DESTHR	A	102	DESIRED TEACHER HIRE RATE (DIMENSIONLESS) <102>

DFXCT	A	25	EFFECT OF TEACHER HIRING ON STUDENT DROPOUT RATE FROM UNDERGRADUATE SED (DIMENSIONLESS) <25>
DGMATP	A	80	DELAY IN MAT CANDIDATES WHILE PREPARING TO GRADUATE (YEARS) <80>
DGSFR	C	64.2	DESIRED GRADUATE FACULTY STUDENT RATIO (YEARS) <64>
DISACT	A	107	DISCREPANCY BETWEEN RECENT AVERAGE SAT OF NEW TEACHER HIRED TO TEACH AND A PRIOR STANDARD (DIMENSIONLESS) <107>
EJPS	A	96	EFFECT OF ALTERNATIVE JOB HIRING OF EDUCATION GRADUATES ON EXIT RATE FROM TJAP (DIMENSIONLESS) <96>
EMAT	A	39	EFFECT OF COMPETITION FOR TEACHER VACANCIES ON FRACTION OF TEACHER POPULATION APPLYING TO GRADUATE SCHOOLS OF EDUCATION (DIMENSIONLESS) <39>
EPOLTA	A	14	EFFECT OF ENTRANCE STANDARDS ON ACCEPTANCE FRACTION AT UNDERGRADUATE LEVEL OF SED (DIMENSIONLESS) <14>
EPOLTB	A	106	EFFECT OF SAT STANDARDS ON TEACHER HIRE RATE (DIMENSIONLESS) <106>
EPOLTC	A	21	EFFECT OF DELAYING BA GRADUATION (POLICY TEST C) (DIMENSIONLESS) <21>
EPOLTD	C	97.2	EFFECT OF ALTERNATIVE CAREER TRAINING ON FRACTION EXITING TJAP FOR ALTERNATIVE CAREERS (DIMENSIONLESS) <97>
ERIF	A	62	EFFECT OF REDUCTION IN FORCE ON SED FACULTY TURNOVER RATE (UNDERGRAD) (DIMENSIONLESS) <62>
ERIFG	A	71	EFFECT OF REDUCTION IN FORCE ON GRADUATE FACULTY TURNOVER (DIMENSIONLESS) <71>
ESDAT	S	175	ESTIMATED DEMAND FOR TEACHERS K-12 (NCES) (PEOPLE) <175>
ESEDC	A	12	EFFECT ON SED ACCEPTANCE FRACTION DUE TO SED CAPACITY (UNDERGRAD (DIMENSIONLESS) <12>
ESNTG	S	174	ESTIMATED SUPPLY OF NEW TEACHERS K-12 (NCES) (PEOPLE/YEAR) <174>
ETHRST	A	163	EFFECT OF TEACHER HIRE RATE ON AVERAGE SCORE OF THOSE MOVING OUT OF TJAP INTO CLASSROOMS (DIMENSIONLESS) <163>
ETJM	A	40	EFFECT OF TEACHER JOB MARKET ON FRACTION OF TEACHERS FROM TEACHER POPULATION APPLYING TO GRADUATE SCHOOLS OF EDUCATION AS PART TIME STUDENTS (DIMENSIONLESS) <40>
ETM	A	153	EFFECT OF TEACHER MARKET ON THE ENTERING AVERAGE SAT OF STUDENTS AFTER FOUR YEARS IN SED (DIMENSIONLESS) <153>
FACSED	A	9	FRACTION OF UNDERGRADUATE APPLICANTS ACCEPTED BY SED (%/YEAR) <9>
FCBSED	A	7	FRACTION OF COLLEGE BOUND POP APPLYING TO SED (%/YEAR) <7>
FCSAT	A	137	FRACTIONAL CHANGE IN RSAT DUE TO FRACTION APPLYING TO SED (%) <137>
FFTOR	C	61.1	NORMAL FRACTION OF SED UNDERGRADUATE FACULTY VACATING FACULTY POSITIONS (%/YEAR) <61>
FGRAD	C	158.3	NORMAL FRACTION OF ARTS AND SCIENCES MAJORS WITH TEACHER QUALIFICATIONS (%/YEAR) <158>

DISAT	A	15	DISCREPANCY BETWEEN CURRENT SAT OF STUDENTS· APPLYING TO UNDERGRADUATE SED, AND A PRIOR STANDARD (DIMENSIONLESS) <15>
DISCF	A	56	DISCREPANCY BETWEEN DESIRED NUMBER OF FACULTY AND ACTUAL NUMBER (UNDERGRAD) (DIMENSIONLESS) <56>
DISCT	A	112	DISCREPANCY BETWEEN DESIRED TEACHERS IN THE SYSTEM AND ACTUAL TEACHERS (DIMENSIONLESS) <112>
DISGCF	A	67	DISCREPANCY BETWEEN DESIRED AND ACTUAL GRADUATE SED FACULTY (DIMENSIONLESS) <67>
DMATP	A	30	ARTS AND SCIENCE GRADUATES ENROLLED IN MAT PROGRAMS DELAYED TO REPRESENT THE TIME TO GRADUATE (PEOPLE/YEAR) <30>
DOR	C	24.1	DROPOUT FACTOR TO ADJUST DROPOUT RATE (%) <24>
DRATHR	A	42	DELAY IN RECENT AVERAGE TEACHERS HIRED IN APPLYING TO ENTER SED GRADUATE SCHOOL (YEARS) <42>
DRTHR	A	169	DELAY IN NEWLY HIRED TEACHERS ENROLLED AS PART-TIME STUDENTS IN GRADUATE SED WHILE WAITING TO GRADUATE (YEARS) <169>
DSATUS	R	154	TOTAL STOCK OF SAT SCORES FOR STUDENTS WHO DROPOUT OF SED (SCORES/YEAR) <154>
DSFR	C	58.2	DESIRED STUDENT FACULTY RATIO (UNDERGRAD) <58>
DT	C	176	CALCULATION INTERVAL (YEARS) <176>
DTHPOP	A	168	DELAY IN TEACHER POPULATION ENROLLED AS PART-TIME STUDENTS IN GRADUATE SED WHILE WAITING TO GRADUATE (YEARS) <168>
DTJAP	S	170	ADJUSTMENT IN PEOPLE APPLYING TO GRADUATE SED FROM TJAP (PEOPLE/YEAR) <170>
DUMP	R	83	OUTFLOW OF NEW CANDIDATES NOT HIRED AS NEW SED FACULTY MEMBERS (PEOPLE/YEAR) <83>
EACF	A	148	EFFECT OF FRACTION OF ACCEPTANCE OF SED (SELECTION STANDARDS) ON AN AVERAGE SAT SCORE OF STUDENTS ENTERING SED (DIMENSIONLESS) <148>
EASED	A	89	EFFECT OF ATTRACTIVENESS OF SED ON NUMBER OF ARTS AND SCIENCE MAJORS WHO SEEK TEACHER QUALIFICATIONS (DIMENSIONLESS) <89>
ECTM	A	47	EFFECT OF SED FACULTY MARKET ON FRACTION OF TEACHERS LEAVING TEACHING APPLYING TO GRADUATE SCHOOLS OF EDUCATION (DIMENSIONLESS) <47>
EDEM	A	119	EFFECT OF ADJUSTMENTS OF DEMOGRAPHIC PROJECTIONS TO CORRECT FOR LOWER THAN EXPECTED BIRTHS (PEOPLE) <119>
EDESGF	A	10	EFFECT OF DESIRED GRADUATE FACULTY POSITIONS ON ACCEPTANCE FRACTION AT UNDERGRAD SED LEVEL (DIMENSIONLESS) <10>
EDISCT	A	131	EFFECT ON TURNOVER DUE TO TEACHERS DESIRED TO FULFILL STUDENT TEACHER RATIO STANDARD AND THE ANNUAL SHORT FALL (DIMENSIONLESS) <131>
EFAP	A	49	EFFECT OF FACULTY AVAILABILITY ON RATE OF TEACHERS LEAVING CLASSROOM TEACHING TO PREPARE FOR FACULTY POSITIONS <49>
EFTH	A	37	EFFECT OF TEACHER HIRE RATE (RAFXCT) (DIMENSIONLESS) <37>
EFXCT	A	99	EFFECT OF TEACHER HIRE RATE FORM TJAP ON TIME TO EXIT TJAP (DIMENSIONLESS) <99>

EGCAP	A	51	EFFECT OF GRADUATE SED CAPACITY ON ACCEPTANCE FRACTION AT GRADUATE LEVEL (DIMENSIONLESS) <51>
FGTHR	A	43	FRACTION OF NEWLY HIRED CLASSROOM TEACHERS APPLYING TO ENTER GRADUATE SCHOOLS OF EDUCATION AS PART- TIME STUDENTS (%YEAR) <43>
FHFR	R	54	FACULTY HIRE/FIRE RATE (UNDERGRAD) (PEOPLE/YEAR) <54>
FHSG	A	5	FRACTION OF SPOP GRADUATING (%/YEAR) <5>
FHSGCB	C	6.2	FRACTION OF HIGH SCHOOL GRADUATES IN COLLEGE BOUND POP (%/YEAR) <6>
FHSGI	C	5.1	INITIAL FRACTION OF HIGH SCHOOL GRADUATES IN COLLEGE BOUND POPULATION (%/YEAR) <5>
FMATP	A	32	EFFECT OF TEACHER HIRE RATE FROM TJAP ON MAT APPLICATIONS TO GRADUATE SED (DIMENSIONLESS) <32>
FREENT	A	93	FRACTION OF RESERVE POOL ACTIVELY SEEKING TEACHING POSITIONS (%/YEAR) <93>
FREENTN	C	94.2	INITIAL FRACTION OF RESERVE TEACHERS POTENTIALLY LOOKING FOR TEACHING JOBS (%/YEAR) <94>
FREGS	A	41	FRACTION OF BA GRADUATES FROM SED WHICH APPLY TO GRADUATE SED AS FULL-TIME STUDENTS (%/YEAR) <41>
FRESED	A	88	FRACTION OF RECENT SED GRADUATES (BACHELORS DEGREE) ENTERING TJAP (%/YEAR) <88>
FRHR	A	109	ACTUAL HIRE RATE AS A RATIO OF TEACHERS SEEKING JOBS (%) <109>
FRIT	A	126	RECENT AVERAGE TEACHERS RIFFED AS A RATIO OF TEACHER POPULATION ·(DIMENSIONLESS) <126>
FRT	A	124	FRACTIONAL RATE OF TEACHERS RIFFED (%/YEAR) <124>
FSEHR	R	82	FRACTIONAL HIRE RATE FROM POOL OF NEW CANDIDATES SEEKING SED FACULTY POSITIONS (PEOPLE/YEAR) <82>
FSPOP	C	120.4	FRACTION OF SPOP SUBTRACTED BY STEP FUNCTION FROM STUDENTS IN GRADES K-12 (%) <120>
FTGRS	A	38	FRACTION OF TEACHER POPULATION APPLYING TO ENTER GRADUATE SCHOOLS OF EDUCATION AS PART TIME STUDENTS (%/YEAR) <38>
FTHAT	A	103	FRACTION OF TIME TO HIRE DESIRED TEACHERS (%/YEARS) <103>
FTHR	A	104	FRACTION OF DESIRED TEACHERS ACTUALLY HIRED (%/YEARS) <104>
FTJGRS	A	44	FRACTION OF POPULATION IN TEACHER JOB APPLICANT POOL APPLYING TO GRADUATE SCHOOLS OF EDUCATION (%/YEAR) <44>
FTOR	R	61	FACULTY TURNOVER RATE (UNDERGRAD) (%/YEAR) <61>
FTRIF	A	125	FRACTION OF RIFFED TEACHERS AS EFFECTED BY PERCENTAGE OF EXISTING TEACHERS BEING RIFFED (%) <125>
FTTOR	C	129.1	FRACTIONAL TEACHER TURNOVER (%) <129>
FXAG	A	45	FRACTION OF POPULATION EXITING TEACHER JOB APPLICANT POOL FOR ALTERNATIVE CAREERS APPLYING TO GRADUATE SCHOOLS OF EDUCATION AS PART TIME STUDENTS (%) <45>
FXAJ	A	98	FRACTION EXITING TJAP FOR ALTERNATIVE JOBS (%) <98>
FXCT	A	100	FRACTION OF JOB POOL WHO ARE HIRED AS TEACHERS (%/YEAR) <100>
FXTP	R	147	STOCK OF SAT SCORES OF APPLICANTS NOT SELECTED BY SED (SCORES/YEAR) <147>

GASEF	A	76	GRADUATES FROM GRADUATE SED SEEKING TO ENTER SED FACULTY RANKS (PEOPLE/YEAR) <76>
GATSED	C	35.2	NORMAL FRACTION OF GRADUATES FROM GRADUATE SCHOOL ENROLLMENTS (%/YEARS) <35>
GCAP	A	52	GRADUATE SED CAPACITY (PEOPLE) <52>
GESATUS	A	157	TOTAL STOCK OF SAT SCORES OF RECENT SED GRADUATES (SCORES/PEOPLE) <157>
GFACSE	A	50	FRACTION OF APPLICANTS ACCEPTED INTO GRADUATE SCHOOLS OF EDUCATION (%/YEAR) <50>
GFACSEN	C	50.1	INITIAL ACCEPTANCE FRACTION INTO GRADUATE SED (%/YEAR) <50>
GFFTO	C	70.1	INITIAL GRADUATE SED FACULTY TURNOVER RATE (%/YEAR) <70>
GFHFR	R	65	GRADUATE SED FACULTY HIRE/FIRE RATE (PEOPLE/YEAR) <65>
GFTO	R	70	RATE OF GRADUATE FACULTY TURNOVER (PEOPLE/YEAR) <70>
GFXAG	R	73	GRADUATES FROM GRADUATE SED WHO ENTERED FOR ALTERNATIVE CAREERS FROM TEACHER RESERVE POOL (PEOPLE/YEAR) <73>
GLSTEF	R	75	GRADUATION RATE OF FULL-TIME TEACHERS WHO LEFT TEACHER FORCE TO ENTER GRADUATE SED (PEOPLE/YEAR) <75>
GMATP	R	79	GRADUATES FROM THE MAT PROGRAM (PEOPLE/YEAR) <79>
GRACSE	R	28	GRADUATE SCHOOL RATE OF ACCEPTANCE (PEOPLE/YEAR) <28>
GRESED	R	34	GRADUATE SCHOOL RATE OF GRADUATION (PEOPLE/YEAR) <34>
GRSDOR	R	36	STUDENT DROPOUT RATE FROM GRADUATE SCHOOLS OF EDUCATION (PEOPLE/YEAR) <36>
GSATUS	R	151	TOTAL SAT SCORES OF GRADUATING STUDENTS FROM SED (UNDERGRAD) (SCORES/PEOPLE/YEARS) <151>
GSDOR	C	36.1	INITIAL GRADUATE SCHOOL STUDENT DROPOUT RATE (%/YEAR) <36>
GSEDSE	L	27	GRADUATE STUDENTS ENROLLED IN SCHOOLS OF
	N	27.1	EDUCATION (PEOPLE) <27>
GSEDSEN	C	27.2	INITIAL LEVEL OF GRADUATE STUDENTS ENROLLED IN SCHOOLS OF EDUCATION (PEOPLE) <27>
GSEFAC	L	64	GRADUATE SCHOOL OF EDUCATION FACULTY (PEOPLE)
	N	64.1	<64>
GTJAP	R	77	RATE OF GRADUATION OF FULL-TIME STUDENTS FROM TEACHER JOB APPLICANT POOL WHO ENTERED GRADUATE SED (PEOPLE/YEAR) <77>
GTPOP	R	74	RATE OF GRADUATION OF PART-TIME TEACHERS IN TEACHER FORCE WHO ENTERED SED GRADUATE SCHOOL FOUR YEARS EARLIER (PEOPLE/YEAR) <74>
GXTJAP	R	86	PEOPLE EXITING TJAP TO ENTER GRADUATE SED AS FULL- TIME STUDENTS (PEOPLE/YEAR) <86>
HFAT	A	59	AVERAGE TIME TO HIRE FACULTY BASED ON NUMBERS TO BE HIRED RELATIVE TO EXISTING FACULTY (YEARS) <59>
HSGPOP	A	4	HIGH SCHOOL GRADUATE POP (PEOPLE) <4>
ICBST	R	133	INCOMING SAT SCORES TO SCORE POOL (COLLEGE BOUND POP) (SCORES/PEOPLE/YEAR) <133>
IPOPHG	A	3	INITIAL POP OF HIGH SCHOOL GRADUATES (PEOPLE) <3>

ISAT	A	135	SAT SCORE FOR AN AVERAGE STUDENT REPRESENTING GRADUAL DECLINE IN OVERALL COLLEGE BOARD SCORES (COLLEGE BOARD) (SCORE/YEARS) <135>
ISATUS	R	144	INCOMING SAT SCORES TO SED APPLICANT POOL (SCORES/PEOPLE/YEAR) <144>
ITHR	C	39.1	INITIAL TEACHER HIRE RATE (PEOPLE) <39>
ITTOR	C	130.1	INCREASE IN TEACHER TURNOVER RATE (%) <130>
LAGSEF	L	81	LEVEL OF NEW CANDIDATES SEEKING SED FACULTY
	N	81.1	POSITIONS (PEOPLE) <81>
LAGSEFN	C	81.2	INITIAL LEVEL OF NEW CANDIDATES SEEKING SED FACULTY POSITIONS (PEOPLE) <81>
LENGTH	C	176.5	LENGTH OF SIMULATION (YEARS) <176>
LGRESE	L	72	LEVEL OF GRADUATES FROM GRADUATE SED (PEOPLE)
	N	72.1	<72>
LGRESEN	C	72.2	INITIAL LEVEL OF GRADUATES FROM GRADUATE SED (PEOPLE) SED <72>
LSTEF	R	46	RATE OF TEACHERS LEAVING CLASSROOM TEACHING JOBS APPLYING TO GRADUATE SCHOOLS OF EDUCATION INTENDING TO ADVANCE TO A HIGHER LEVEL OF THE SYSTEM AS FACULTY (PEOPLE/YEAR) <46>
MATP	R	29	MASTERS IN TEACHING PROGRAM RATE OF ADMISSION TO SED GRADUATE SCHOOL (PEOPLE/YEAR) <29>
MED	S	173	
METJM	A	33	EFFECT OF TEACHER HIRING FROM TJAP ON MAT APPLICATIONS TO GRADUATE SED (DIMENSIONLESS) <33>
MGRAD	C	89.2	FUNCTION TO ADD TO EDUCATION MAJORS (RESED) GRADUATES IN ARTS AND SCIENCE WHO QUALIFY FOR TEACHING CERTIFICATES (UNDERGRAD) (%/PEOPLE/YEAR) <89>
NACT	A	166	AN AVERAGE SAT SCORE OF NEW TEACHERS ACCEPTING ALTERNATIVE EMPLOYMENT (SCORE/PEOPLE/YEARS) <166>
NFGTH	C	43.1	NORMAL FRACTION OF NEWLY HIRED TEACHERS APPLYING TO GRADUATE SCHOOLS OF EDUCATION AS PART TIME STUDENTS (%/YEAR) <43>
NFMAT	C	33.3	NORMAL FRACTION OF ARTS AND SCIENCES MAJORS SEEKING ADMISSION TO SED GRADUATE SCHOOL (%/YEAR) <33>
NFNTGS	C	41.1	NORMAL FRACTION OF NEW BA GRADUATES APPLYING TO GRADUATE SCHOOLS OF EDUCATION AS FULL TIME STUDENTS (%/YEAR) <41>
NFPCT	C	46.1	NORMAL FRACTION OF THE TEACHER TURNOVER RATE SEEKING ENTRY TO GRADUATE SED TO PREPARE FOR ADVANCED POSITIONS (%/YEAR) <46>
NFTGRS	C	39.3	NORMAL FRACTION OF TEACHERS IN TEACHER POPULATION APPLYING TO GRADUATE SED AS PART-TIME STUDENTS (%/YEAR) <39>
NFTJG	C	44.1	NORMAL FRACTION OF POPULATION OF TEACHER JOB APPLICANT POOL APPLYING TO GRADUATE SCHOOLS OF EDUCATION (%/YEAR) <44>
NFXAG	C	45.1	NORMAL FRACTION OF POPULATION EXITING TEACHER JOB APPLICANT POOL FOR ALTERNATIVE CAREERS APPLYING TO GRADUATE SCHOOLS OF EDUCATION (%/YEAR) <45>
NFXAJ	C	98.1	NORMAL FRACTION EXITING TJAP FOR ALTERNATIVE JOBS (%) <98>

NTSAT	A	165	AN AVERAGE SAT SCORE OF NEW TEACHERS HIRED TO TEACH (SCORE/PEOPLE/YEARS) <165>
PLTPER	C	176.2	PLOTTING PERIOD IN DYNAMO (YEARS) <176>
PRTPER	C	176.1	PRINTING PERIOD IN DYNAMO (YEARS) <176>
PTGS	C	45.2	FRACTION TO CONVERT PART TIME STUDENTS IN GRADUATE SED TO FULL-TIME EQUIVALENT ENROLLMENTS (%) <45>
RACSED	R	2	RATE OF ACCEPTANCE OF SED (UNDERGRADUATE) (PEOPLE/YEAR) <2>
RACTSAT	A	160	SMOOTH OF RECENT AVERAGE SAT SCORES OF NEWLY HIRED TEACHERS (SCORES/YEARS) <160>
RAFTOR	A	55	RECENT AVERAGE FACULTY TURNOVER RATE (UNDERGRAD) (%/YEARS) <55>
RAFXCT	A	8	RECENT AVERAGE FRACTION EXITING TEACHER JOB APPLICANT POOL FOR CLASSROOM TEACHING POSITION <8>
RAGFTO	A	66	RECENT AVERAGE GRADUATE FACULTY TURNOVER (PEOPLE/ YEARS) <66>
RANTSAT	A	108	RECENT AVERAGE SAT SCORE OF NEW TEACHERS HIRED
	N	108.1	TO TEACH (USED IN POLICY TEST B) (SCORE/PEOPLE/ YEAR) <108>
RASEDG	A	69	RECENT AVERAGE SED GRADUATE FACULTY (PEOPLE) <69>
RASEDS	A	58	RECENT AVERAGE NUMBER OF STUDENTS IN SED (UNDERGRAD) (PEOPLE) <58>
RATHR	A	110	RECENT AVERAGE TEACHER HIRE RATE <110>
	N	110.1	
RATPOP	L	91	RECENT AVERAGE TEACHER POPULATION IN RESERVE
	N	91.1	POOL (PEOPLE) <91>
RATPOPN	C	91.2	INITIAL RECENT AVERAGE TEACHER POPULATION (PEOPLE) <91>
RATRIF	A	127	RECENT AVERAGE TEACHER RIF (PEOPLE/YEAR) <127>
	N	127.1	
RATTOR	A	111	RECENT AVERAGE TEACHER TURNOVER RATE (PEOPLE/ YEAR) <111>
RDFXCT	A	26	RECENT AVERAGE EXIT FRACTION FROM TJAP HIRED AS TEACHERS (%/YEAR) <26>
RDUMP	A	84	MAXIMUM OUTFLOW OF NEW CANDIDATES NOT HIRED AS NEW SED FACULTY MEMBERS (PEOPLE/YEAR) <84>
RECAP	A	60	SED CAPACITY (UNDERGRAD) (DIMENSIONLESS) <60>
REENT	R	90	TEACHERS PREVIOUSLY IN THE SCHOOL SYSTEM WHO SEEK TO RETURN TO TEACHING (PEOPLE/YEAR) <90>
RESED	R	17	RATE OF EXIT FROM SED DUE TO GRADUATION (UNDERGRAD) (PEOPLE/YEAR) <17>
RETJM	A	94	REENTRY EFFECT OF TEACHER JOB MARKET (DIMENSIONLESS) <94>
RGRAD	R	87	RATE OF GRADUATION FROM COLLEGE WITH TEACHER QUALIFICATIONS (UNDERGRAD) (PEOPLE/YEAR) <87>
RGSEDSE	A	35	RECENT AVERAGE ENROLLMENTS IN GRADUATE SED (PEOPLE) <35>
RGTJAP	A	78	MAXIMUM FULL-TIME STUDENTS WHO EXIT TJAP TO ENTER GRADUATE SED <78>
RSAT			RECENT EFFECT ON SAT SCORE OF AN AVERAGE COLLEGE BOUND STUDENT APPLYING TO ARTS AND SCIENCE DUE TO ATTRACTIVENESS OF ARTS AND SCIENCE RELATIVE TO SED OF COLLEGE BOUND STUDENTS APPLYING TO SED
	A	136	(DIMENSIONLESS) <136>

RSDOR	R	24	RATE OF SED DROPOUTS BEFORE GRADUATION (UNDERGRAD) (PEOPLE/YEAR) <24>
RXAJ	R	95	RATE OF EXIT FROM TEACHER JOB POOL INTO ALTERNATIVE CAREERS (PEOPLE/YEAR) <95>
SAT	A	134	SAT SCORE FOR AN AVERAGE COLLEGE BOUND STUDENT (COLLEGE BOARD) (SCORE/YEAR) <134>
SATATS	A	161	AVERAGE SAT SCORE OF STUDENTS IN MASTERS OF TEACHING PROGRAM (SCORE/PEOPLE/YEAR) <161>
SATCBN	C	132.2	INITIAL TOTAL SAT SCORE POOL FOR COLLEGE BOUND STUDENTS (COLLEGE BOARD) (SCORE/YEAR) <132>
SATCBS	L N	132 132.1	TOTAL SAT SCORE POOL FOR COLLEGE BOUND STUDENTS (SCORES/PEOPLE) <132>
SATEP	A	140	SAT SCORE OF AN AVERAGE STUDENT APPLYING TO SED FROM COLLEGE TALENT POOL (SCORE/PEOPLE/YEARS) <140>
SATGCP	A	141	SAT SCORE OF AN AVERAGE STUDENT APPLYING TO ARTS AND SCIENCE FROM COLLEGE TALENT POOL (SCORE/PEOPLE/YEARS) <141>
SATJP	L N	158 158.1	TOTAL STOCK OF SCORES IN TEACHER JOB POOL (SCORES) <158>
SATJPN	C	158.2	INITIAL TOTAL STOCK OF SCORES IN TEACHER JOB POOL (SCORES/PEOPLE/YEARS) <158>
SATN	C	134.1	INITIAL TOTAL AVERAGE SAT SCORE OF A COLLEGE BOUND SENIOR (COLLEGE BOARD) (SCORE/YEARS) <134>
SATNECP	S	142	AN AVERAGE SAT SCORE OF NEW ENTRANTS TO COLLEGE BOUND POPULATION (SCORE/PEOPLE/YEARS) <142>
SATRVS	R	159	SAT SCORE POOL OF TEACHERS SEEKING TO REENTER TEACHING (SCORES/PEOPLE/YEAR) <159>
SATSE	A	149	AN AVERAGE SAT SCORE OF STUDENTS SELECTED BY SED (SCORE/PEOPLE/YEARS) <149>
SATUSE	L N	150 150.1	TOTAL SAT SCORES OF STUDENTS IN SED (UNDERGRAD) (SCORES/PEOPLE/YEAR) <150>
SATUSI	C	150.2	INITIAL TOTAL SAT SCORES OF STUDENTS IN SED (UNDERGRAD) (SCORES/PEOPLE/YEARS) <150>
SAXTE	S	156	AVERAGE SAT SCORE OF GRADUATES OF SED (UNDERGRAD) (SCORE/PEOPLE/YEARS) <156>
SDOR	C	24.2	STUDENT DROPOUT RATE (UNDERGRADUATE) (%/YEAR) <24>
SEDFAC	L N	53 53.1	SED FACULTY (UNDERGRAD) (PEOPLE) <53>
SEDSAT	R	139	OUTFLOW OF SCORES FOR STUDENTS APPLYING TO SED (SCORES/PEOPLE/YEAR) <139>
SEDSE	L N	1 1.1	SED STUDENT ENROLLMENT (PEOPLE) <1>
SEDSEN	C	1.2	INITIAL SED STUDENT ENROLLMENT (UNDERGRADUATE) (PEOPLE) <1>
SEDTP	L N	143 143.1	TOTAL SAT SCORE POOL FOR ALL SED APPLICANTS (UNDERGRAD) (SCORES/PEOPLE/YEARS) <143>
SEDTPN	C	143.2	INITIAL TOTAL SAT SCORE POOL FOR ALL SED APPLICANTS (UNDERGRAD) (SCORES/PEOPLE/YEARS) <143>
SNTG	S	23	SUPPLY OF NEW TEACHER GRADUATES (PEOPLE/YEAR) <23>
SNTSAT	C	108.2	TIME TO AVERAGE RECENT AVERAGE SAT SCORES OF NEW TEACHERS HIRE TO TEACH (YEARS) <108>

SPOP	A	117	STUDENT POPULATION GRADES K-12 (PEOPLE) <117>
SPOPN	C	120.2	INITIAL STUDENT POPULATION (PEOPLE) <120>
STDEM	C	118.1	TIME TO IMPLEMENT ADJUSTMENT TO STUDENT POPULATION DUE TO LOWER THAN EXPECTED BIRTHS (YEARS) <118>
STFTOR	C	55.1	SMOOTH TIME FOR GRADUATE FACULTY TURNOVER (YEARS) <55>
STFXCT	C	8.1	SMOOTH TIME TO AVERAGE FXCT (YEARS) <8>
STHR	C	110.2	TIME TO AVERAGE HIRE RATE OF TEACHERS (YEARS) <110>
STJAP	A	167	AVERAGE SAT SCORE IN TJAP (SCORE/PEOPLE/YEARS) <167>
STR	A	114	STUDENT TEACHER RATIO (YEARS) <114>
STRIF	C	127.2	TIME TO AVERAGE RECENT TEACHER RIF RATE (YEARS) <127>
STRT	C	116.2	TIME TO IMPLEMENT CHANGE IN STUDENT-TEACHER RATIO (YEARS) <116>
STSEDS	C	58.1	TIME TO AVERAGE SEDSE (UNDERGRAD) (YEARS) <58>
STTOR	C	111.1	TIME TO AVERAGE RECENT TEACHER TURNOVER RATE (YEARS) <111>
STT5	C	120.5	TIME IMPLEMENT STEP CHANGE IN STUDENT POP (YEARS) <120>
SW100	C	19.2	SWITCH TO TURN OR OFF POLICY TEST C <19>
SW20	C	135.2	SWITCH TO TURN ON OR OFF SAT CONSTANT <135>
SW21	C	135.3	SWITCH TO TURN ON OR OFF SAT CHANGE FUNCTION <135>
SW3	C	128.3	SWITCH TO TURN ON OR OFF TEACHER POP AS A FUNCTION OF STUDENT-TEACHER RATIO <128>
SW30	A	13	SWITCH TO TURN ON OR OFF POLICY TEST A (RAISING STANDARDS AT ENTRANCE TO SCHOOLS OF EDUCATION) <13>
SW35	A	105	SWITCH TO TURN ON OR OFF POLICY TEST B <105>
SW4	C	128.4	SWITCH TO TURN ON OR OFF TEACHER POP AS A CONSTANT <128>
SW40	A	20	SWITCH TO TURN ON OR OFF POLICY TEST C (RAISING CERTIFICATION STANDARDS WHICH DELAY GRADUATION OF NEW TEACHER CANDIDATES FROM BACCALAUREATE PROGRAMS BY 2 YEARS) <20>
SW5	C	120.3	SWITCH TO TURN ON OR OFF STEP CHANGE IN SPOP <120>
SW50	A	97	CLIP FUNCTION TO IMPLEMENT POLICY TEST D <97>
SW59	C	119.2	SWITCH TO TURN OR OFF SPOP AS A TABLE FUNCTION <119>
SW60	A	120	TABLE FUNCTION TO GENERATE SPOP BASED ON DEMOGRAPHY <120>
SW61	C	119.3	SWITCH TO TURN ON OR OFF ADJUSTMENT TO SPOP DUE TO <119>
SW63	C	117.1	SWITCH TO TURN ON OR OFF DEMOGRAPHIC EFFECTS ON SPOP DUE TO LOWER THAN EXPECTED BIRTH RATE <117>
SW64	A	118	TABLE FUNCTION TO ADJUST SPOP DUE TO BIRTH RATE <118>
SW70	C	3.1	SWITCH TO TURN ON OR OFF FIXED HIGH SCHOOL GRADUATE FRACTION <3>
SW75	C	3.2	SWITCH TO TURN ON OR OFF HIGH SCHOOL GRADUATES AS A TABLE <3>

SW80	C	45.3	SWITCH TO TURN ON OR OFF POLICY TEST D (INCREASING THE ATTRACTIVENESS OF GRADUATE SCHOOLS OF EDUCATION TO POPULATION SEEKING ALTERNATIVE CAREERS) <45>
SW99	A	130	SWITCH TO TURN ON OR OFF CHANGE IN TEACHER TURNOVER RATE <130>
TACSE	T	11.1	TABLE OF EFFECT OF COLLEGE BOUND FRACTION APPLYING TO SED ON SED ACCEPTANCES (UNDERGRAD) <11>
TBSSED	T	172.1	TABLE OF BACHELORS DEGREES AWARDED <172>
TCSTR	A	116	TABLE OF CHANGES IN STUDENT-TEACHER RATIO <116>
TDEM	T	120.1	TABLE GENERATING SPOP BASED ON HISTORICAL AND PROJECTED DATA <120>
TDFXCT	T	25.1	TABLE OF EFFECTS ON STUDENTS REMAINING IN SED DUE TO TEACHER HIRE RATE FROM TJAP <25>
TDMAT	C	33.2	TIME FOR ARTS AND SCIENCES MAJORS TO COMPLETE UNDERGRADUATE STUDIES (YEARS) <33>
TDRTHR	C	42.1	TIME FOR NEW TEACHERS TO BE EMPLOYED BEFORE SEEKING ADMISSION TO AND BEING ADMITTED TO SED GRADUATE SCHOOL (YEARS) <42>
TDSATA	C	161.1	TIME TO DELAY AN AVERAGE SAT SCORE OF STUDENTS MAJORING IN ARTS AND SCIENCES (YEARS) <161>
TDTRP	C	90.1	TIME FOR TEACHERS LEAVING TEACHING TO REENTER SYSTEM (YEARS) <90>
TDUMP	C	84.1	TIME TO DUMP PEOPLE REMAINING IN LEVEL OF NEW GRADUATES OF GRADUATE SED (YEARS) <84>
TEACF	T	148.1	TABLE REPRESENTING EFFECT OF SELECTION STANDARDS ON AN AVERAGE SCORE <148>
TEASED	T	89.1	TABLE OF EFFECT OF SED ATTRACTIVENESS ON ARTS AND SCIENCES MAJORS WHO SEEK TEACHER QUALIFICATIONS <89>
TECTM	T	47.1	TABLE OF EFFECT OF SED FACULTY MARKET ON FRACTION OF TEACHERS LEAVING TEACHING APPLYING TO GRADUATE SCHOOLS OF EDUCATION <47>
TEDEM	T	119.1	TABLE OF EFFECT OF BIRTH RATE ON ADJUSTING SPOP PROJECTIONS <119>
TEDESF	T	10.1	TABLE OF EFFECT OF DESIRED EDUCATION SCHOOL GRADUATE FACULTY ON ACCEPTANCE FRACTION AT UNDERGRADUATE LEVEL <10>
TEDISCT	T	131.1	TABLE OF EFFECT OF DISCREPANCY BETWEEN ACTUAL AND DESIRED TEACHERS ON TEACHER TURNOVER RATE <131>
TEFAP	T	49.1	TABLE OF EFFECT OF FACULTY AVAILABILITY ON RATE OF TEACHERS LEAVING CLASSROOM TEACHING TO PREPARE FACULTY POSITIONS (DIMENSIONLESS) <49>
TEFTH	T	37.1	TABLE OF EFFECT OF FRACTION OF EXITING TEACHERS FROM TJAP FOR CLASSROOM TEACHING POSITIONS <37>
TEFXCT	T	99.1	TABLE OF EFFECTS OF FRACTION HIRED FROM TJAP AS TEACHERS <99>
TEGCAP	T	51.1	TABLE OF EFFECT OF GRADUATE SED CAPACITY ON ACCEPTANCE FRACTION AT GRADUATE LEVEL <51>
TEJPS	T	96.1	TABLE OF EFFECTS OF HIRING TEACHERS ON DELAY IN LEAVING TEACHER MARKET <96>

THFAT	T	59.1	TABLE OF TIME TO HIRE OR FIRE FACULTY MEMBERS (UNDERGRAD) <59>
THR	R	101	TEACHER HIRE RATE (PEOPLE/YEAR) <101>
THSAT	C	108.3	INITIALIZED AVERAGE SAT SCORE FOR COLLEGE BOUND SENIORS <108>
TIME	N	176.3	DYNAMO FUNCTION FOR RECORDING TIME <176>
TIMEN	C	176.4	DYNAMO FUNCTION FOR RECORDING TIME (INITIAL TIME) <176>
TITTOR	C	130.2	TIME TO INITIALIZE CHANGE IN TEACHER TURNOVER RATE (YEARS) <130>
TJAP	L	85	TEACHER JOB APPLICANT POOL (PEOPLE) <85>
	N	85.1	
TJAPN	C	85.2	INITIAL TEACHER JOB APPLICANT POOL (PEOPLE) <85>
TLB	A	6	TABLE FUNCTION TO PRODUCE HIGH SCHOOL GRADUATES BASED ON HISTORICAL AND PROJECTED DATA <6>
TMED	T	175.2	CONTROL STATEMENTS <175>
TMETJM	T	33.1	TABLE OF EFFECTS OF TEACHER HIRING FROM TJAP <33>
TPOLD	C	97.1	TIME TO IMPLEMENT POLICY TEST D <97>
TPOLTA	C	13.1	TIME POLICY TEST A IS IMPLEMENTED <13>
TPOLTB	C	105.1	TIME TO IMPLEMENT POLICY TEST B <105>
TPOLTC	C	20.1	TABLE OF EFFECT OF DELAYING BA GRADUATION <20>
TPOP	L	128	TEACHER POPULATION IN CLASSROOM TEACHING JOBS
	N	128.1	(PEOPLE) <128>
TPOPN	C	128.2	INITIAL TEACHER POPULATION IN CLASSROOM TEACHING JOBS (PEOPLE) <128>
TRETJM	T	94.1	TABLE OF REENTRY EFFECT OF TEACHER JOB MARKET <94>
TRIF	R	122	TEACHER REDUCTION IN FORCE (PEOPLE/YEAR) <122>
TRPX	R	92	TEACHERS WHO HAVE LEFT THE SYSTEM ENTERING THE TEACHER JOB APPLICANT POOL (PEOPLE/YEAR) <92>
TSAT	T	135.1	TABLE OF CHANGE IN AVERAGE SAT OF COLLEGE BOUND SENIORS <135>
TSATSE	C	152.1	TIME TO DELAY INITIAL SATS OF SED UNDERGRADUATES UNTIL GRADUATION FOUR YEARS AFTER ENTRANCE TO SED (YEARS) <152>
TSGSE	C	69.1	TIME TO SMOOTH RECENT AVERAGE GRADUATE SED FACULTY (YEARS) <69>
TSGSED	C	35.1	TIME TO AVERAGE GRADUATE SED ENROLLMENTS (YEARS) <35>
TSM	C	160.1	TIME TO SMOOTH RECENT AVERAGE SATS OF CLASSROOM TEACHERS AS AN INPUT TO TJAP SATS FROM REENTERING TEACHERS (YEARS) <160>
TSMDFXCT	C	26.1	TIME TO SMOOTH RECENT AVERAGE FRACTION OF TEACHERS HIRED FROM TJAP (YEARS) <26>
TTCSTR	T	116.1	TABLE OF CHANGES IN STUDENT-TEACHER RATIO BASED ON HISTORICAL DATA <116>
TTLB	T	6.1	TABLE OF HIGH SCHOOL GRADUATES <6>
TTOR	R	129	TEACHER TURNOVER RATE (PEOPLE/YEAR) <129>
TXAJ	C	95.1	TIME TO EXIT TJAP FOR ALTERNATIVE JOBS (YEARS) <95>
TXRAT	C	92.1	TIME FOR TEACHERS TO PERMANENTLY LEAVE SYSTEM (YEARS) <92>

Bibliography

Adams, Jane Meredith, and Claudia M. Christie. 1938. "The Changing Relations between Business and Education." New England Business (May 16): 12-14.

American College Testing Program. 1980. College Student Profiles: Norms for the ACT Assessment, 1980-81 ed. Iowa City, Iowa: American College Testing Program.

_____. 1978. College Student Profiles: Norms for the ACT Assessment, 1978-79 ed. Iowa City, Iowa: American College Testing Program.

_____. 1976. College Student Profiles: Norms for the ACT Assessment, 1976-77 ed. Iowa City, Iowa: American College Testing Program.

_____. 1972. Assessing Students on the Way to College. Vol. II. College Student Profiles: Norms for the ACT Assessment. Iowa City, Iowa: American College Testing Program.

_____. 1966. College Student Profiles: Norms for the ACT Assessment, 1966-67 ed. Iowa City, Iowa: American College Testing Program.

American Council on Education. 1966-80. The American Freshman. National Norms. Annual Reports. Washington, D.C.: American Council on Education.

American School Board Journal. 1930. "The Problem of Teacher Surplus and Unemployment." 81 (September): 68.

_____. 1920a. "Teacher Crisis." 60 (January): 41-42.

_____. 1920b. "The Salary Situation with Remedies." 61 (October): 40.

_____. 1920c. "Status of the Teacher Shortage." 61 (November): 53.

_____. 1918a. "For Busy Superintendents." 57: 58.

_____. 1918b. "To Relieve the Teacher Shortage." 57 (December): 47.

_____. 1918c. "The Teacher Shortage in the High Schools." 57 (December): 49.

American Society for Training and Development. 1983. ASTD Directory of Academic Programs in Training and Development/Human Resource Development. Washington, D. C.

_____. 1981. Models and Concepts for T&D/HRD Academic Programs. Paper presented at the Second Invitational Conference on the Academic Preparation of T&D/HRD Practitioners. Washington, D. C.

Anderson, Earl W. 1939. "Teaching Opportunities in 1938." Educational Research Bulletin 18 (March 1): 68-71.

_____. 1930. "Supply and Demand in High School Teaching in Ohio 1929-30." Bureau of Educational Research, Ohio State University, October. Cited in Review of Educational Research 1 (April 1931): 137.

_____. 1929. "A Study in Supply and Demand." Educational Research Bulletin 7 (December 4): 339-403.

Anderson, Earl W., and Reuben H. Eliassen. 1952. "Teacher Supply and Demand." Review of Educational Research 22 (June): 219-23.

_____. 1943. "Teacher Supply and Demand." Review of Educational Research 13 (June): 213.

_____. 1940. "Teacher Supply and Demand." Review of Educational Research 10 (June): 179-84.

Baugh, William, and J. A. Stone. 1981. Trends in the Education Labor Market. ED 197490. Washington, D. C.: U. S. Department of Education, National Institute of Education.

_____. 1980. Simulation of Teacher Demand Demographics and Mobility—A Preliminary Report. ED 197491. Washington, D. C.: U. S. Department of Education, National Institute for Education.

Berg, I. 1970. Education and Jobs: The Great Training Robbery. New York: Praeger.

Bestor, Arthur. 1955. The Restoration of Learning: A Program for Redeeming the Unfulfilled Promise of American Education. New York: Knopf.

_____. 1953. Educational Wastelands. Urbana: University of Illinois Press.

Bethune, S. B. 1981. "Factors Related to White Females' Choice of Education as a Field of Study during College: An Analysis of the National Longitudinal Study of the High School Class of 1972." Doctoral dissertation, University of North Carolina.

Blau, P. M., and O. D. Duncan. 1967. The American Occupational Structure. New York: Free Press.

Bloom, B. S. 1976. Human Characteristics and School Learning. New York: McGraw-Hill.

Bloom, Benjamin, et al. 1965. Taxonomy of Educational Objectives. Handbook I: Cognitive Domain. New York: Longmans, Green.

Borinsky, Mark. 1978. Survey of Recent College Graduates. Washington, D. C.: National Center for Educational Statistics, January.

Bowers, Harold J. 1941. Teacher Certification in 1941. Columbus, Ohio: State Department of Education.

Bowles, S., and H. Levin. 1968. "The Determinants of Scholastic Achievement: An Appraisal of Some Recent Findings." Journal of Human Resources 3 (Winter).

Brookover, W. B., et al. 1978. "Elementary School Social Climate and School Achievement." American Educational Research Journal 15: 301-18.

Buehler, Vernon M., and Y. Krishna Shetty, eds. 1981. Productivity Improvement, Case Studies of Proven Practice. New York: AMACOM.

Burack, Elmer H., and Nicholas J. Mathys. 1980. Human Resource Planning: A Pragmatic Approach to Manpower Staffing and Development. Lake Forest, Ill.: Brace-Park Press.

Carnegie Commission. 1973. College Graduates and Jobs: Adjusting to a New Labor Situation. New York: McGraw-Hill.

Carroll, Stephen J. 1979. "Past and Likely Future Trends in the Labor Market for Teachers." Research in Education. ED 168967. August.

_____. 1974. "Analysis of the Educational Personnel System: VIII." The Market for Teachers. R-1344-HEW. Santa Monica, Calif.: Rand Corporation, February.

Cartter, A. M. 1976. Ph.D.'s and the Academic Labor Market. New York: McGraw-Hill.

_____. 1972. "Faculty Needs and Resources in American High Education." Annals of the American Academy of Political and Social Science 404 (November): 71-88.

Cebula, Richard J., and J. Lopes. 1982. "Determinants of Student Choice of Undergraduate Major Field." American Education Research Journal 19 (Summer): 303-12.

Chapman, B. R. 1980. "Supply of Physics Teachers—Into the 1980's." Physics Education 15 (May): 136-43.

Chapman, David W., and Sigrid M. Hutcheson. 1982. "Attrition from Teaching Careers—A Discriminant Analysis." American Education Research Journal 19 (Spring): 93-105.

Charters, W. W. 1970. "Some Factors Affecting Teacher Survival in School Districts." American Educational Research Journal (7): 1-27.

_____. 1963. "The Social Background of Teaching." In Handbook of Research on Teaching, edited by N. L. Gage. New York: Rand McNally.

Clauset, K. H., Jr. 1982. "Effective Schooling: A System Dynamics Policy Study." Doctoral dissertation, Boston University.

Coffman, Lotus D. 1912. "The Relation between Supply and Demand for High School Teachers." Addresses and Proceedings of the National Education Association, 50th Annual Session, p. 682. Cited by Maaske (1950).

Coleman, James, et al. 1966. Equality of Educational Opportunity. Washington, D.C.: Government Printing Office.

College Entrance Examination Board. 1977. On Further Examination (Wirtz Report). New York.

_____. 1975-76. National Report, College-Bound Seniors. Waltham, Mass.

_____. 1973-80. Admissions Testing Program. Summary Reports. Princeton, N.J.: Educational Testing Service.

Collins, John F. 1976. "A Perspective on Criminal Justice, Remarks to the M.I.T. Club of Boston." Mimeographed. March 24.

Comptroller General for the U.S., 1974. Report to the Congress. Supply and Demand Conditions for Teachers and Implications for Federal Programs. DHEW Publication No. (OE) B-164031 (1). Washington, D.C.: General Accounting Office, March 8.

Conant, James Bryant. 1963. The Education of American Teachers. New York: McGraw-Hill.

Cook, Katherine M. 1928. State Laws and Regulations Governing Teachers' Certificates. U.S. Department of the Interior, Bureau of Education, Bulletin 1927, no. 19.

_____. 1920. "Certification by Examination—The Open Door to the Teaching." American School Board Journal 61 (July): 29-31.

Corrigan, Dean. 1974. "Do We Have a Teacher Surplus?" Journal of Teacher Education 25 (Fall): 196-200.

Courtis, S. A. 1929. "Identifying and Eliminating the Unfit in Teachers Colleges." Nations Schools 4 (September): 21-26.

Cowley, W. H., and Albert Grant. 1929. "A Technique for Analyzing Supply and Demand for Educational Workers." School and Society 29 (May): 618-20.

Craft, Maurice. 1971. "A Broader Role for Colleges of Education." In The Future of Teacher Education, edited by J. W. Tribble. London: Routledge and Kegan Paul.

Crockett, D. S. 1975. "Survey of ACT-Participating Colleges." Iowa City, Iowa: American College Testing Program.

Davis, Frank G. 1932. "Trends in the Education of Teachers." Educational Administration and Supervision 18 (May): 366-81.

Davis, George S. 1908. "The Supply of Teachers and Their Training after Appointment." Addresses and Proceedings of the NEA, 46th Annual Session, p. 274. Cited by Maaske (1950).

Davis, J. A. 1964. Great Aspirations. Chicago: Aldine.

Davis, R., and G. Lewis. 1976. "The Demographic Background to Changing Enrollments and School Needs." Cambridge, Mass: Center for the Study of Public Policy, February.

DeWitt, I. B., and A. Dale Tussing. 1971. The Supply and Demand for Graduates of Higher Education: 1970-1980. Syracuse, N.Y.: Educational Policy Research Center.

Downes, F. E. 1920. "Teacher Crises." American School Board Journal 60 (January): 41-42.

Dreeben, R. S. 1970. The Nature of Teaching. Glenview, Ill.: Scott, Foresman.

Drucker, Peter F. 1968. The Age of Discontinuity, Guidelines to Our Changing Society. New York: Harper & Row.

Ducharme, E., and R. Nash. 1975. "Humanizing Teacher Education for the Last Quarter of the Twentieth Century." Journal of Teacher Education 26 (Fall): 222-28.

Edmonston, Barry, and T. R. Knapp. 1979. "A Demographic Approach to Teacher Supply and Demand." American Education Research Journal 16: 351-66.

Education Daily. 1983. "State Officials Should Not Set Teacher Standards, Says College Group." March 2.

Education U.S.A. 1983. "Houston Teacher Test Erupts into Chaos." 25:29 (March 14): 226.

Education Week. 1983. "Many Prospective Teachers Fail Colorado Test, State Education Chief Said 'Disappointed.'"

_____. 1983. "Merit Pay Denounced by N.E.A., But Shanker Willing to 'Consider' It." (May 18): 11.

_____. 1983. "New Criteria Agreed to For Ala. Teacher Training." (February 23): 11.

Educational Research Bulletin. 1928. "The Demand and Supply of Teachers." 7 (October): 282.

Educational Testing Service. 1983. "A Summary of Data Collected from Graduate Record Examination's Test-Takers during 1981-82." Data Summary Report no. 7, prepared by Marlene B. Goodison, Princeton, N.J.

Eisenberg, J. Linwood. 1926. "Provisions for the Added Supply of New Teachers and for the Training of Teachers in Service." Thirteenth Annual Schoolmen's Week Proceedings, Philadelphia, University of Pennsylvania, pp. 119-21.

Elementary School Journal. 1927. "Certification of Teachers and Supply of Teachers" 48 (December): 255.

Eliassen, R. H., and Earl W. Anderson. 1931. "Teacher Supply and Demand." Review of Educational Research 1 (April): 69-72.

Encyclopedia of Educational Research. 1982. 5th ed. American Educational Research Association. New York: Free Press.

_____. 1969. 4th ed. American Educational Research Association. New York: Macmillan.

Eurich, Alvin C. 1969. Reforming American Education. The Innovative Approach to Improving Our Schools and Colleges. New York: Harper & Row.

Evenden, E. S., Guy C. Gamble, and Harold G. Blue. 1935. "Supply and Demand Studies." Teacher Personnel in the U.S. U.S. Department of the Interior, Office of Education Bulletin, 1933, no. 10, vol. II. Part I, chap. 5, pp. 74-102. Cited in Review of Educational Research 7 (June 1937): 317.

Fahey, Sarah H. 1919. "Some Causes of the Present Decline for High School Teachers." Addresses and Proceedings of the National Education Association, p. 383, vol. LVII, 1919. Cited by Maaske (1950).

Farr, Roger, and Jill Edwards Olshavsky. 1980. "Is Minimum Competency Testing the Appropriate Solution to the SAT Decline?" Phi Delta Kappan 61 (April): 528-30.

Forrester, Jay W. 1968. "Market Growth, as Influenced by Capital Investment." Industrial Management Review 9: 83-105.

Forrester, Jay W., Nathaniel J. Mass, and Charles J. Ryan. 1976. "The System Dynamics National Model: Understanding Socio-Economic Behavior and Policy Alternatives." Technological Forecasting and Social Change 9: 51-68.

Foster, Clifford D. 1967. "Teacher Supply and Demand." Review of Educational Research 37 (June): 260-71.

Foster, Richard R. 1931. "Continuous Employment for the Teacher." Journal of the National Education Association 20 (December): 343-44.

Frankel, Martin. 1982. Special Report. Teacher Shortage May Occur in the Late 1980's. Washington, D.C.: U.S. Department of Education, National Center for Educational Statistics, February.

_____. 1979. Projections of Enrollments and Classroom Teacher Staffing in Elementary and Secondary Schools. ED 165304. Washington, D. C.: U.S. Department of Education, National Center for Educational Statistics.

Frasier, George Willard. 1935. "Do We Need More Teachers?" Phi Delta Kappan 18 (April): 182-83.

_____. 1931. "Selective Admission of Students: Its Philosophy." Journal of the National Education Association 20 (December): 341-42.

Frazier, Benjamin W. 1941. "Teacher Supply and the Defense Program." School Life 27 (December): 71-74.

_____. 1940. "Education of Teachers as a Function of State Departments of Education." Studies of State Departments of Education, Bulletin 1940, no. 6. Monograph no. 6. Cited in Review of Educational Research. "Selection Placement, Administrative Relocations" 13 (June 1943): 249.

_____. 1933. "History of the Professional Education of Teachers in the United States." Special Survey Studies. U.S. Department of the Interior, Office of Education Bulletin 1933, no. 10, vol. 5, pp. 1-86. Cited in Review of Educational Research 7 (June 1937): 326.

_____. 1932. "Professional Education of Teachers." Biennial Survey of Education in the United States, 1928-30. U.S. Department of the Interior, Office of Education Bulletin 1931, no. 20, vol. 1, pp. 501-40. Cited in Review of Educational Research 4 (June 1934): 327.

_____. 1929. Teacher Training, 1926-28. USOE Bulletin no. 17. Cited in Review of Educational Research 1 (April 1931): 142.

Freeman, Richard B. 1976. The Over-educated American. New York: Academic Press.

_____. 1975a. "Legal 'Cobwebs': A Recursive Model of the Market for New Lawyers." Review of Economics and Statistics 57 (May): 171-79.

_____. 1975b. "Supply and Salary Adjustments to the Changing Science Manpower Market: Physics, 1948-73." American Economic Review 65 (March): 27-39.

_____. 1971. The Market for College-Trained Manpower. A Study in the Economics of Career Choice. Cambridge, Mass.: Harvard University Press.

Freeman, Richard B., and Herbert Holloman. 1975. "The Declining Value of College Going." Change (September).

Friedman, Myles L., et al. 1980. Improving Teacher Education. Resources and Recommendations. New York: Longman.

The Future for Teaching Education in Ontario. 1978. Simulation Experiments to Examine the Impact of Environmental Factors and Policy Decisions on Ontario Teacher Education Institutions 1978-2000. Mississaugo, Ont.: The Hansen Group, Management Consultants, for Commission on Ontario. Working Paper no. 35. September.

Gage, N. L. 1972. Teacher Effectiveness and Teacher Education: The Search for a Scientific Basis. Palo Alto, Calif.: Pacific Books.

Gagné, Robert M. 1965. The Conditions of Learning. New York: Holt, Rinehart & Winston.

Galambos, Eva C. 1983. Communication. Council of Graduate Schools in the United States (March): 2-4.

_____. 1980. The Changing Labor Market for Teachers in the South. ED 186419. Research in Education. September.

Gardner, William E., and John R. Palmer. 1982. Certification and Accreditation: Background, Issue Analysis and Recommendations. Prepared for the National Commission on Excellence in Education, August.

Gaynor, Alan K., and Karl H. Glauset. 1983. "Organizations and Their Environments: A System Dynamics Perspective." Paper presented to the Annual Meeting of the American Educational Research Association, Montreal, April.

Gilbert, Thomas. 1978. Human Competence. New York: McGraw-Hill.

Gillis, Cynthia. 1976. Special Education Manpower in Massachusetts. Status Report and Recommendations. Boston: Massachusetts Department of Special Education, July.

Goldman, Roy, Donald Schmidt, Barbara Hewitt, and Ronald Fisher. 1974. "Grading Practices in Different Major Fields." American Educational Research Journal 11 (Fall): 343-58.

Goodman, Michael R. 1974. Study Notes in System Dynamics. Cambridge, Mass.: Wright-Allen Press.

Graybeal, W. 1974. "States and Trends in Public School Teacher Supply and Demand." Journal of Teacher Education 25 (Fall): 200-8.

Green, Thomas F. 1980. Predicting the Behavior of Educational Systems. Syracuse, N.Y.: Syracuse University Press.

_____. 1971. The Activities of Teaching. New York: McGraw-Hill.

Griffith, H. M. 1926. "Social Problems in the Supply of Teachers." Thirteenth Annual Schoolmen's Week Proceedings. Philadelphia, University of Pennsylvania, pp. 69-73.

Guiwits, Emily. 1927. "What about the Left Overs?" American School Board Journal 75 (November): 45.

Guthrie, J., et al. 1971. Schools and Inequality. Cambridge, Mass: MIT Press.

Hagen, Elizabeth, and Robert C. Thorndike. 1960. Characteristics of Men Who Remained in and Who Left Teaching. ED 0027902. Research in Education.

Hanushek, Eric. 1970a. "The Production of Education, Teacher Quality, and Efficiency." In Do Teachers Make a Difference? DHEW OE-58042. Washington, D. C.: Government Printing Office.

_____. 1970b. The Value of Teachers in Teaching. Santa Monica, Calif.: Rand Corporation.

_____. 1968. "The Education of Negroes and Whites." Ph.D. dissertation, Massachusetts Institute of Technology.

Harden, Frances E. 1931. The Economic Welfare of Teachers. Washington, D. C.: National Education Association, Sixth Yearbook of the Department of Classroom Teachers.

Hardin, Garrett. 1968. "The Tragedy of the Commons." Science 162: 1243-48.

Harper, Charles A. 1939. A Century of Public Teacher Education. Originally published by the American Association of Teachers Colleges, Washington, D. C. Reprinted by Greenwood Press, 1970.

Hart, F. W. 1934. "A Proposal to Spread Employment in the Teaching Profession by a Sabbatical Stagger Plan." American School Board Journal 87 (March): 28, 72.

Hausman, Howard. 1978. "Supply and Demand for High School Teachers in 1985." ED 160412. Washington, D. C.: National Institute for Education.

Hausman, Howard J., and Arthur H. Livermore. 1978. "Supply and Demand for High School Science Teachers in 1985." Washington, D. C.: National Institute for Education.

Heath, R. W., and M. A. Nielson. 1974. "The Research Basis for Performance-Based Teacher Education." Review of Educational Research 44 (Fall): 463-84.

Immig, David. 1975. "Alternatives for Schools of Education Confron fronted with Enrollment and Revenue Reductions." ED 008012. Washington, D. C.: National Institute for Education.

Katz, Michael. 1975. Class, Bureaucracy and Schools: The Illusion of Educational Change in America. New York: Praeger.

Kinney, Lucien B. 1964. Certification in Education. Englewood Cliffs, N.J.: Prentice-Hall.

Klonower, Henry. 1930. "Demand versus Supply among Teachers in the Public High Schools." Report of the Seventh Annual Meeting of the National Association of Placement and Personnel Officers, pp. 10-12.

Koerner, J. D. 1963. The Miseducation of American Teachers. Boston: Houghton Mifflin.

Kuuskraa, Vello A., et al. 1978. "Condition of Teacher Education— 1977 Summary Report." ED 143644. Research in Education. January.

LaBue, Anthony C. 1960. "Teacher Certification in the United States: A Brief History." Journal of Teacher Education 11: 147-72.

Lambert, Sam M. 1963. "Angry Young Men in Teaching." NEA Journal 52 (February): 17-20.

Learned, W. S., and Ben D. Wood. 1938. The Student and His Knowledge: A Report to the Carnegie Foundation on the Results of the High School and College Examinations of 1928, 1930 and 1932. Study of the Relations of Secondary and Higher Education in Pennsylvania. Bulletin No. 29. New York: Carnegie Foundation.

Levin, H. M. 1970. "A Cost Effectiveness Analysis of Teacher Selection." Journal of Human Resources 5 (Winter): 24-33.

Levinson, J., L. B. Henderson, J. A. Riccobono, and R. P. Moore. 1979. National Longitudinal Study Base Year, First, Second, and Third Year Follow-up Data File Users' Manual, vols. 1 and 2. No. 017-080-01983-3. Washington, D.C.: National Center for Educational Statistics.

Lieberman, Myron. 1976. "The Future of the Custodial School." Phi Delta Kappan 58 (September): 122-25.

Lockhart, A. V. 1978. "The Present Teacher Surplus." American School Board Journal 76 (May): 40.

Lortie, D. C. 1975. Schoolteacher. Chicago: University of Chicago Press.

Los Angeles Times. 1983. "State Stands by New Teacher Exams," March 16.

Lutz, Sandra. 1968. "Do They Do What They Say They Will Do?" ACT Research Report no. 24. Iowa City, Iowa: American College Testing Program.

Lyons, G. 1980. "Why Teachers Can't Teach." Phi Delta Kappan 62: 108-12.

Maaske, Roben J. 1951. "Analysis of Trends in Teacher Supply and Demand." Journal of Teacher Education 2 (December): 263-68.

McCain, Jane Hamilton. 1929. "Too Many Teachers." Educational Journal 9 (October): 55.

McClellan, James E. 1968. Toward an Effective Critique of American Education. Philadelphia: Lippincott.

Madaus, G., T. Kellaghan, and E. Rakow. 1975. "A Study of the Sensitivity of Measures of School Effectiveness." Report submitted to the Carnegie Corporation of New York. Dublin: Educational Research Centre, St. Patrick's College; and Chestnut Hill, Mass.: Boston College.

Madaus, G., T. Kellaghan, E. Rakow, and D. King. 1979. "The Sensitivity of Measures of School Effectiveness." Harvard Educational Review 8: 207-32.

Mager, Robert. 1962. Preparing Objectives for Programmed Instruction. San Francisco: Fearon.

Manuel, H. T. 1932. "On the Oversupply of Teachers." School and Society 35 (February 6): 178-79.

Maryland State Board of Education. 1982. Final Recommendations of the Commission on Quality Teaching. Annapolis, Maryland.

Mason, W. S. 1961. The Beginning Teacher. Circular no. 644. Washington, D.C.: U.S. Department of Health, Education and Welfare, Office of Education.

Massachusetts, Commonwealth of. 1979. "Certification of Educational Personnel." Chapter Number and Heading 603 CMR 7.00. Boston: Massachusetts State Board of Education, Department of Education.

Maul, Ray C. 1966. "Where Is the Teacher Shortage?" Wisconsin Journal of Education 98 (March): 14-15.

_____. 1965. "A Turning Point in Teacher Supply." Journal of Teacher Education 16 (September): 275-80.

_____. 1961. "Can the Teacher Shortage Be Solved?" American School Board Journal 142 (May): 17-19.

_____. 1960a. "A Changing Trend in Teacher Supply." NEA Journal 491 (October): 37.

_____. 1960b. "Staff-Supply and Demand." Encyclopedia of Educational Research, rev. ed., pp. 1378-82. New York: Macmillan.

_____. 1960c. "The Teacher Shortage Persists." American School Board Journal 140 (May): 17-19.

_____. 1954. "The Long-Range Demand for Teachers in the United States." Educational Outlook 28 (May): 137-48.

_____. 1951. Teacher Supply and Demand in the United States. Washington, D. C.: National Commission on Teacher Education and Professional Standards.

_____. 1950a. "Implications of the 1950 National Study of Teacher Supply and Demand." Journal of Teacher Education 1 (June): 95-102.

_____. 1950b. "Overview of the Situation in Teacher Supply and Demand." Third Yearbook, 1950. American Association of Colleges for Teacher Education and NEA.

_____. 1950c. "The Supply and Demand for Teachers." North Central Association Quarterly 24 (April): 386-94.

_____. 1950d. Teacher Supply and Demand in the United States. Washington, D. C.: National Commission on Teacher Education and Professional Standards.

Maxey, James E., et al. 1976. ACT Research Report No. 74: Trends in the Academic Abilities, Background Characteristics, and Educational and Vocational Plans of College-Bound Students: 1970-71 to 1974-75. Iowa City, Iowa: American College Testing Program, May.

Miller, Clyde R. 1935. "Report of the Director of the Bureau of Educational Service for the Year Ending June 30, 1935." Report of the Dean of Teachers' College, pp. 129-34. New York: Columbia University, November. Cited in Review of Educational Research 7 (June 1937): 317.

_____. 1930. "Present Problems in Teacher Placement." Report by the Seventh Annual Meeting of the National Association of Placement and Personnel Officers, pp. 15-16.

_____. 1929. "Too Many Teachers." High School Teacher 5 (June): 186-87.

Montgomery, J., et al. 1973. "The Teacher Surplus: Facing the Facts." Phi Delta Kappan 54: 627.

Moritz, R. D. 1937. Annual Report of the Department of Educational Services. Bulletin of the University of Nebraska, Series XIII, no. 2, October 29.

_____. 1929. "Report of the Department of Education Service of the University of Nebraska." Educational Research Record 11 (December): 49-66.

Morra, Frank. 1977. "The Supply and Demand for Beginning Teachers—Past, Present and Future." ED 157864. Washington, D.C.: U.S. Department of Education, National Center for Educational Statistics.

Morrison, Peter. 1976. "The Demographic Context of Educational Policy Planning." Occasional Paper of the Aspen Institute for Humanistic Studies Program on Education for a Changing Society. First published by Rand Corporation as Rand P-5592.

Moses, Stanley. 1970. "The Learning Force." Working paper, Educational Policy Research Center, Syracuse, N.Y.

Myers, Alonzo F. 1932. "Teacher Demand and the Supply." School and Society 35 (February): 210-15.

Nadler, Leonard. 1980. Corporate Human Resource Development: A Management Tool. Madison, Wisc.: American Society for Training and Development and Van Nostrand Reinhold.

National Center for Educational Statistics. 1982. Projections of Educational Statistics to 1990-91. Vol. 1. Analytical Report. NCES 82-402-A. Washington, D.C.: USGPO.

_____. 1980. Digest of Educational Statistics. NCES 80-401. Washington, D.C.: USGPO.

_____. 1979. Digest of Educational Statistics. NCES 79-401. Washington, D.C.: USGPO.

_____. 1978. Digest of Educational Statistics. NCES 78-402. Washington, D.C.: USGPO.

_____. 1978. Projections of Educational Statistics to 1986-87. NCES 78-403. Washington, D.C.: USGPO.

_____. 1975. Digest of Educational Statistics. NCES 75-210. Washington, D.C.: USGPO.

_____. 1975. Projections of Educational Statistics to 1983-84. NCES 75-209. Washington, D.C.: USGPO.

_____. 1973. Digest of Educational Statistics. DHEW Publication no. (OE) 73-11103. Washington, D.C.: USGPO.

_____. 1973. Projections of Educational Statistics to 1981-82. DHEW Publication no. (OE) 73-11105. Washington, D.C.: USGPO.

_____. 1972. Projections of Educational Statistics to 1980-81. DHEW Publication no. (OE) 72-79. Washington, D.C.: USGPO.

_____. 1968. Statistics of State School Systems 1967-68. DHEW Publications no. (OE) 20020, USGPO No. HE 5.220: 20020-68. Washington, D.C.: USGPO.

National Education Association. 1981. Research Division. Teacher Supply and Demand in Public Schools, 1980-81. Research Memo. Washington, D.C.

_____. 1980. Teacher Supply and Demand in Public Schools, 1979. Research Memo.

_____. 1979. Teacher Supply and Demand in Public Schools, 1978. Research Memo.

_____. 1978. Teacher Supply and Demand in Public Schools, 1977, with Population Trends and Their Implications for Schools, 1978. Research Memo.

_____. 1977. Teacher Supply and Demand in Public Schools, 1974, 1975, 1976, with Population Trends and Their Implications for Schools, 1976-1977.

_____. 1974. Teacher Supply and Demand in Public Schools, 1973.

_____. 1972. Teacher Supply and Demand in Public Schools, 1971. Research Report 1972-R4.

_____. 1972. Teacher Supply and Demand in Public Schools, 1972. Research Report 1972-R8.

_____. 1970. Teacher Supply and Demand in Public Schools, 1969. Research Report 1969-R14.

_____. 1970. Teacher Supply and Demand in Public Schools, 1970. Research Report 1970-R14.

_____. 1969. Teacher Supply and Demand in Public Schools, 1968. Research Report 1969-R4.

_____. 1966a. "A New Look at Teacher Supply and Demand." NEA Research Bulletin 44 (December): 117-23.

_____. 1966b. Rankings of the States, 1966. Research Report 1966-R1. Washington, D.C. January.

_____. 1966c. Teacher Supply and Demand in Public Schools, 1966. Research Report 1966-R16. October.

_____. 1963a. "Interesting Facts and Figures on American Education." NEA Research Bulletin 41 (February): 3-9.

_____. 1963b. Rankings of the States, 1963. Research Report 1963-R1. Washington, D.C. January.

_____. 1962a. Estimates of School Statistics 1962-63. Research Report 1962-R13. Washington, D.C. December.

_____. 1962b. "Teacher Supply and Demand in Public Schools." NEA Research Bulletin 40 (October): 93-95.

_____. 1962c. Teacher Supply and Demand in the Public Schools, 1962. Research Report 1962-R8. April.

_____. 1961. "Ten Years of Population Growth." NEA Research Bulletin 39 (December): 104-6.

_____. 1960a. "The Teacher Shortage Analyzed." NEA Research Bulletin 38 (October): 68-74.

_____. 1960b. Teacher Supply and Demand in Public Schools, 1960. Research Report 1960-R7. April.

National Longitudinal Study. 1978. NLS JT EST, J 965A. U.S. Office of Education. Washington, D.C.: National Center for Educational Statistics, May 2.

Nation's Schools. 1930. "Combatting the Problem of Too Many Teachers." 5 (January): 31-36.

Neal, A. O. 1920. "The Shortage of High School Teachers." American School Board Journal 61 (August): 72.

New York Times. 1966. "Editorial." 10:1 (September 4).

New York Times. 1966. "Governor Rockefeller's Plan." September 25, p. 1.

Nolfi, George, et al. 1977. Experiences of Recent High School Graduates: The Transition to Work or Postsecondary Education. Cambridge, Mass.: University Consultants.

Pauley v. Kelley. 1979. 225 S.E.2d 859.

Pavalko, R. M. 1970. "Recruitment to Teaching: Patterns of Selection and Retention." Sociology of Education 43: 340-55.

Pennsylvania Department of Education. 1976. Division of Research. The Preparation and Occupational Pursuits of Elementary, Secondary and Ungraded Teachers, 1974-75. Harrisburg.

_____. 1975. Postbaccalaureate Activities of the Class of 1974 in Pennsylvania. Harrisburg.

Pfeifer, Herman. 1930. "Some Determinants of Teacher Supply and Demand." Washington Educational Journal IX (March): 202. Cited in Review of Educational Research 1 (April 1931): 138.

Phi Delta Kappan. 1966. "Teacher Shortage: Even More Severe?" 48 (October): 95-96.

Picardi, Anthony, and W. Seifert. 1976. "A Tragedy of the Commons in Sahel." Technology Review 78 (May): 1-10.

Pillich, Lisa S. 1980. "The Job Market for Teachers in the 80's." Occupational Outlook Quarterly 24 (Fall): 22-27.

Pinto, Patrick, and James Walker. 1978. A Study of Professional Training Development Roles and Competencies. Washington, D.C.: American Society for Training and Development, May.

Pipho, Chris. 1983. "Stateline, Differential Pay Schedules: A Solution to the Teacher Shortage?" Phi Delta Kappan (March): 453-54.

Randall, Donald, and Felix Zollo. 1974. Teacher Supply and Demand. Boston: Massachusetts Teachers Association.

Reinhart, G. R. 1981. The Persistence of Occupational Prestige. Paper presented at the Southern Sociological Society. Louisville, Ky. Personal communication.

Review of Educational Research. 1931. "The Preparation of Teachers" 1 (April): 79.

Richmond, Barry M. 1977. "Toward a Structural Theory of Cancer." System Dynamics Group, Alfred P. Sloan School of Management, Massachusetts Institute of Technology. Mimeographed.

Robinson v. Cahill. 1973. 306A.2d 65.

Rosenberg, Harry M., et al. 1976. "U.S. Fertility Trends: What Birth Rates Specific for Age and Parity of Women Tell Us." In Proceedings of the American Statistical Association, Social Statistics Section.

Rosenshine, B. , and N. Furst. 1971. "Research on Teacher Per-
    formance Criteria." In Research in Teacher Education,
    edited by B. O. Smith. Englewood Cliffs, N.J.: Prentice-Hall.

Roth, Robert A. 1981. "A Comparison of Methods and Results of
    Major Teacher Supply and Demand Studies." Journal of Teacher
    Education 32: 43-46.

Ryan, Kevin, D. Phillips, and C. E. Peters. 1982. "A Multidimen-
    sional Profile of Pre-Service Teacher Characteristics."
    Columbus: Ohio State University, April.

Ryans, D. G. 1960. Characteristics of Teachers. Their Descrip-
    tion, Comparison and Appraisal. Washington, D.C.: Ameri-
    can Council on Education.

Schlechty, P. S. , and V. S. Vance. 1982. "Recruitment, Selection
    and Retention: The Shape of the Teaching Force." Paper pre-
    sented at the National Institute of Education's conference Re-
    search in Teaching: Implications for Practice. February 25-27.

_____. 1981. "Do Academically Able Teachers Leave Education?"
    Phi Delta Kappan 63 (October): 101-12.

School and Society. 1919. "Societies and Meetings, the National
    Education Association, How to Secure an Adequate Supply of
    Trained Teachers for the Public Schools of the United States"
    10 (September): 299-300.

_____. 1918. "Quotations—The Shortage of Teachers" 8 (July): 52-54.

Sharp, L. M., and S. B. Hirshfield. 1975. "Who Are the New
    Teachers: A Look at the 1971 College Graduates." Washing-
    ton, D.C.: Bureau of Social Science Research.

Sklar, June, and Peter Berkov. 1975. "The American Birth Rate:
    Evidence of a Coming Rise." Science 189 (August 29): 693-700.

Slack, Warner, and Douglas Porter. 1980. "The Scholastic Aptitude
    Test: A Critical Appraisal." Harvard Educational Review 50
    (May): 154-75.

Stinnett, T. M. 1967. "Teacher Certification." Review of Educa-
    tional Research 37 (June): 248-59.

Stone, James C. 1963. "Teacher Certification, Supply and Demand." Review of Educational Research 33 (October): 343-54.

Summers, A. A., and B. L. Wolfe. 1975. "Which Resources Help Learning? Efficiency and Equity in Philadelphia Public Schools." Federal Reserve Bank of Philadelphia. January 28.

Tarkington, R. N. 1939. "Supply and Demand for Commercial Teachers in the High Schools of the United States." Balance Sheet 21 (October): 67-68, 95. Cited in Review of Educational Research 10 (June 1940): 267.

Teacher Preparation: Problems and Prospects. 1982. Hearings before the Subcommittee on Postsecondary Education of the Committee on Education and Labor, House of Representatives, Ninety-seventh Congress. First Session. September 9-November 10, 1981. 86-5850. Washington, D.C.: USGPO.

Thorndike, R. L., and E. Hagen. 1960. Characteristics of Men Who Remained in and Left Teaching. Cooperative Research Project no. 574 (SAE 8189). Washington, D.C.: U.S. Office of Education.

Toch, T. 1982. "Number of Blacks Entering Teaching Declines Dramatically." Education Week 1 (March 10): 24.

Tractenberg, Paul L. 1978a. "Evaluating Student Competency: The Legal Issues." Paper prepared for the Conference on Issues in Competency Based Education, Georgia State University, Atlanta, October 25-26.

_____. 1978b. "Testing for Minimum Competency: A Legal Analysis." Paper prepared for the American Educational Research Association Topical Conference on Minimum Competency Achievement Testing, October 12-14.

_____. 1978c. "Who Is Accountable for Pupil Illiteracy." Paper prepared for the 1978 National Right to Read Conference, May 30.

_____. 1977. "The Legal Implications of Statewide Pupil Performance Standards." Rutgers University Law School, Newark, N.J. September.

_____. 1973. Testing the Teacher. How Urban School Districts Select Their Teachers and Supervisors. New York: Agathon Press.

Training Magazine. 1982. "Special Issue. A Comprehensive Overview of Training and Employee Development Activity in Organizational America." October.

Turk, D. C., and M. D. Litt. 1982. Stress, Dissatisfaction and Intention to Leave Teaching among Experienced Connecticut High School Teachers. Report submitted to State of Connecticut Department of Education. June.

U.S. Bureau of the Census. 1977. Current Population Reports. Population Estimates and Projections. Series P-25, no. 704. Washington, D. C.: Government Printing Office.

_____. 1975. Historical Statistics of the United States, Colonial Times to 1970. Part 1. Bicentennial Edition. Washington, D. C.

U.S. Office of Education. Biennial Survey of Education. Washington, D. C.

Useem, Elizabeth. 1982. "Education in a High Technology World: The Case of Route 128." Boston: Institute for the Interdisciplinary Study of Education, Northeastern University. June.

_____. 1981. "Education and High Technology: The Case of Silicon Valley." 404 UO. Boston: Institute for the Interdisciplinary Study of Education, Northeastern University. August.

Vance, V. S. 1981. "The Ready, Willing and Academically Able: A Longitudinal Study of Retention and Attrition among North Carolina's New Classroom Teachers from 1973 to 1980." Doctoral dissertation, University of North Carolina, Chapel Hill.

Vance, V. S., and P. C. Schlechty. 1982. Who Enters and Who Leaves Teaching? The Case of the High School Graduating Class of 1972. ED 221 541. Washington, D. C.: NIE, U. S. Department of Education.

Vlaanderen, Russ. 1982. "Testing for Teacher Certification." School Products News 21 (October): 27. Originally prepared for Education Commission of the States.

Wall Street Journal. "Minus Numbers, Math, Science Teachers Are in Short Supply; One Solution: Money, to Compete with Industry, Houston Urges Bonus Plan and Fills Most Vacancies." December 21, p. 1.

Waller, W. 1961. The Sociology of Teaching. New York: Russell and Russell.

Ward, Dwayne. 1975. "Labor Market Adjustments in Elementary and Secondary Teaching: The Reaction to the 'Teacher Surplus.'" Teacher's College Record 77 (December): 189–218.

Warner, Pearl E. 1930. "Teacher Training in the High Schools of Missouri, 1927–29." School and Community 16 (January): 22–24.

Weaver, W. Timothy. 1982a. The Contest for Educational Resources. Equity and Reform in a Meritocratic Society. Lexington, Mass.: Lexington Books.

_____. 1982b. "Supply/Demand of Vocational Educators." Research in Education. ED 211740. June.

_____. 1981a. "The Talent Pool in Teacher Education." Journal of Teacher Education 62 (May–June): 32–36.

_____. 1981b. "The Tragedy of the Commons: The Effects of Supply and Demand on the Educational Talent Pool." ED 204261. Research in Education. November.

_____. 1979. "In Search of Quality: The Need for New Talent in Teaching." Phi Delta Kappan 61: 29–46.

_____. 1978. "Educators in Supply and Demand: Effects on Quality." School Review 86 (August): 552–93.

_____. 1977. "Educators in Supply and Demand: Effects on Quality." Paper presented at American Education Research Association Annual Meeting, New York City, April.

Whyte, W. H. 1956. The Organization Man. New York: Simon & Schuster.

Wilde, A. H. 1927. "Demand, Supply and Preparation of High School Teachers." American Education 30 (January): 139–43.

Wiley, Will E. 1926. "Teachers Salaries v. Teacher Surplus." American School Board Journal 73 (October): 47–48.

Williams, Robert T. 1981. "Beneath the Surface of the Mathematics Teacher Shortage." Mathematics Teacher (December): 691–94.

Zerfoss, E., and Leo T. Shapiro. 1972. The Supply and Demand for Teachers and Teaching. Lincoln, Nebr.: Study Commission on Undergraduate Education and Education of Teachers.

Index

About the Author

W. TIMOTHY WEAVER is a professor of education at Boston University. Before coming to Boston University in 1974, he was a research Fellow and manager of educational services at the Educational Policy Research Center, Syracuse University. He received the Ph.D. from Syracuse University in 1969. He was awarded a Ford Foundation grant to study educational policy in Japan in 1971. His work on social class and educational resources was supported by a grant from the National Institute of Education in 1979. That work resulted in a book by Dr. Weaver entitled The Contest for Educational Resources (Lexington, Mass.: Lexington Books, D. C. Heath, 1982). His work with Ross M. Zerchykov on a handbook on the management of declining enrollment was also supported by the National Institute of Education. Dr. Weaver perhaps is best known to American educators for his studies of teacher quality, which began in the mid-1970s and culminate with the publication of this volume.